ALSO BY DAVID W

THE MAGNIFICENT MRS ᴛᴇɴɴᴀɴᴛ

"Thackeray at his best." - *The Independent*

"Waller's story has terrific pace and wit. It is rich in period detail and places events unobtrusively in context. It is a real discovery." - Valerie Grove

"David Waller has written an engaging biography about the marvellous Gertrude Tennant. We all need someone like Gertrude in our lives; failing that, having her for a quiet hour or two is a delicious treat." - Amanda Foreman

"How did the self-educated daughter of a penniless, half-pay naval officer become one of Victorian England's great hostesses? In scenes worthy of a Balzac novel, David Waller recreates Gertrude Tennant's character-forming struggles in post-Revolutionary Paris, and brings to life her close and immensely touching friendship with Gustave Flaubert. This sparked her lifelong passion for the company of great men - a hunger not even appeased when Henry Morton Stanley became her son-in-law. Only by creating her own salon in Whitehall would she find fulfilment. An unusual and involving story, impressively researched and vividly told." - Tim Jeal

"Some historians have all the luck: David Waller's *Magnificent Mrs Tennant* starts off as a literary-detective novel, with the author finding caches of letters from the likes of Flaubert and Browning in a farmhouse attic, and goes on to illuminate mid-Victorian Britain and France from the refreshing perspective of a gaggle of irrepressibly eccentric and confident women. Scholarly and alive to the perils and passions of the era, it breathes fresh life into the supposedly corsetted and cossetted world of 19th century literary high society." - Ian Kelly, biographer of *Beau Brummell* and *Sunday Times* Biography of the Year, 2008, *Casanova*

"Thoroughly engaging and extremely well written. *The Magnificent Mrs Tennant* is not only the story of a fascinating woman's rise through intelligent Victorian Society, but an eye-opening portrait of life amongst the great men of the day." - Frances Osborne, author of *The Bolter*

The Perfect Man

The Muscular Life and Times of Eugen Sandow, Victorian Strongman

by David Waller

'His life was gentle, and the elements so mix'd in him that Nature might stand up and say to the world, "This was a man."', *Julius Caesar*

'Mr Waller[1] was very sonorous throughout, and his forearm would have won an approving nod from Sandow.' *Penny Illustrated Post*, 11 February 1891

Published by

Victorian Secrets Limited
32 Hanover Terrace
Brighton BN2 9SN

www.victoriansecrets.co.uk

The Perfect Man: The Muscular Life and Times of Eugen Sandow, Victorian Strongman by David Waller

Cover design by Mathew Keller (www.mathewkeller.com)
Composition by Catherine Pope

All internal images from the author's own collection.

A catalogue record for this book is available from the British Library.

ISBN 978-1-906469-25-2

CONTENTS

INTRODUCTION

One winter's day in 1904, Arthur Conan Doyle steered his Wolseley Motoring Machine too quickly into the drive of his Surrey country home. The car clipped a gatepost and ran up a high bank before overturning completely. Doyle's passenger was thrown clear but the author was pinioned by the heavy vehicle. "The steering wheel projected slightly from the rest," he wrote later, "and broke the impact and undoubtedly saved my life, but it gave way under the strain, and the weight of the car settled across my spine just below the neck, pinning my face down onto the gravel, and pressing with such terrible force as to make it impossible to utter a sound..."

The creator of Sherlock Holmes remained under the car until a crowd gathered and was able to lift the vehicle from him. "I should think there are few who can say that they have held up a ton weight and lived unparalysed to talk about it," he recalled. "It is an acrobatic feat which I have no desire to repeat." In correspondence, Doyle subsequently attributed his narrow escape to a course of muscular development he had undertaken with Eugen Sandow, the world-famous strongman and music-hall performer who provided personal fitness coaching from his Institute of Physical Culture at 33a St James's Street, in the heart of London's fashionable Clubland.[2] The training had left Doyle in superb physical condition and provided Sandow with what today we call "celebrity endorsement" for the near-miraculous efficacy of his method.

Readers who come across this anecdote in a biography of Conan Doyle may be forgiven for regarding Eugen Sandow (pronounced "You-jean Sand-ow" to rhyme with "how" or "now") as a mere footnote in late Victorian and Edwardian cultural history. Sandow (1867-1925) is now almost totally forgotten by the broader public by whom he was once adored. The man who rose from humble origins in

Prussia to become internationally famous as the literal embodiment of masculine perfection a century ago – the possessor of the most famous male body in the world – lay for more than 80 years in an unmarked grave in Putney Vale Cemetery. Only recently has his great-grandson erected a memorial, ending more than three-quarters of a century of ignominious anonymity. He is remembered today chiefly by body-building enthusiasts, for whom a statuette of Sandow is the coveted first prize in the International Federation of Body Building & Fitness Mr. Olympia competition. (Arnold Schwarzenegger won one of these figurines in 1980).[3] Not surprisingly for so good-looking a man, who posed near-naked for photographs long before pornography entered the mainstream, Sandow has also become an icon of homosexual culture: the various Sandow artefacts (such as bill-posters, dumb-bells, cigar-boxes and indeed semi-nude photographs) that regularly come up for sale on eBay tend to be flagged as "gay int.," i.e. of special interest to the gay community. Even in his lifetime, he was a pin-up for a circle of covertly homosexual intellectuals such as the author and critic Edmund Gosse and J. Addington Symonds, the consumptive art historian who moved from Victorian England to Switzerland in search of health and athletic young boys. In 1889, barely weeks after the strongman made his music hall debut, Gosse sent pictures of Sandow to Symonds at his home in Davos as a Christmas present and Symonds wrote a drooling thank-you note by return. "They are very interesting," he gushed. "The full length studies quite confirm my anticipations with regard to his wrists and ankles & feet. The profile and half-trunk is a splendid study. I am very much obliged to you for getting them to me."[4]

In his heyday in the late Victorian and Edwardian era, Sandow's appeal was very much broader: he was a music hall celebrity and an international sex symbol. Early accounts of his performances suggest that he was capable of stirring up an erotic frenzy akin to the impact of The Beatles on their female audiences 75 years later. When Sandow appeared on stage, according to an 1890 newspaper account, "semi delirium seized the delighted dames and damsels. Those at the back of the room leapt on the chairs: paraquet-like ejaculations, irrepressible, resounded right and left; tiny palms beat till...gloves burst at their wearer's energy. And when Sandow, clad a little in black and white, made the mountainous muscles of his arms wobble! Oh ladies!" "He was a handsome, beautifully proportioned man, and a born showman," enthused Vesta Tilley, his friend and fellow music hall celebrity. "The ladies were particularly attracted by his performance, and he once showed me a good size box containing all sorts of jewellery – rings, brooches, bracelets, etc, which had been thrown on to the stage by ladies attending his performance."[5] Later, in North America, society ladies paid a surcharge to attend private viewings backstage after the show, where they were encouraged to fondle his muscles.

Kings and crowned princes beat a path to the door of his fitness salon in St James's. Tens of thousands who could not afford his personalised attention subscribed to his mail-order fitness courses. Scientists and artists studied him, deeming him not merely strong, but the perfect specimen of male beauty. Before Sandow, nobody believed that a human body could copy the perfection of classical art. Artists clamoured to paint him, sculptors to model him. The Natural History Museum took a plaster cast of his body as representing the ideal form of Caucasian manhood, the remnants of which are still in the basement of that institution, long hidden from view. On an early visit to the US, Thomas Edison filmed him – one of the first moving pictures – and postcard images of his near-naked body were circulated by the thousand.

According to his own account, he was born in Königsberg in Prussia (now Kaliningrad, part of Russia) as Friedrich Wilhelm Müller, the son of a jeweller. He ran away from home and made a living as a circus strongman, wrestler and artist's model in Belgium, Holland, France and Italy before being plucked out of impoverished obscurity by an Anglo-American artist by the name of E. Aubrey Hunt. In a gloriously camp encounter, Hunt is said to have spotted Sandow walking along the beach at the Lido in Venice in nothing but his bathing shorts. The sight was so impressive that Hunt hired Sandow to be the model for

his portrait of a Roman gladiator in the arena.[6] Hunt told him about
a contest at the Royal Aquarium Music Hall in Westminster, in which
a strongman by the name of Sampson was issuing challenges to find
the mightiest man in the world. Sandow travelled to London, won
the contest and was promptly signed up for a three-month show at
the Alhambra Music Hall in Leicester Square. In the course of the
next two years, he became a music hall sensation, regularly topping
the bill in London and in Liverpool, Manchester and Birmingham and
other provincial cities. Wearing little more than a fig-leaf and a pair
of tights, Sandow would ape the poses of Greek and Roman statues,
demonstrating his strength by tearing apart packs of cards, bending
iron bars, snapping chains and supporting horses and a squadron of
soldiers on his back.

As with a modern-day rock-star or promising screen actor, his
agents saw the North American market as the key to greater fortune
and Sandow opened in New York in the sweltering summer of 1893.
There, he encountered Florenz Ziegfeld (later to achieve fame as the
promoter of the eponymous Ziegfeld Follies), who brought Sandow
to Chicago at the time of the World's Columbian Exposition. Sandow
triumphed again and spent the next seven years in North America,
where he set a new benchmark for American virility.

Despite his successes in North America, he chose to settle in
London, marrying an English wife and eventually (in 1906) taking
British citizenship. In 1896, he established his Institute of Physical
Culture in London's St James's, where ladies and gentlemen would go
for the late-Victorian equivalent of a workout. He wrote a number
of best-selling books, starting with *Strength and How to Obtain It*. First
published in 1897, this went into four further editions during his lifetime
and was translated into many languages. From 1898-1907, he edited
and published *Sandow's Magazine of Physical Culture*. At a time when most
men were sedentary and unhealthy, constitutionally disinclined to take
any kind of exercise, and when British and indeed much of European
society feared the onset of physical and moral degeneration, Sandow's
self-improvement system claimed to be able to transform weaklings

into paragons of health and strength. One famous, albeit fictional, follower of his method was Leopold Bloom, the hero of James Joyce's *Ulysses*, who took up Sandow's regime in search of "relaxation … and the most pleasant repristination of juvenile agility." An early example of a David Beckham- or Claudia Schiffer-style personal brand, he developed a chain of licensed fitness training schools and a mail-order business selling everything from Sandow's stretching equipment to cigars, Sandow's cocoa, chocolate powder and branded body-lotion. Although the chocolate powder failed to catch on, he was initially successful in business and became every well-toned inch the prosperous Edwardian gentleman, a patron of Ernest Shackleton, a friend of Lord Esher and Sir Arthur Conan Doyle. In March 1911, he was appointed Professor of Scientific and Physical Culture to King George V. He and his family lived in Dhunjibhoy House, a substantial residence in Holland Park Avenue in west London, named in honour of an Indian benefactor whom Sandow claimed to have cured of elephantiasis during a tour of the sub-continent.

In his lifetime, Sandow was a famous figure throughout the British Empire and North America, an idol to generations of young men and women and companion and fitness advisor to an impressive list of Kings, Emperors and Prime Ministers. In the 1890s, he was an early champion of physical culture, an emblem of masculinity and a symbol of human perfectibility. By the 1920s, he still had many thousands of adherents around the world, but his fame was much diminished. He was the subject of several biographies during his own lifetime, but the first and only modern one appeared in the US in 1994, when David L. Chapman rescued Sandow from almost total obscurity, demonstrating in his *Sandow the Magnificent* how Sandow invented the oddball sport of bodybuilding. This assessment of his influence, while undoubtedly correct, is far too narrow: he is not just the "father of bodybuilding" and thus initiator of a cult where men and women do freakish things to their bodies and end up with limbs and torsos that look like condoms stuffed with walnuts. He deserves to be resurrected as a significant cultural figure in his own right. Sandow straddled the Victorian world and the modern, like Oscar Wilde helping us to understand the birth of modern manhood. He also deserves credit for initiating the very modern craze for physical fitness.

Beyond the determination to restore Sandow's reputation, there is a personal motivation for this book: Eugen Sandow is a very distant relative. For those prompted to search for comparisons between my own physique and Sandow's, there is sadly no possibility of any genetic influence as he was merely a sort of great-great uncle by marriage. Growing up, I heard stories of his life, and, as I learned of his feats, I had visions of him juggling ancient aunts and lifting my great-grandfather's grand piano onto his back. However, I noted that adults tended to clam up when children came into earshot and I suspected that there was some scandal associated with a man who brought a tincture of glamour to my otherwise entirely pedestrian ancestors (the others of that generation were accountants, engineers and shop-keepers.) So for the last decade or so I have been investigating his life, getting to the bottom of the family scandal (as revealed in the epilogue) and rooting out a great deal of new facts and stories about great uncle Eugen. I even acquired a set of his patented dumb-bells and tried to follow his training regime, with indifferent results as we will see.

Sandow remains something of a conundrum for a biographer and although I can unveil for the first time the secret of his origins, I cannot prove or disprove conclusively that he was a bisexual philanderer, as some have claimed. There is frustratingly little intimate biographical information: neither diaries, nor scrapbooks or archive, as if after his early demise his widow and daughters held an enormous bonfire and destroyed all records relating to the man whose memory they wished to obliterate. Certainly within days of his funeral they held an auction to sell off anything with a valuable association. To compound the problem further, the many who encountered Sandow tended to be viscerally impressed by his muscles and typically recorded what they thought of them rather than him. In a sense, this book is a biography of one remarkable body and all that it stood for, as well as of the fascinating but inscrutable man to whom the body belonged.

- 1 -

FROM PRUSSIA WITH MUSCLES

A s will become only too apparent, Sandow was an unreliable witness, especially when telling stories about himself. Early in his life, he was not above telling starry-eyed maidens and potential financial backers that he was of aristocratic descent, but by the time he set down the official version of his origins in his early 20s, he chose a more credible tale of respectable middle-class origins. According to G. Mercer Adam, the author of an authorised Sandow biography published in 1894, he was born Friedrich Wilhelm Müller, in Königsberg in East Prussia, on 2 April 1867, the child of a prosperous tradesman and former officer in the Prussian army. His father served five years in the army "like all patriotic Germans," before setting himself up as a jeweller and dealer in precious stones and metals. Perhaps Müller senior served in the war with Denmark in 1864, or with Austria a couple of years later, before returning home to trade Baltic amber, then much prized as the perfect material for pipe-stems and still found in abundance on the spectacular Baltic beaches nearby? According to this official account, his mother was of Russian stock, her family name Sandov, which in due course would be Germanised to provide the future athlete with his stage name. During the First World War (a time when Germany had become the arch enemy of his adoptive homeland) Sandow went so far as to claim that both his parents had been Russians – a desperate and not entirely successful attempt to distance himself from his Prussian origins.

However, this official version is a farrago of invention, as is clear from a candid account of his family circumstances contained in a hitherto unpublished document in the National Archives at Kew. In a side-letter submitted as part of Sandow's application to become a British citizen in 1906, Guilford Lewis, the strongman's solicitor, wrote to Mr Akers Douglas, Principle Secretary of State for the Home Department, to explain the delicate matter of Sandow's birth parents:

> I wish to draw your attention to the omission of any statement concerning his actual parentage. This is due to the fact that he is the natural son of his parents [i.e. illegitimate] and I have under these circumstances refrained from stating what had I done so [would have become public.] In order to comply with your rules, I would ask for you to permit me to state by letter, although Mr Sandow will if requested depose to this fact, that his mother's name was Wilhelmina Elizabeth Kresand and that she was a German subject and died in the year 1876. Mr Sandow informs me that he was in early infancy adopted and that he assumed his present name of "Sandow"…

While there is every possibility that elements of this account are just as fabricated as the sanitised version – the facts would have been difficult to verify then as now – the story has the ring of truth: Sandow was illegitimate and given up for adoption, perhaps in early childhood. He knew his mother's name – her Christian name was a stoutly respectable and Teutonic one at that – and her surname did indeed provide the basis for his stage name. (Kresand is an unusual German surname and seems to be Slavic in origin, suggesting again that there was some truth in his claim that his mother was originally Russian.) It appears that he did not know his father's name, although like many adopted children he may have had an inkling and from time to time was tempted to create a fanciful paternal lineage. Here is the definitive explanation for his perennial shiftiness about his origins and his reluctance ever to return to Königsberg, or even Germany, for any length of time. The stigma of illegitimacy was profound and for personal and professional reasons Sandow maintained a permanent cover-up. Shamed by his origins, he simply did not want people to know the truth. He was no doubt also acutely aware that his credibility as an apostle of healthy living would be undermined had his customers known that he was tainted by bastardy. Further sleuthing is in vain, as the place of his birth, and all the records that it contained, no longer exists.

Located some 340 miles to the north-east of Berlin and 680 miles west of Moscow, the ancient city of Königsberg was obliterated in the latter stages of the Second World War. American and British planes attacked at the end of August 1944, turning the lattice of medieval streets, churches, museums, universities, gymnasia, royal palaces and the cathedral that Sandow would have known as a child into a fireball, destroying the 700-year-old inner city in two nights of bombing. Five months later, at the end of January 1945, the last train left for Berlin and Königsberg was left to its unenviable fate as the first important German city to face the vengeful Red Army, with a pathetically inadequate garrison of just 30,000 soldiers.[7] After the war, Königsberg was ceded to the Soviet Union at the Potsdam Conference and, three years later, those Germans who had not been killed were expelled – physically driven back to Germany in an example of what we would now call ethnic cleansing – and the city was renamed Kaliningrad, after Michail Ivanovich Kalinin, a Bolshevik statesman. Sandwiched between Poland and Lithuania, the province of Kaliningrad was 200 miles to the west of the Soviet Union's main frontier, its geographic isolation exacerbated by its status as a military exclusion zone, closed to westerners for more than 25 years.[8] Yet its isolation and its status as an "exclave" detached from the geographic mass of modern Russia and the rest of Europe are in historical terms recent phenomena.

In Sandow's day, Königsberg was a thriving cultural, administrative and commercial centre, the capital of the province of East Prussia and the second Prussian city after Berlin itself, enjoying the prestige of long association with the Prussian Royal Family. It was here in 1701 that Elector Frederick III assumed the title of King of Prussia and Fredrick William III retreated here with his court just over a century later after Prussia's defeat at the hands of Napoleon. Everywhere in the city of Sandow's origins were impressive reminders of the imperial connection. Set on the Pregel river, the city was celebrated for its seven bridges, which gave rise to a notorious problem in the history of mathematics – try as one might, it was impossible to walk through the city and cross all the bridges only once.[9] The chief buildings were the Royal Palace and the cathedral, both forbidding Gothic constructions erected by Hohenzollern ancestors in the distant past. It was a centre of austere, Pietistic learning – a Grand Duke had founded a Lutheran university in 1544 – and its most celebrated son was Immanuel Kant (1724-1804), the philosopher of pure reason who had no inclination to cultivate his body. Kant, in contrast to Sandow, never ventured far from Königsberg and was an unimpressive physical specimen, hollow-chested and only five feet tall.

Sandow grew up at a time when Prussia was going through a strikingly self-confident and expansionary phase. This was the era of Prince Otto von Bismarck, the Iron Chancellor, who fought a sequence of brilliantly executed military campaigns to establish Prussia as Europe's leading power, culminating in the Franco-German war of 1870-1871. Königsberg was a vital component of Bismarck's military machine, the headquarters of the 1st Corps d'Armée and the home of a substantial garrison, with some 7,000 soldiers stationed there at any one time. More were based in a string of 12 subsidiary forts that encircled the city. A strategically important port (which had the advantage of being navigable in winter), Königsberg held the key to the defence of Germany's eastern frontier.

There are few anecdotes of his early life in this ancient and prosperous city. The surviving stories seem to be as much part of Sandow's personalised creation myth, as a true reflection of his childhood. He attended school and was good at mathematics, he told interviewers years later. His parents – presumably his adoptive parents – were strict and loving but misjudged their son's character in hoping that he might enter the Lutheran church as a minister. His true vocation was for the body, not the spirit. Sandow would explain to those who would listen that he had displayed no special physical promise as a child and until his mid-teens had a slight build and a delicate constitution. He insisted that anyone could have a body like his, providing only that they worked at it. There was no question of inheriting special genes: his father and a half-brother were of modest stature. "There prevails a rather general impression that in order to become strong, one must be born strong," he wrote many years later. "I can put forward no greater proof of the error of this idea than my own case. As a child I was pale, frail, delicate, even weakly…"[10] (Of course, being adopted, he could only guess at his genetic inheritance.) The proposition that one did not need to be born strong to become strong certainly helped open the market for his system and there may well have been some truth in it so far as Sandow was concerned. A picture that was often published

alongside accounts of Sandow's early life shows a wimpish, Teutonic
lad, clad in lederhosen, bearing out the assertion that the young Müller
was not especially strong or handsome. Many celebrated fitness
enthusiasts, from US President Theodore Roosevelt to Charles Atlas,[11]
tell a similar story of personal self-transformation through exercise
and application. Sandow promoted, and later exploited for commercial
purposes, a powerful personal narrative of self-improvement.

"Contemporary with his college-days," his Victorian biographer
wrote, "he devoted himself with great ardour to all forms of gymnastic
exercises and athletics…so successful was his training that he soon
distinguished himself in all sports, and feats of agility." He would
have attended the local Turnhalle, the gym established on the precepts
laid down by Friedrich Ludwig Jahn (1778-1852), the controversial
so-called *Turnvater* or father of gymnastics, whose system of exercise
originated as a form of resistance to the Napoleonic occupation of the
country earlier in the century. Sandow forged himself into a capable
athlete by his early teens, but the discovery of his true calling, he would
always claim, came at the age of around 15 when he went on holiday
with his father to Rome and there confronted for the first time the
statues of ancient wrestlers and deities: "[Their] sculptured beauty…
bespeaking power and beauty in every limb, appealed so strongly to
my juvenile imagination and aroused my youthful appreciation of
the bodily strength and natural grace of these heroes of a long-lost
civilisation." Looking down at his own weedy frame, and all the ill-
developed specimens of living modern manhood all around him, he
asked his father why men of the 19th century were so different from
the heroes of the ancient world in terms of strength and stature. "The
heroes of old, my little Eugen," his father is supposed to have replied,
"never lolled at ease in a carriage or railway train. Either they walked or

rode on horseback. They were ever active, ever exercising their bodies. But nowadays the brain is cultivated and the body neglected."[12]

One may doubt whether the conversation ever took place, at least in this form, for there is no way that his stepfather would have addressed him as "little Eugen," as he would not take on this name until after he had left Germany for good. But there is truth in the anecdote, nonetheless, for from an early age Sandow was impressed, indeed obsessed, by the degeneration of health and strength from the noble ideals of classical times. Sandow looked at his own body, after his father had explained how the sordid habits and indolence of modern society was in danger of creating a race of weaklings, and contrasted his pathetic figure with the thews and graceful figures of the statued forms around him. Little Friedrich, as he must then have been addressed, conceived there and then of the notion of training himself to "the utmost pitch of perfection". He returned home, redoubled his exercises and, as a photograph taken at the age of 18 bears witness, his frame filled out and his strength and skill as wrestler and all-round gymnast improved dramatically. He spent all his free time at the gym or the circus, where he would jump into the ring and pit his strength against the professionals. His mania for physical fitness, and his love of the circus, put him on a collision course with his adoptive parents, who were horrified at the thought of him becoming a showman. According to Sandow's version of events, the looming conflict abated when he was sent away to study at the University of Göttingen in southern Germany and subsequently in Brussels. He spent all his time in anatomy classes. "Here the reader will perceive the undeviating bent of the young athlete's purpose," noted his first biographer in 1894. "Yet more valuable…was the intimate knowledge he gained of structure and muscle ramification of the human frame." Certainly, his later codification of his exercise system suggested more than a passing acquaintance with the basics of anatomy.

In his late teens, there came a permanent rupture with his parents. His stepfather cut off his allowance and he was left to fend for himself. As Sandow tells it, the cause was a principled dispute over his emerging choice of vocation, but there was probably a less noble reason for the break with family and fatherland. He wanted to avoid the lengthy military service that was the duty of every young Prussian of the time. Having had a taste of the bohemian freedoms of the circus, the wilful young Sandow had no desire to submit himself to the rigours of Prussian martial discipline. So around 1885, when he was 18 years old, he ran away from Königsberg as a tumbler or acrobat with a travelling circus – such is the inglorious start to his career. He spent the next three years of his life as a journeyman strongman, acrobat and artist's model, a period of his life that he would always present as a kind of rite of passage, akin to the *Wanderschaft* or wandering journey traditionally undertaken by German apprentices as they roamed from city to city, even country to country, as they sought to perfect their trade.

Around 1887, at the age of 20, Sandow found himself marooned in Brussels after the circus company ran out of money and was forced to disband. Far from home and desperate for funds, Sandow here encountered Louis Durlacher, alias Professor Attila, another German exile who became a father figure to the young Sandow and would appear at various times in Sandow's career.[13] Attila had opened what he called an "athletic saloon" in the city, a gymnasium frequented chiefly by university students. "One day some of them brought to me a young man, who is now known as Sandow, then not quite twenty years of age," the older man related in a long interview on 28 January 1890. "They did so because without training he had been able to equal them in their athletic pastimes. As soon as I had put him through a few exercises I saw that a little of my training would make a remarkable man of him, and I said: 'Attend to my instructions and I shall be able to make you the strongest man in the world'." Sandow followed Attila's advice and, in a few weeks, the two of them went on the stage and so great was Sandow's success that he was "carried shoulder-high by the students through the streets of Brussels."[14]

Attila was himself a showman credited with inventing many of the formalised poses of the strongman's routine, including the so-called "bent press" (by bending one's hip outwards as one jerks a dumb-bell off the ground, thus deploying the muscle of the back leg, it is possible to lift a prodigious weight) and the Roman Column, where the strongman dangles himself upside down from a column while hefting immense dumb-bells and doing sit-ups. Born in Karlsruhe in 1844, Durlacher-alias-Attila ended up running a gym in New York City, but not before he had performed in front of Queen Victoria (at the time of her Golden Jubilee in 1887) and administered lessons in physical training to a number of crowned heads and other potentates, from Alexander III, Tsar of Russia, to Kings George of Greece and Haakon of Norway, and the millionaires Baron Rothschild and Cornelius Vanderbilt. As a young man, he had supposedly saved the son of the Duke of Baden from drowning and the royal gratitude was such that he had been given an introduction to the courts of Europe. A mere 5' 4" high, Attila was an accomplished linguist and a gifted sportsman who contrived to earn a handsome living from his stage career. While there was no doubting that he had a magnificent physique, the nickel-plated weights that he threw around the stage were rumoured to be lighter than they looked. He was also hot-tempered: during a later sojourn in London he faced two summonses for using abusive language and was bound over to keep the peace for two months at the Marlborough St. police court.[15] His bad language notwithstanding, Attila was a role model for the young Sandow who (according to less-than-flattering later accounts) was at the time of their first meeting reduced to earning a living as a stable-boy and *Kermesse* performer – a species of fairground strongman.

Having impressed Attila with his physique, Sandow was taken on as a pupil and janitor in Attila's gym before becoming a full partner in a music hall act. "We travelled together through Belgium, Holland and Denmark," recalled Attila, "and at each place our performances were received with the greatest astonishment. Everywhere the strongest men were pitted against him, and on every occasion he was victorious". With Attila's encouragement, Sandow met, and made an impression on, Charles Batta, the legendary French strongman, who briefly took the young Prussian under instruction. It was Attila, alert to the need to "sex up" his dowdily named protégé, who most likely encouraged Herr Müller to follow his own example and take on an arresting stage-name. "Sandow", as we have seen, was a Germanised version of his birth mother's name. It also pays oblique homage to a famous German fairy story: his name sounds identical to that of Countess Sandau, heroine of Wilhelm Hauff's *Wirtshaus in Spessart* which chronicles the adventures of three young men setting out to make their fortune in the world. In this story, the Countess is waylaid by robbers in a forest and the young men help set her free. She becomes godmother to one of the lads, an apprentice goldsmith, and has a wonderfully beneficent influence on his life. Müller may have modified his real mother's surname to that of this aristocratic benefactress to bring himself luck as he himself left home to find his fortune. Eugen, meanwhile, simply means "good" in Greek and was supposedly adopted as tribute to the ideas of Sir Francis

Galton, the cousin of Charles Darwin, who invented the science of eugenics. It seems unlikely that Galton's erudite publications would as yet have been familiar to the young performer, as they had only recently appeared in English (which of course Sandow could not read or speak at the time) but many years later the two men would become acquainted. Galton returned the compliment and paid court to Sandow. In due course, many thought the term eugenics derived from Eugen Sandow's name. But that is to look a decade ahead.

Attila had plans to introduce Sandow to the London market, placing the following advertisement in British show-business magazine *The Era*:

> "They are coming!
> Who's Coming?
> ## ATTILA and SANDOW,
> The two World Renowned Athletes, the Two Unsurpassed Wonders of Strength and undoubtedly strongest men of the universe."

The notice goes on to explain that Attila is desirous of accepting engagements in London and the provinces in partnership with his pupil Sandow:

"The Great Muscular Phenomenon of the Century, the Statue of Hercules Alive; declared by H.M. The Emperor of Russia to be the Strongest and Best Developed Man HM had ever seen, and defies any Hercules or Amateur of the United Kingdom for the sum of £500 to equal him in Real Feats of Strength and Endurance and that their Show (never before seen anything like it in England) would be a Mighty Attraction.

MR SANDOW has been for the past twelve months the object of
the greatest admiration on the part of the Greatest Living Painters,
Sculptors, Professors of Anatomical Development, Great Travellers
on the Continent, and specially retained by Universities for Medical
Lectures on his unique et non plus ultra Muscular Development."[16]

They would be appearing with the finest and most costly apparatus
ever seen on stage, the advertisement averred, and guaranteed to
make good any damages should they inadvertently drop a bar-bell on
someone or something.

They secured some bookings but the tour had to be called off after
Prof. Attila fractured a bone in his arm when an act went wrong at
Crystal Palace. Sandow was obliged to part company with his mentor
and resume his peripatetic career, with limited success. Once again,
he found himself alone and short of funds, obliging him to resort to
ingenious tricks to get noticed. In Amsterdam, for example, Sandow
contrived to be arrested. He recounts how the city was full of strength
machines, contraptions that allowed young men to test the strength of
their grip. Sandow himself was so strong that he smashed all the city's
machines and, after contriving to be caught in the act of breaking one
of these devices, he was taken into custody on suspicion of belonging
to a gang of vandals. He was freed only after he lifted the arresting
officer into the air with one hand, a party trick that made him the toast
of the constabulary and earned him local celebrity and a contract at
the theatre.

Sandow went on to practise as a professional wrestler in Italy,
where he trounced three contenders singlehandedly and defeated the
national champion Basilio Bartoletti, exponent of the especially brutal
so-called Greco-Roman school of wrestling, in which flesh-gouging,
finger-snapping and rib-crushing were all positively encouraged. For

this feat, the Athletic Club of Milan awarded him the veritable Platonic ideal of bespangled gold medallions, which for many years afterwards he disported proudly on his many-muscled chest. "I like wrestling better than any other physical pastime," he told a reporter from the *New York Herald*, musing on this time many years later. "Not a muscle of the body, but it catches hold of and improves: calves, thighs, arms and back – every little bit of human band and strap – are used. Not only that, but it also does one's wit good. Patience, nerve, endurance, agility, quickness, and coolness are all involved." And, of course, the ability to squeeze your opponent half to death, which is what Sandow achieved with Bartoletti.

At the Riviera resort of San Remo, he performed in front of the ailing Crown Prince Frederick of Prussia, the heir to the Prussian Empire who was married to Queen Victoria's first and favourite daughter Vicky. Frederick was to disappoint all those (including his mother-in-law) who hoped that he would rule over a peaceable and liberal Germany allied with Great Britain. As Sandow told the story, the Prince tore apart a pack of 52 cards to demonstrate his own strength. To this display from His Imperial Majesty, Sandow responded by ripping apart two packs. ("To tear two packs requires considerable strength of grip or very large hands," observed one investigator of such feats, "but to tear a single pack is extremely easy when the mode of procedure is known.") On watching Sandow in a wrestling match, the Prince is supposed to have said that he would exchange his royal position for the strongman's rude health. At the time, which must have been in the winter of 1887-1888, the Prince was already suffering from the throat cancer that would kill him after reigning for just 99 days and thus could have but croakily entered into the conversation that the strongman proudly related. Maybe Sandow's recollection captured the spirit of the encounter even if the Prince could not fully vocalise his admiration; certainly he awarded the strongman and Prussian subject an imperial presentation ring (made out of worthless crystal rather than precious stones as Sandow would always claim) which is in the possession of Sandow's descendants to this day.[17] After this encounter, Sandow toured France as one half of a circus act called Les Frères Rijos, but he eventually found his way back to Italy.

Despite the victories and moments of glory, Sandow often came close to destitution: an opponent in a much later court case (Sandow proved as combative in the courtroom as in the wrestling ring) suggested that at this phase of his career, he often had no money, nothing to eat – and, more shamefully still given that he was at least professionally obliged to take his clothes off, no suit, boots or hat to put on when his performances were finished. He denied these accusations strenuously, but however picaresque and formative these early adventures, however wholesome his dedication to the cause of physical culture, there is more than a hint of the illicit about these early wanderings at the margins of European popular culture. Circus artistes and artists' models were traditionally morally suspect, beyond the pale of respectability. Earlier in the century, there was an Earl of Warrington who married a circus performer and as a result was shunned by polite Cheshire society despite his title and the ample acres of the Dunham Massey estate: the parishioners of Bowdon refused to allow the church bells to be rung in honour of the wedding and the new Countess was shunned at the races. One must question the lengths to which Sandow needed to go in order to keep body and soul together and indeed the purity of the motives inspiring some of his patrons.

Sandow relates, for example, with no apparent sense of impropriety, how on one occasion in Paris he was obliged to perform a near striptease for a sculptor by the name of Gustave Adolphe Crauck. When Sandow pitched up at Crauck's atelier in search of modelling work, the sculptor was initially inclined to turn him away and tried to shut the door against him. Sandow noticed that Crauck was working on a statue of Hercules and thrust his arm through the door and forced his way into the studio. Crauck was impressed enough at this initial demonstration of strength and muscle to invite the Prussian to take his clothes off. On seeing Sandow's naked torso for the first time, the sculptor "launched himself upon me," the strongman recollected, "and embraced me in his wild enthusiasm, kissing me on both cheeks…his eyes agleam with excitement". Sandow was taken on as a model and the result of their cooperation is the massive *Combat du Centaure*, a statue in Carrara marble which to this day is housed in the courtyard of the *Mairie* of the 6th Arrondissement on the Parisian Left Bank. In this monumental work, which reputedly took 30 years to complete, Sandow is clearly recognisable as the giant Lapith battling amid a tangle of limbs with the Centaur, which is itself wrestling with a beautiful young woman. The statue would be suggestive of rampant bisexual couplings, were the overall effect not so ponderous.

Other sculptures dating from this early phase of Sandow's professional existence include the Flemish artist Jef Lambeaux's *Le Dénicheur d'Aigles* (in which he is robbing an eagle's nest) and *St Michael's Vanquishing of Satan*. "At the Hotel de Ville of Brussels there is a group of a fallen angel overthrown by St Michael," noted the deathless Belgian magazine *Le Biceps*, "and it was Sandow who posed for the torso and legs of this fallen angel."[18]

On the beach at Venice, Sandow emerged from the sea, near naked like a male version of Botticelli's *Venus*, and attracted the attention of an English gentleman sauntering nearby. Like Gustav von Aschenbach in Thomas Mann's *Death in Venice*, the painter Aubrey Hunt was transfixed by this vision of male beauty and stopped to compliment Sandow on his "perfect physique and beauty of form". According to Sandow's account, the artist expressed a desire to paint the view from the strongman's villa, but Sandow was too poor to be residing in a villa. Hunt would in time paint a portrait of Sandow as a Roman gladiator, but not before he had tipped off this well-built young Tadzio about an opportunity to make his name and fortune in late Victorian London. Sandow and Attila made contact and a plot was hatched.

Sandow went back to Germany at least once for a holiday and was describing himself as a native of Königsberg as late as January 1896.[19] Even in 1902-1903, shortly before he became a British citizen, he carried and displayed pictures of the three Kaisers on his grand tour of Australasia. But at no point in his long career did he return to his homeland for professional reasons. The Berlin *Wintergarten* hosted W.C. Fields, the Tiller Girls, Little Tich, Houdini and Marie Lloyd – but not Eugen Sandow. Wary of the consequences of shirking his national service, he feared conscription – and perhaps exposure of his origins. Later in life, he became a naturalised English citizen and fanatical patriot, helping the British counter the militarism of his abandoned homeland. By the time he achieved celebrity in his early 20s, his parents were supposed to be dead and all personal connections with Germany severed. The most enduring trace of his origins would be the heavy accent that survived long after he had turned himself into an irreproachable English gentleman.

EUGEN SANDOW.

- 2 -

A LATE-VICTORIAN CELEBRITY

The Music Hall, the Royal Aquarium, Westminster, 28 October 1889

S andow is dressed in full evening attire and wearing a monocle as he makes his way on to the stage of the Royal Aquarium Music Hall in Westminster, a massive and long-since destroyed temple to popular culture adjacent to Westminster Abbey and a stone's throw from the Houses of Parliament. The Prussian is greeted by whoops of derisive laughter by unruly members of the audience. They cannot believe that this curly blonde-haired youth of average height, with an almost girlishly sweet and smiling face, dressed as a conventional English gentleman, is really trying to prove himself the strongest man in the world. He has taken up the challenge laid down by Charles Sampson (a debonair showman from Alsace) and Franz Bienkowski (alias Cyclops, a bull-necked 19 year old from Hamburg), two dubious professional strongmen who have entertained Londoners for months with their bogus feats of strength.

As Sandow's patron Aubrey Hunt has told him, they are offering £100 to anyone who can beat Cyclops in a trial of strength and a further £500 to anyone who can beat Sampson himself (in later accounts, Sandow typically rounded the figure up, to a full £1,000, but with or without the exaggeration, there was a great deal of money at stake – even the initial £100 was several times the annual income of a servant or working man). Having rushed to London from Italy the very moment he heard of the challenge, Sandow is feeling fitter and stronger than ever before. He is the first to accept the challenge. Sampson posts £100 in cash with Captain Molesworth, the manager of the Aquarium, and the contest is poised to begin. Sandow stumbles, his monocle appearing to impede his vision as he trips over the weights and other paraphernalia that litter the stage. More laughter and the rowdy, cigar-smoking bucks in the audience shout that Sampson should ignore the challenger and get on with his performance. Sampson himself guffaws at the sight of so unequal a contender.

All of a sudden, the boisterous young men in the audience are hushed as Sandow rips apart the front of his evening suit and the shirt beneath to reveal a magnificently muscled body dressed in athletic tights. The laughter suddenly changes into a hum of appreciation: "Before they had all been shouting and laughing, but the enormous development of his biceps, forearm and breadth of chest changed all that, and they remained dumb with amazement." "He is an immensely powerful young fellow…something enormous for his age," noted another stunned observer. "His muscles stand out like iron bands," gasped another. "When he takes off his coat and prepares for action," wrote a deeply impressed correspondent for the *Daily Telegraph*, "the muscles stand out under a clear white skin in high relief, and suggest the gnarled roots of old trees." Sampson turns pale at this transformation, while a frenzy of gambling gets under way, with bets taken and offered as on a racecourse. The contest takes place under the watchful eyes of Professor Attila (who has come to London with Sandow to act as his manager) and representatives of the National Sporting Club, a Victorian institution whose members include the Marquess of

Queensberry, the man who systematised the rules for the sport of boxing, and the Prince of Wales, the future King Edward VII, who, despite an aversion to exercise, was fascinated by competitive sports and would take a special interest in Sandow. Having witnessed a private display of his strength, they have lent their official support to Sandow's challenge and are there to ensure the competition is fairly fought.

There are several tests: first, Cyclops lifts over his head two weights of 56lbs each, lowering them with arms fully extended. This is the equivalent of picking up two substantial sacks of potatoes and, although this test would defeat most ordinary mortals, it is no challenge for Sandow, who repeats the challenge with ease. Then, Cyclops takes a 240lb bar-bell – about the weight of a grown man – and lifts it above his head. Sandow once again betters the challenge, lifting the weight above his head with just one hand. Then Cyclops takes a 150lb dumb-bell with one hand and another weighing 100lbs with the other. Sandow lifts the weights effortlessly above his head and, after pausing for dramatic effect, lifts them a further six times (according to a breathless account in the London *Sportsman*).[20] Cyclops cannot compete and the audience is provoked to fury when Sampson tries to wriggle out of his obligation to hand over the money which has manifestly been won by the young contender. Sandow agrees to undertake two further tests. So Cyclops lies on his back and raises a 240lb weight with two men sitting on it; the men get off and Cyclops stands up with the weight. Sandow repeats this easily. The evening concludes when Sandow successfully lifts a 500lb stone block, on which are placed the two 56lb weights, using just his middle finger.

Sandow is declared the winner, leaving with just £100 in cash, and the promise of a comprehensive rematch in a few days time, on Saturday 2 November. "If the fate of the Empire had hung in the balance," noted one newspaper ahead of the event, "more keenness in the coming match could not have been shown." On the day itself, crowds started to gather around midday, eager multitudes pushing their way in through the turnstiles, seats changing hands for up to five pounds, a multiple of the usual price of seven or eight shillings. Sandow arrived 20 minutes before the performance began and could not make his way through the eager multitude. Meanwhile, Sampson, prancing around the stage in tights, boots and a cloak, medallions arrayed around his neck, mocked his opponent's apparent capitulation. The hour of the challenge came and went and Sampson said he would wait a further ten minutes. Sandow and his party could not prevail upon the door-keeper to let them in, so Sandow broke down the stage door (tipping the injured doorman ten pounds for his pains) – he would always affect embarrassment when he had to use his strength in acts of actual violence against property or men – and burst forth into the theatre wearing a plain pink sleeveless under-vest and a pair of black evening trousers, arriving just seconds before the contest was due to be cancelled. The Marquess of Queensberry and Lord de Clifford sat as judges at the centre of the stage.

In the first test, Sampson took an iron bar and bent it over his arms, calf, chest and back, with apparent ease. Sandow, who claimed never to have performed this feat before, just managed to repeat the trial. Then Sampson took a chain, wrapped it around his chest and under his arms and broke it by simultaneously inflating his lungs and contracting the muscles of his chest – a well-practised routine that owed as much to technique as strength. This Sandow was able to repeat (albeit with some difficulty) as again he had never done the trick before. Then, Sampson wrapped a short length of chain about his arm and snapped it by expanding his muscles. Sandow found he could not replicate the feat, as the proffered chain was too small to go round his own arm – but the Prussian had come prepared. Out of his trouser pocket, he produced an armlet of the correct size, apparently made to identical specifications, as was later vouchsafed by a representative of the manufacturer who just happened to have been in the audience.

It was later alleged that Sandow had brought accomplices into the theatre to help him with his challenge, arranging to substitute the chain for "one prepared earlier". "Sandow connived with a confederate," Sampson asserted. "And when my honest chains were passed around the audience for inspection the confederate substituted in their place false chains, previously filed and prepared by Sandow, and he succeeded in breaking these counterfeits." We will examine this accusation in a later chapter. For now, the judges examined the chain and declared that the performance was to continue. Sandow broke it effortlessly and, having matched Sampson in three chosen feats, was technically the winner, but Sampson refused to concede defeat. Through an interpreter, Sandow made the offer that if either Sampson or Cyclops could repeat his performance with a vast dumb-bell, which was at that moment brought onto the stage, the contest should be declared a draw. There followed a vintage Sandow stage display. "With one hand I lifted up [this 280lb weight]," Sandow recalled, "then lay down, and finally stood up with it." He then took another, somewhat less heavy dumb-bell and raised it to his chest, fastened some chains about his arms and burst them asunder before releasing the weight. Sampson refused to accept any of the challenges and the aristocratic judges declared Sandow the winner, to the delight of the by-now frenzied crowd. Sampson and Cyclops left London that night without paying over the prize money. But Sandow received a special payment of £350 from the management of the theatre and the contest attracted an audience of at least a thousand, many of whom accompanied the victorious Prussian on his journey back to his rooms in the West End.

Soon after besting Sampson, he and Attila signed a £150-a-week contract for a show at the Alhambra Theatre (one of the more salubrious music halls in London, located on the east side of Leicester Square and built in the style of a Saracen temple). His fortunes were transformed – the strongman had thus become "the subject of as much public talk as if he were some royal personage whom the clubs, the privileged class and society in general had agreed to treat as the lion of the season." His performances at the Alhambra were attended by "not only all athletic and would-be athletic London, but royalty, also, and the flower of the nobility, plus the elite of Mayfair and Belgravia." The Prince of Wales attended at least one performance, on 29 November, when Sandow started with manipulation of a two-handed dumb-bell, went on to lift various enormous weights above his head with one or two hands and concluded with his enactment of the death of Hercules, which involved bearing a weight of 1,500lbs on his chest. The future King Edward VII visited Sandow in his dressing room on this occasion and he and his son, the future King George V, would in later years patronise Sandow's establishment in St James's. Even allowing for the hyperbole of a sympathetic biographer concerned to demonstrate his subject's appeal to high society, Sandow had become, within days of his arrival in London, a late-Victorian celebrity.

In highbrow English-lit circles, the 1890s are remembered as the time of a *fin-de siècle* flourishing. This was the decade of *The Yellow Book*, of Henry James and Thomas Hardy, Oscar Wilde and the two Georges,

Meredith and Gissing – and of Robert Louis Stevenson and H.G. Wells, who both wrote parables of modern manhood in decline (*Dr Jekyll and Mr Hyde* and *The Time Machine*). But for every man or woman who had read or even heard of Henry James or puzzled their way through the convoluted prose of Meredith or laughed at Wilde's risqué satires, there were thousands who knew and admired Eugen Sandow and, from the moment he took to the stage, Sandow eclipsed these figures in terms of fame. A point made obliquely by the popular novelist Walter Raleigh in 1901 when he wrote of his rival that: "I suppose Meredith is the cleverest novelist who has ever written [whereas] I am no more like a great novelist than I am like Sandow..." Sandow belonged fairly and squarely to popular culture, the culture of the masses and the new entertainment industries, rather than the elite who read sophisticated novels or attended fashionable West End theatre.

By the 1890s, music hall had evolved from its mid-century roots in the pub concert rooms of working class England into a sophisticated mass leisure industry, distinct from highbrow theatre and subject to its own internal stratifications between West End, East End, up-market, low-brow, London and regional establishments. It was a highly urbanised and sophisticated industry targeted at the lower and lower-middle classes – a new mass audience that had money and leisure and political clout for the first time in British history, following successive extensions of the franchise and the opening up of education to all. There were all the trappings of the modern entertainment and leisure industry: show-business impresarios and agents, well-capitalised chains of theatres such as (the future Sir) Horace Edward Moss's Empire Palaces, and a definite move towards highly paid celebrities, spectacular stage effects and bombastic architecture. These music hall business empires were as organised as modern mass leisure attractions such as

Disneyworld. "What strikes one on and after entering [one of Moss's establishments] is the organisation which prevails in every part of the building," noted one contemporary. "In this lies the secret of Mr Moss's success. Every official knows his business, and does it with a quiet unobtrusive ease and politeness. The same scientific system is evident in the working of the stage…and altogether the eye must rest with pleasure on a place of amusement whose arrangement and working are smooth and complete."

Even today as one looks around and in particular above one's head in the Leicester Square area of west London, one will see the relics of this splendiferous age – for example the revolving globe atop the Coliseum, now the home of the English National Opera but first erected in 1904 by Oswald Stoll as an emporium of popular culture, or the horses on top of the Hippodrome. As the name suggests, this establishment really was a place where horses raced around the stage. The Saracenic ramparts of the Alhambra can be identified hidden behind the hoardings gaudily advertising the popular movies of today, watched by the descendants of those who came to the same identical spot over a hundred years ago to seek similar distractions and gratifications. Towards the end of the 19th century, music hall had thus entered its period of "maximum prosperity and influence," according to the historian Peter Bailey.[21] There were nearly 500 music hall establishments in London alone and thousands more in provincial cities. Music hall was a dominant form of popular culture for at least a century, dying out in Great Britain only at the time of the Second World War, evolving over time into variety theatre, as indeed the fun for the audience was the sheer variety of the entertainment on offer. There was considerable overlap between British music hall and American vaudeville: in both countries offering the public everything from trick cyclists and trained seals, to opera singers and slapstick comedians.

For the late-Victorian elite, the vitality and amorality of music hall culture were a source of appalled fascination, tempered by hypocrisy. Writers such as Arthur Symons and F. Anstey ventured to the music halls of the East and West Ends, exalting in the tawdriness of the experience, just as contemporary social explorers experienced a frisson when they visited the slums of London. Publicly, they denounced the licentiousness and drunkenness of the clientele and expressed horror at the sheer number of prostitutes who none too discreetly advertised their availability (the convention was that they never approached the men for custom, but rather milled about in the aisles); privately, they boasted of their sexual conquests and sat themselves close to the stage so they could look up the skirts of the chorus-girls and ballet dancers. The top class of halls, such as the Alhambra or the Empire Theatre in Leicester Square, were large, brash and gaudy. "Huge cressets in classical tripods flare between the columns of the façade," noted the humorist F. Anstey. "The windows and foyer glow with stained glass, the entrance hall, lighted by softened electric lamps, is richly and tastefully decorated. You pass through wide, airy corridors, and down stairs, to find yourself in a magnificent theatre, and the stall to which you are shown is wide and luxuriously fitted. Smoking is universal, and a large proportion of the audience promenades the outer circles, or stand in groups before the long refreshment bars which are a prominent feature on every tier."[22] As for the Empire, noted another observer, "it was to [its Victorian and Edwardian patrons], men about town, gallants from Ouida or Kipling almost a club...the most celebrated rendezvous in the world. It bordered on Bohemia and its social amenities, if such they could be called, included the notorious Promenade where ladies of the town consorted with the dandies of the time and shocked the entire nation." In 1894, the London County Council insisted on modifications to this promenade as a condition for renewing the theatre's music and dancing licence, having denounced the theatre as "the habitual resort for prostitutes in search of their traffic."

As another contemporary poetically observed:

> "The low and soft luxurious promenade,
> Electric light, pile carpet, the device
> Of gilded mirrors that repeat you thrice,
> The crowd that lounges, strolls from yard to yard.
> The calm and brilliant Circes who retard
> Your passage with the skirts and rouge that spice
> The changeless programme of insipid vice…"[23]

The suburban and bourgeois music halls were dingier and gaudier than these magnificent West End establishments, but in a curious way more wholesome. "You will see little family parties – father, mother, and perhaps a grown-up daughter or a child or two – in the stalls." Large ham sandwiches were handed round by cooks in white blouses while young men taking a break from their work in nearby shops and factories treated their sweethearts to a glass of port. Or perhaps:

> "She wouldn't call for sherry; she wouldn't call for beer;
> She wouldn't call for Cham, because she knew 'twould make her queer;
> She wouldn't call for brandy, rum or anything they'd got;
> She only called for Bovril – hot! Hot! Hot!"

A glance at the front pages of the major newspapers gives a flavour of the programme at the more salubrious establishments. For example, you could see a fish ballet complete with elaborately costumed molluscs, whelks, oysters, and fish and chips, or a complete recreation of the Epsom Derby. "Today – Royal Aquarium – The Talking Horse," reads an advertisement in a random copy of the *Daily Telegraph* from the early 1890s. The show that night was to include: Fuller's miraculous dives through the roof; Adelina Ontonio's wonderful mid-air feats with a double-backward somersault from the roof; Baum's Monte Cristo Sack Feat; the two marvellous flying girl Fitzroys; the Wonderful Performing Dog; the murder, capture, burial &c., the widow's grief, the return to life; the 1,052nd extraordinary performance of the original boxing kangaroo and a multitude of others including Spanish dancers, a man emerging from an egg, a lady saxophonist, a pair of sleigh-bell soloists, the three sister Slaters' Banjo and Skipping Rope dance, and Sloman, the bird and animal impersonator.

In its quick-change variety, the music hall show catered to the late Victorians' lust for sensation and immediacy, calling to mind the modern age of reality TV and cable television. The speedy transition from one act to another catered to those with a very low attention span and a desire for instant thrills and gratification. While you couldn't flick through the channels, you could at least engage in conversation or stroll to the bar until something more entertaining came along. "In the upper parts of the house the conversation renders it impossible to hear distinctly anything that is said or sung…stage footmen…slip a giant card bearing a number into a gilded frame on either side of the proscenium before each item of the programme. The electric bell tings, the lights are raised, the orchestra dashes into a prelude, and the artiste whose 'turn' it is comes on…"

The whooping of the crowds provided a form of audience interaction that would delight the producers of modern "reality TV" shows and, as with modern TV culture, the events and personalities were subject to a constant process of media recycling. Within days of his arrival in London, Sandow became a darling of the press, the perfect subject for a feature article whether the tone was admiring or, on occasions, gently mocking. Accordingly, stories about Sandow's body and his exploits appeared in many leading newspapers and magazines, from the highbrow such as *The Times* and the *Daily Telegraph* to middle-brow publications such as *The Strand Magazine* (where many of the *Sherlock Holmes* stories by his friend Conan Doyle would later be published) and the purely popular such as *Ally Sloper's Half-Holiday*, where Sandow was "interviewed" by this rapscallion, fictitious character.

Ally Sloper was an impish, down-at-heel representative of the lower middle-classes – slightly further down the social scale than another fictional creation, his near contemporary Mr Pooter – who seeks to emulate Sandow as a way of restoring his strength and masculinity. As the cartoon narrative relates, Sloper hopes that through diligent training he will be strong enough to fight off the bailiffs, who have come to collect his grand piano. "I will at once to Sandow," Sloper reflects, "he shall make a strong man of me, and then ruiners of other men's houses, beware!" Sloper meets Sandow and tears come to his eye as the strongman clasps his hand. Start with this 500lb dumb-bell, Sandow counsels. Like tens of thousands of late Victorians of all social classes, Sloper becomes an enthusiastic practitioner. However, he can't afford the dumb-bells, so uses household objects such as his son's rocking horse instead. Declaring that his great ambition is to have a band playing on his chest, he tries the experiment with the ironing board, a few flatirons and his young son. "A. Sloper doubts not he will, in course of time, succeed in becoming as strong as Sandow himself."[24]

DISTINGUISHED PEOPLE INTERVIEWED BY A. SLOPER.—SANDOW.

Ally Sloper's Half-Holiday, 21 November 1891

The cartoon mocks both Ally Sloper's pretensions and Sandow's sales pitch, but still speaks to the wide appeal of the young Prussian. Sandow himself is portrayed in the skimpiest of costumes, his medallion displayed on his naked chest, wearing harlequin socks and a gentle smile on his mildly moustachioed face. He is angelic, rather than bulky, sweet-tempered, not violent. The press nevertheless gleefully reported a real-life altercation between Sandow and his landlady, after Sandow was alleged to have smashed the ceiling of his apartment while doing his exercises.

More typically, journalists were impressed by his quiet manner and the sheer ordinariness that belied his physical prowess. "The strongman is a young German who speaks English fairly well [this interview dates to December 1891, so he has acquired more than the rudiments of the language], with light curly hair and a fair moustache," noted one who visited him in his rented accommodation at 170 Warwick Street, Pimlico. "He is singularly modest in manner, and our representative could hardly believe that the young Prussian who entered the room (he is not yet 24) was the splendid athlete who defeated Sampson at the Aquarium some months ago." The only evidence of his strength was Aubrey Hunt's portrait of the athlete as a Roman Gladiator, which Sandow had hung on his dining-room wall, thus showing off his muscles to great advantage. Sandow puffed insouciantly on a huge Havana cigar throughout the interview.

The strongman's stage performances lasted no more than 20 minutes and in that time it was imperative to pack in as much novelty and excitement as possible. At the Alhambra and on the regional tour that followed it, the audience was first treated to conjuring tricks performed by a magician called Charles Bertram. ("How neat he is, how delightful in manner!") Then Attila would appear, clad in a vivid scarlet bodysuit "which was close drawn to his figure as an eel's skin to his sinuous body". Sandow's mentor would raise and manipulate 56lb weights and then perform the musketry drill of the German army with a 90lb steel bar instead of a rifle. Undoubtedly impressive – Attila deftly manipulated this very heavy weight – but nothing compared to the performance that followed. "When at last [Sandow] came on the stage and advanced to the footlights the roar which greeted him made the reception of his tutor seem as a Fifth of November cracker in comparison." Sandow would start with a revealing warm-up act, followed by poses designed to exhibit his musculature and then feats of strength. These might include lifting a (quite genuine) horse above his head, or cartwheeling across the stage with dumb-bells attached to his arms and legs, and turning a somersault with 56lb weights in each hand. He would break an English penny in half between his finger and thumb, or tear apart a pack of cards or two, or sometimes three in one go. He lifted up fully grown men with one hand, his arm outstretched. He had a special set of hollow dumb-bells with large spheres at each end. He would lift these above his head with one hand and, to the audience's delight, a fully-grown man would emerge from each of the spheres.

"It is a much more difficult thing to lift a weight than to support it," he would explain. To demonstrate his extraordinary strength in this regard, he made a bridge of himself on the stage, supporting his body, chest upwards, with his arms and knees. His assistants would strap a board on top of his chest, pierced with three holes, one which encircled his neck, the others fitting around his knees. Then all manner of heavy objects and living creatures would be heaped on top of him, as for example when a horse and its rider were led onto the platform, while assorted stagehands, weights and paraphernalia were added to make up the ballast. Once he supported a grand piano with an orchestra of eight performers on top of it and it was calculated that he could hold a total weight of some 2,400lbs in this way – more than a ton and about the same as a small vehicle such as a Mini. He would polka step across the stage with an ordinary piano strapped to his back, together with a pianist who sat at the instrument and played and sang. His trademark act was the so-called Roman Column display, imparted to him by his mentor Prof. Attila, in which he strapped himself upside down to a steel pole, supported only by his legs, and then bent down backwards until his hands touched the stage; then he would pick up a big dumb-bell and proceed to draw it up with enormous effort, his muscles protruding (as one journalist noted) "like lianas on a forest tree", until his body was at right angles to the pole, the weight held triumphantly at arm's length above his head.

Sandow's first run of London engagements lasted until late January 1890. Then, together with Prof. Attila and Charles Bertram the magician, he went on a tour of the provinces, visiting: Bristol, Bradford, Nottingham, Manchester, Oxford, Sheffield, Leeds, Halifax, Huddersfield, Boston, Preston, Liverpool, Hull, Newcastle, York, Chester, Lancaster, Burnley, Rochdale and Derby. While in the north of England he watched a football game for the first time in his life and was deeply impressed by the muscularity, mental strength, coolness, quickness and judgement of the players (perhaps he saw Newton Heath FC, the forerunners of Manchester United?). And, at some point, he made friends with the Manchester photographer Warwick Brookes, who took his portrait in his studio at 350 Oxford Road and whose daughter Blanche he would eventually marry. Although he was by now on familiar terms with Royalty and aristocrats, and would become good friends with music hall celebrities like Marie Lloyd (who performed at the Alhambra at the same time as Sandow), he clearly felt an affinity with the energetic and enterprising northern businessmen he met on these early travels: he married into this community and, in due course, one of his daughters would marry a prosperous Manchester department store owner. In later life he would join the ranks of frock-coated late-Victorian entrepreneurs. But this is to look a long way ahead: he had as yet to conceive of a career beyond the music hall stage.

In the autumn of 1890, he returned to London where he ditched Attila and began his solo career with a season at the Royal Music Hall, Holborn, drawing massive crowds, particularly when he shared the stage with Karl Westphal, a 6' 2", 27 stone German giant, nicknamed "Goliath", whose bulk provided a fitting contrast with Sandow's more elegant frame (Sandow was a modest 5' 9" tall and weighed a mere 15 stone). Sandow had stumbled upon the giant on holiday in the Black Forest and brought him back to London. On arrival at Charing Cross station, Goliath could not fit into a cab and so he and Sandow had to lumber up Haymarket to their rooms in Piccadilly, followed by a large crowd. Goliath, a quarryman by profession, had little to do but pose as a galumphing foil for his infinitely more elegant and intelligent stage companion. "Goliath is huge, lumbering and unprepossessing," noted one observer, "Sandow medium-sized, agile, and a model of compactness and symmetry." Goliath would pick up a 400lb cannon and then Sandow would pick *him* up, reportedly with one finger. Here is an account from the *Sunday Times* of 30 September 1890:

As I am standing on the Royal Music Hall, chatting with Captain Taylor, the courteous manager, a young man, clad in a dark tweed suit, with a buff waistcoat, emerges from the wing, and stands, cigarette in mouth, watching the motions of the stage carpenters setting the stage. Captain Taylor introduces him as Mr. Sandow. The abnormal muscular development which makes him unique among living men is hidden in his street attire, and in his face, or in what is visible of his figure, there is nothing to speak of his extraordinary strength. The face and figure both look a little boyish. After a minute's chat on indifferent subjects he invites me to his dressing room, on a level with the stage, in which the paraphernalia used in his performance are kept. In the corner is his "dumb-bell," two huge masses of metal united by a steel bar, and weighing in all 312lbs…this he invites me to examine. With considerable difficulty I manage to support it, staggering under its weight, when he insinuates a casual forefinger about the bar and relieves me of the burden. Various other of the weights which figure in his performance are standing about the room, and he chats with me as he performs, in an easy manner, various feats with them, and ends by getting me to stand on the palm of one of his hands while he lifts me on to the dressing table. He dissipates the wonder of this performance by saying he is going to do the same with Goliath, the new giant, who weighs 27 stone. 'I am expecting him any minute,' he says. 'Come back to the stage,

perhaps he is here now.' We go back and there, sure enough, stands
Goliath, a huge mountain of flesh and bone, standing well over six feet,
with a chest measurement of Heaven knows how many inches, and
huge face like a pantomime mask. This gentleman's hand measures over
twelve inches from the tip of the thumb to that of the little finger, and
the silver ring on the index of his right hand slides easily, with room
to spare, over any two of my fingers. His hat covers my head and rests
upon my shoulders. He bestrides the narrow stage like a Colossus, and
Sandow, standing beside him, is a mere pigmy, though he is almost as
much Goliath's superior in mere brute force as he is in deftness. Goliath
speaks no English, but has a fashion of expressing friendly interest in
anything going forward by a sort of grunt, which shakes the building...

Sandow's...performance is really marvellous: Goliath, girt by a
leathern band, stands upon a raised platform which brings his waist
about on a level with his companion's elbow; in the easiest manner
possible, Sandow puts his hand under the belt and walks off with his
huge companion held at arm's length."

"From head to heel there is not a bad point in him," the *Newcastle
Chronicle* noted after a similar performance. "His features are of a bold
classical type; his head is well-shaped and balanced upon a white and
muscular neck; his shoulders are immensely broad; and in every limb
– from mighty arm to shapely calf – the muscles stand out firm and
rounded as bosses of steel."

During the course of 1890-1892, Sandow performed in Birmingham
and Edinburgh and appeared at other leading London halls such as
the Pavilion and the Tivoli. He varied the routine to include special
exhibition performances and there were at least two professionally
judged weight-lifting competitions. In the first of these, which took
place on 10 December 1890 at the Royal Music Hall, Holborn, the
contest consisted of six genuine feats of strength, three selected by
Sandow and three by his challenger Hercules McCann. The stakes
were £100 a side. In addition, Sandow was offered £50 if he could lift

a weight of 250lbs with one hand, from the shoulder to a position at arm's length from his head. This Sandow achieved without the slightest difficulty and proceeded to carry out four further feats of strength, two of his own and two of McCann's. McCann himself performed only three feats and so Sandow supporters were outraged when the Marquess of Queensberry quixotically declared McCann the winner instead of the young Prussian (when Sandow protested, Queensberry haughtily declared that he was disappointed at the "un-English way" that the decision of the judges had been challenged).

Sandow made amends a few weeks later, on 29 January 1891 at the International Hall of the Café Monico near Piccadilly Circus, when he became the first man in the world to lift a 250lb weight. As *Sporting Life* described the scene, Sandow was worried that the stage would collapse under the combined 400lb weight of man and long-handled dumb-bell:

> Steadying himself, Sandow lifted the bell on to his chest, then pushed it half-way up, straightening his arms as the bell rose. He stood with the enormous mass fully extended. Dropping the bell shoulder high, he again pushed it up and tried the performance again, but the bell turned his hand when it was halfway up, and he dropped it to the floor with a crash that made everyone's teeth jar. Next the bell was stood endwise, and with two hands Sandow lifted it to his shoulder, steadying it for a moment, and then gradually pressing the bell up, he achieved one of the grandest pieces of dumb-bell lifting ever seen...

He went on to impress his audience by lifting a 177lb bar-bell. He raised a 70.5lb weight in one hand and a 56lb weight in the other – at the same time. "The ease and the coolness of the performance electrified everyone…"

Despite these and other prodigious feats of strength, Sandow himself carefully never claimed to be the strongest man in the world (although his promoters would often make that claim on his behalf). He knew that others were stronger, including the French-Canadian Louis Cyr (1863-1912) and the Frenchman Louis Uni, alias Apollon (1862-1928). Cyr was capable of picking up horses *à la* Sandow, lifted 18 men on a platform on his back, hefted a 1000lb weight with his finger (that one sounds especially improbable) and pushed a freight car up a hill. He beat Sandow's record for a one-handed lift by two pounds, but his most celebrated feat was to stand fast while resisting the pull of four horses, two held in each hand, while grooms cracked their whips in a vain attempt to pull his arms asunder. "It is generally conceded that Louis Cyr was, in his best days, the strongest man in the known world for straight weight-lifting," said Harry Houdini, who made a study of strongmen. "[But] Cyr did not give the impression of being an athlete, nor a man of training, for he appeared to be over-fat and not particularly muscular."[25] There was talk of a weight-lifting contest between Cyr and Sandow, but this never came to pass, as the two men could never agree on the rules for such a competition. Some thought Apollon stronger still, lazily snapping iron bars and juggling axle wheels, but both men were large and ungainly, neither possessing Sandow's matchless combination of strength *and* elegance. As we will consider in a later chapter, it was this yoking of power and beauty that his contemporaries found staggering.

Sandow also dispensed instruction in physical fitness training to individuals and institutions. For example, on 12 December 1892, he was the subject of a lecture at the Royal Military Academy, Woolwich. Sandow gave his audience of cadets and officers a demonstration of his physique. "Stripped to the waist, he was able to demonstrate by different movements how great was the command he had over various muscles," related a contemporary account taken from the pages of the *Lancet*, the authoritative medical journal. "Clasping his hands behind his head, he was able to make his biceps rise and fall in time to music. Walking around the audience, he displayed various muscles in action as they were separately named." He allowed the troops to run their hands over his body "with the result that a young fellow described the sensation as being like that of 'moving your hand over corrugated iron'." He then carried out a series of exercises that made the muscles of his back look like "snakes coiling and uncoiling themselves under his skin." The evocative language suggests the strength and sinuosity of serpents and the power of a machine. With the music and the ritualised display of his muscles, followed by feats of strength, this was as much of a performance as any of his on-stage routines. The demonstration to soldiers, medical men and respectable members of the community would become a key part of the off-stage Sandow act. He would also try in vain throughout his career to get his system adopted officially by the military. Although individual soldiers such as Col Sir George Malcolm Fox, Inspector of Army Physical Training from 1890-1897, became declared followers of Sandow, his system was never taken up by the military as a whole. But it certainly suited Sandow to promote his close association with the patriotic endeavours of the armed forces.

As a star catering to the late-Victorian desire for spectacle, Sandow was by now more than an especially successful strongman. Eclipsing the likes of Prof. Attila, Batta, Cyr and Apollon, he belonged to an elite of music hall performers who had transcended their specialisations to become big-name attractions popular enough to anchor a season's entertainment. To adopt modern parlance, he was an A-list celebrity and his illustrious peers included Marie Lloyd (1870-1922), the singer who became Sandow's friend,[26] and Vesta Tilley (1864-1952), "the

Irving of the halls" who made her career impersonating men on stage (and ended up buried in the same Putney Vale Cemetery as Sandow, albeit with a proper memorial to her achievements). Other deities in the music hall firmament included Dan Leno, the cockney comedian, and Little Tich, the midget pantomime artiste whose most famous routine was "an acrobatic feat in which he balanced on boots which were nearly as long as he was tall," and who died after a mop fell on his head during an act (Tich was an early inspiration to Charlie Chaplin – who began his own career in music hall as a member of Fred Karno's Sketch Company – and Jacques Tati). And as for so many of these heroes of popular culture, from the actress Lillie Langtry to Charles Blondin the tight-rope walker and Buffalo Bill Cody, the hero of the Wild West turned showman, there was a lively international market for Sandow's talents: in due course, he was spotted in London by the impresario Henry S. Abbey and signed up for a tour of North America. But before we follow Sandow's move to 1890s America, let's consider just why Sandow's body had such an impact on his late-Victorian audiences.

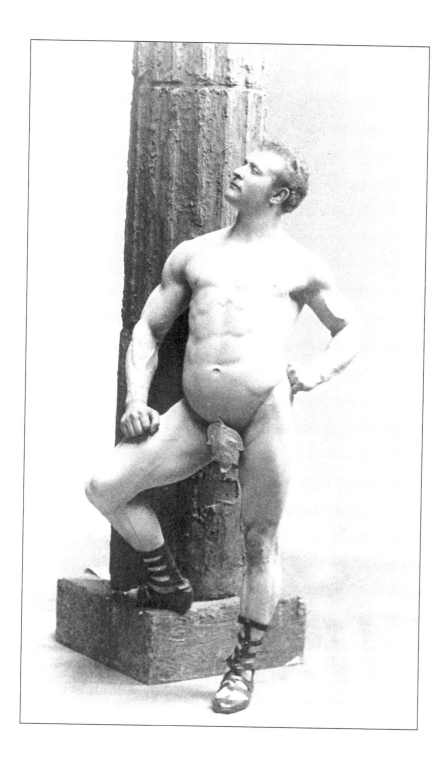

- 3 -

MANHOOD ON TRIAL

S andow's contemporaries were acutely conscious of living in a time of rapid change and preternatural stress. In the overheated but exceedingly influential words of the Austro-Hungarian writer Max Nordau:

> Our epoch of history is unmistakeably in its decline, and another is announcing its approach. There is a sound of rending in every tradition, and it is though the morrow would not link itself with today. Things as they are totter and plunge, and they are suffered to reel and fall, because man is weary, and there is no faith that it is worth an effort to uphold them...such is the spectacle presented by the doings of men in the reddened light of the Dusk of the Nations.[27]

Nordau's book *Degeneration* was published in Germany in 1892 and appeared in English three years later and its period of influence overlapped with Sandow's early career in London and the US. The author lamented the impact of so-called civilisation on health and life expectancy. "The dead carried off by heart and nerve diseases are the victims of civilisation," Nordau argued, blaming fatigue and exhaustion on "the vertigo and swirl of our frenzied life, the vastly increased number of sense impressions and organic reactions, and therefore of perceptions, judgements and motor impulses, which at present are forced into a given unity of time." Nervous diseases and bodily decrepitude are "exclusively a consequence of the present conditions of civilised life". Nordau mounted a generalised critique of modern, urban society, but he detested modern art in particular (Zola, Ibsen, Wagner and Tolstoy were special targets), and he singled out railway travel for vilification, alleging that the instability of modern man was at least partially attributable to the "vibrations undergone in railway travelling".[28]

Such eccentricities notwithstanding, Nordau's apocalyptic rant resonated acutely with his readers all around Europe. Everywhere, men and women were struggling to come to terms with the pace of social, political and technological change as the 19th century drew to a close. With the benefit of hindsight, one can indeed see empires swirling in the vertigo of forces that led to the conflagration of the First World War: mounting economic and political competition between nations; unrelenting industrialisation bringing an end to traditional economic production, driving millions from the countryside into factories and cities. By the early 20th century, more than three quarters of the population lived in towns and cities, compared to just over half in 1850. This process is poignantly evoked in the novels of Thomas Hardy and later by E.M. Forster, who described one character in *Howard's End* as "the third generation shepherd or ploughboy whom civilisation had sucked into the town…one of the thousands who have lost the life of the body and failed to reach the life of the spirit". The evolution of mass democracies went hand in hand with the disintegration of traditional, patriarchal modes of social control. The rise of new media such as Alfred Harmsworth's *Daily Mail*, first launched in 1896, was every bit as destabilising as the arrival of the Internet in our own age. "There was a mass readership eager to read the popular press, while technical advances in telegraphy and news gathering had transformed the methods and scope of the British newspaper industry," notes historian Kenneth O. Morgan. "Instead of the traditional, restrained reporting of such newspapers as *The Times* or the *Daily News*, there was now a vibrant press catering for the masses, and one less elitist and deferential."[29] The flourishing of periodicals fostered new literary genres, notably the short story, but it also spelt the end of traditional forms such as the triple-decker novel and Mudie's Circulating Library.

To cap it all, men had to face the emergence of the "New Woman" in the 1890s. Women enjoyed greater social, political and indeed sexual freedom than their mothers had enjoyed and their fathers and brothers wanted them to have. Satirised unrelentingly in the conservative press, they rode bicycles, wore rational, i.e. comfortable, clothes and insisted on their right to go to work and earn a living, or to pick a husband on their own terms, or even not choose a husband at all. "Her brow is serious," lamented one typical male observer, "for the brain behind is crammed full of high projects as is the satchel she carries of pamphlets on the missions, rights, grievances and demands of her sex…if she assumes certain aspects of masculine garb on occasion, it is solely on account of their superior utility; if she rides out on a bicycle it is for the purpose of strengthening her muscles and expanding her muscles and expanding her lungs for the great work she has before her."[30] Some wrote novels, others sought to reform their menfolk, while still others wanted the vote. This new assertiveness was expressed in the protests of the proto-suffragettes and the literature of early feminists such as Mona Caird, Sarah Grand or Olive Schreiner – and also more prosaically in the high street. One symptom of the new freedom enjoyed by women was the phenomenon of frenzied shopping:

"Now once again the old familiar frenzy
Stirs in the breasts of agitated females,
Now are the sales on, and the air is thick with
Rumours of remnants.
Down from the heights of Highgate and of Hampstead,
Up from the wilds of Camberwell and Brixton,
Come they by hansom, omnibus or railway,
Thirsting for bargains.
Packed are the halls of Maple and of Shoolbred,
Fierce is the fray where flies the flag of Whitely,
Scarce shall a Sandow penetrate the throng at
Marshall and Snelgrove's…"[31]

Meanwhile, in the United States, the end of the frontier removed a field of masculine endeavour from American life, while growing industrialisation and urbanisation brought their own strains. France had to deal with the impact of a declining population and the humiliation of the 1870-1871 War with Prussia, which after a series of punishing military defeats led to the loss of Alsace-Lorraine and the self-laceration of the Commune and its suppression. Germany was unified under Prussian domination in the Hall of Mirrors in Versailles, but despite its new political power, the country was itself in the throes of rapid industrialisation and destabilising social change. And Britain, which as the 19th century drew to a close possessed the largest and most powerful Empire the world had ever known, and ought to have been profoundly self-confident, endured the same problems of "imperial overreach" experienced by the US a century later. Its imperial and industrial dominance was under threat on many fronts. Insecurity gnawed at the bowels of empire and, wherever you turned in the modern world, men suffered agonies of emasculation. They found themselves carried along on powerful currents that led they knew not whither; the old patterns of authority and control had broken down, in the home and in the workplace.

In the early chapters of his book, Nordau extrapolated from the fitness of the individual body to the health of the race and nation as a whole. To paraphrase the argument, western civilisation was doomed because individual westerners were weak. This weakness would be transmitted from generation to generation, further enfeebling the health of the race and leading to the long-term decline of western civilisation. The word that encapsulated this process, for Nordau and his contemporaries, was *degeneration*, indicating what was felt to be an inexorable process of moral as well as bodily weakness and corruption. *Degeneration* originated as a scientific concept invented in part as a response to the theories of Charles Darwin, posited as one of the ways in which evolution might take place, alongside balance and elaboration. So the distinguished zoologist (and later admirer of Sandow) Prof Roy Lankester concluded in a study of barnacles and soon expanded his definition to describe a sort of unfitness that befell all species when they found themselves with too much to eat and drink and did not have to compete to survive. "Any set of conditions which render [a species'] food and safety very easily obtained, seem to lead to degeneration," he argued.

It did not take too big a leap of the imagination to extrapolate from the behaviours of molluscs to men and women in modern western society. In December 1888, the year before Sandow came to London, *The Lancet* found that degeneration was "undoubtedly at work among town-bred populations as the consequence of unwholesome occupations, improper [diet], and juvenile vice…[and] it would be wrong to ignore the existence of widespread evils and dangers to the public health."[32] The concept helped explain a bitter contradiction at the heart of British society: never had the British Empire enjoyed so much power and prestige and yet this imperial domination went hand in hand with domestic poverty and squalor, living proof that the notions of progress that inspired earlier generations of Victorians did not extend to the working classes that lived on one's doorstep. It was a stark fact that, in the heart of the great metropolis of London, a "residuum" of unredeemable *untermenschen* lived in conditions of depravity and destitution, moments in a hackney cab from the mansions of the rich and the music halls of the West End. "Overcrowding is the great cause of degeneracy," concluded Charles Booth in his study of *Life and Labour in London*. Visit Southwark, for example, just across the river from the Houses of Parliament, or Colliers Rents (in the Seven Dials area of Covent Garden) or Saffron Hill, not to mention the East End, and the eyes, nostrils and conscience would be affronted by places "compared with which the lair of a wild beast would be a comfortable and healthy spot". In his pamphlet *The Bitter Cry of Outcast London*, journalist Andrew Mearns wrote:

> Few who will read these pages have any conception of what these pestilential human rookeries are, where tens of thousands are crowded together amidst horrors which call to mind what we have heard of the middle passage of the slave ship. To get into them you have to get into courts reeking with poisonous and malodorous gases arising from accumulations of sewage and refuse scattered in all directions and often flowing beneath your feet...every room in these rotten and reeking tenement houses a family, often two...[33]

The contradictions between imperial splendour and domestic squalor inspired some memorable polemics, notably General William Booth's *In Darkest England*, a book which appeared in 1890 as an answer to the explorer Henry Morton Stanley's *In Darkest Africa*, an account of his epic expedition to rescue Emin Pasha. The founder of the Salvation

Army asked whether "as there is a darkest Africa is there not also a darkest England? Civilisation, which can breed its own barbarians, does it not breed its own pygmies?". "The Equatorial Forest traversed by Stanley," the General wrote, "resembles the Darkest England of which I have to speak, alike in its vast extent ... its monotonous darkness, its malaria and its gloom, its dwarfish and dehumanised inhabitants, the slavery to which they are subjected, their privations and their misery."

The poor physical state of proletarian man was deemed to be at the very root of Great Britain's decline. However, it became alarmingly and perversely clear that the underclass was flourishing. Far from exterminating itself under the weight of its inherited defects and criminality, the underclass appeared to be prospering not merely in spite of the terrible conditions of modern industrial society, but because of them – benefiting from a mutant fecundity like some undesirable organism reproducing itself in a sewer. Karl Pearson (1857-1936), a brilliant mathematician and pioneer of the new science of statistics, calculated that half of each generation was the product of one quarter of its predecessor and that this prolific quarter was in turn drawn disproportionately from the "unfit". This meant: "the habitual criminal, the professional tramp, the tuberculous, the insane, the mentally defective, the alcoholic, the diseased from birth or from excess."[34] As his mentor Galton observed, they seemed better adapted to the circumstances of modern living: "sickly-looking and puny residents in towns may be better knit and do more work and live longer than much haler men imported from elsewhere." Only by facing up to these problems would British society avoid "degeneration of type, that is, race degeneration, if not race suicide," the socialist Sidney Webb later argued.[35]

These preoccupations reflect confusedly the ideas of Jean-Baptiste

Lamarck (1744-1829) who had developed a pre-Darwinian theory of evolution. According to his "theory of adaptation," acquired characteristics could be passed on from generation to generation (one example was the blacksmith's strong arm, acquired during a lifetime at the forge and supposedly capable of being passed on from father to son.) The Austrian monk Gregor Mendel (1822-1884) had already carried out the research to prove that this was not the way heredity actually worked, but his findings, based on a study of pea plants, did not become current in the scientific community until well after the pseudo-science of eugenics had taken root. Eugenicists deemed it in the interest of society as a whole to improve the "racial stock" of the nation, through either *positive* eugenics (which sought to promote the breeding of desirable characteristics) or the negative variety, which aimed to eliminate negative qualities through intervention – for example, sterilisation, euthanasia and ultimately murder.

Few legacies of the late Victorian era are so reviled today, primarily because of the terrible efficiency with which the Nazi government of the 1930s promoted eugenicist policies.[36] In the 1890s and the early 20th century, however, the doctrine of eugenics was respectable, promoted by some of the brightest scientific minds of the era. Pioneers included Francis Galton, a gentleman explorer and talented mathematician, who invented not merely the forensic science of fingerprinting but also the modern field of statistics, as he sought ways of making sense of the large volumes of data acquired in the process of his research into heredity. He coined the term in 1883 and later founded first a research laboratory and then a professorial chair in the subject at University College, London.[37] Galton had no doubt that the pick of the British race were as capable human animals as the world at present produced. Deficient though they may have been in terms of Sandowesque grace and sympathy, Galton found them to be "strong in mind and body, truthful and purposive, excellent leaders of the people of lower races".[38] This favourable judgement was confined to the upper classes: those who "are selected to go abroad in various high capacities, whether by Government or by firms to carry out large undertakings under circumstances when they have to depend much on themselves." His view of the masses was predictably far less favourable. "He finds the average holiday-maker and cheap excursion tourist unprepossessing as compared to the like section of other European races," noted Karl Pearson, Galton's friend and disciple. "We may superficially, perhaps, but nevertheless with some justification, sum them up as mentally and physically litter-scatterers."[39]

In addition to extensive "socio-medical" writings, there are plentiful literary examples that cast light on this central cultural preoccupation of the 1890s. The decaying Oxford colleges in Thomas Hardy's *Jude the Obscure* evoke the decadence of the ruling classes. In Stevenson's *Dr Jekyll and Mr Hyde*, Mr Edward Hyde "bears the imprint of deformity and decay" and is thus a degenerate alter ego to the impeccably civilised Dr Henry Jekyll. In *The Nether World* by George Gissing, the figure of Clem embodies a strong, lusty but ultimately degenerate and criminal physical strength: she "had all her charms in apparent maturity, and they were of the coarsely magnificent order …[she was] an embodiment of fierce life independent of morality…one would have compared her, not to some piece of exuberant normal vegetation, but to a rank, evilly fostered growth." A biologist by training, H.G. Wells rather admired the urban underclass, as from his own experience he knew life in the countryside was far worse. "To my mind, the English townsman even in the slums is infinitely better spiritually, more courageous and more imaginative and cleaner, than his agricultural cousin," he wrote in

The Secret of Tono-Bungay. But his *Time Machine* (published in 1895) is more than an enduring popular science fiction fable: to contemporary readers it was biting social satire, a parable of the decadent ruling class (the effete, pleasure-seeking, physically weak "Eloi"), and the preternaturally physically robust members of the industrial proletariat who prey murderously on their social superiors (the "Morlocks"). Wells, like Nordau, believed that the upper classes were degenerating more rapidly than the rampant proles.

Sandow's body had a visceral impact on contemporary audiences. He was the embodied rebuke to all those who argued that manhood was in decline, the incarnate proof that the tide of degeneration could be reversed. His brand of masculinity was the antithesis of the slothful *flaneur* or the effete, feminised dandy so often associated with the 1890s: he was energetic, purposive, disciplined. He represented an ideal of male physical perfection that reached back into the classical past and appropriated the influential ideals of an earlier generation of 19th century sages. In 1831, Thomas Carlyle had argued in *Sartor Resartus*, that society as a whole was comparable to a body that needed to be kept healthy through hard work. This evolved into the mid-century doctrine of "muscular Christianity," under which influential figures such as Thomas Arnold, Thomas Hughes and Charles Kingsley held that a man could not lead a useful and righteous life without strength and physical fitness. In contrast to 18th century ideals, where idleness was the mark of a true gentleman, Victorians were expected to put their bodies to work and pursue what Kingsley called a "healthy and manful Christianity". The author of *The Water Babies* and *Westward*

Ho!, vicar of Eversley in Hampshire, and subsequently Professor of History at Oxford, Kingsley was a quintessentially hyperactive, reforming Victorian of the mid-century: he captained both football and rugby at Rugby school, boxed and rowed and played cricket and ran the steeplechase. He swam naked in freezing streams, went on extravagantly energetic walking tours of Germany that left his limbs knotty and as "hard as iron." As one contemporary observed, "his ideal is a man who fears God and can walk a thousand miles in a thousand hours…who breathes God's free air on God's rich earth, and at the same time can hit a woodcock, doctor a horse and twist a poker around his finger." Muscular Christians such as Kingsley did not believe in strength for its own sake. Bodily power needed to be deployed in the service of righteousness.

"The muscleman seems to have no belief whatever as to the purpose for which his body is given him, except some hazy idea that it is to go up and down the world with him, belabouring men and captivating women," explained Thomas Hughes, author of *Tom Brown's Schooldays* and one of Kingsley's disciples, "whereas the least of the muscular Christians has hold of the old chivalrous and Christian belief, that a man's body is given him to be trained and brought into subjection, and then used for the protection of the weak, the advancement of all righteous causes".[40] Matthew Arnold was equally clear that the cultivation of bodily health and vigour needed to be conjoined to "the idea of a perfect spiritual condition" if it were not to be deemed unintelligent and vulgarising. Arnold, son of the founder of Rugby School and inspector of schools as well as poet and polemicist, knew well that one practical application of this ideology was the rise of competitive games in the British public school system. "The physical training of a public school," noted a *Quarterly* reviewer in 1860, "is

by no means the least important part of the system: combined with
the field-sports of the holidays…it goes far to make the Englishman
what he is". The domination of British rowers, cricketers and even
mountaineers over their French, German and American counterparts
was taken as crucial evidence of national superiority.

Later in the century, intellectuals such as Sir Leslie Stephen
continued to be fanatical about fitness: in his youth, the man now
remembered chiefly as the father of Virginia Woolf and Vanessa Bell
was celebrated throughout England for his athletic prowess: he walked
the 55 miles from London to Cambridge in 12 hours flat, leaving
after breakfast and arriving in time for dinner; he won the mile race in
five minutes and four seconds; later he graduated to mountaineering
and was a President of the Alpine Club as well as the first man to
climb the Schreckhorn in the Swiss Alps, a feat celebrated in a poem
by Thomas Hardy. But, by this time, the alliance between Christianity
and robust physical exercise had been severed: while Stephen enjoyed
quasi-religious experiences when contemplating a sublimely beautiful
alpine sunrise from atop a precipice, he had long since abandoned his
faith. He and other irreligious intellectuals enjoyed fitness and exercise
for their own sake.

In the decadent 1890s, Sandow's brand of muscularity, in all its
supple, secularised carnality, pointed the way towards a regenerate
future. His potency derived from the fact that he was both strong *and*
beautiful, an astonishing combination, according to contemporary
accounts. "It is a sad proof of our physical decadence that beauty
is no longer found allied with strength," lamented Hugues Le Roux
and Jules Garnier in their influential survey of the circus *Acrobats and
Mountebanks* (published in English in 1890 as Sandow was performing
in London). "The two qualities, formerly blended like metals in an

alloy, are now entirely separated."[41] In Sandow's body, these qualities appeared to be marvellously recombined. As we have seen, when he appeared on stage alongside the mountainous Goliath a few months later, observers were struck by the "extreme contrast" between Goliath's bulk and Sandow's graceful, well-proportioned form and his deftness of movement. "There is a conspicuous absence of the brutal proportions supposed to accompany muscular power," commented a Liverpool newspaper after Sandow performed in that city. "Sandow [possesses] one of the most symmetrical figures it is possible for the developed male to be endowed with." Sandow's symmetry was more than a neutral, anatomical descriptor: it was a culturally loaded concept that implied the antithesis of degeneration. Indeed Nordau, citing the Italian criminologist Cesare Lombroso, identified asymmetry of body and facial features as a prime indication of degeneracy.

The Victorians had never seen anything quite like his body. Or rather, if they had, it was in a picture or a statue rather than a real-life human body. "A good many people…are fond of insisting that the mighty men of muscle which were portrayed in the marble by the sculptors of the classical age were simply products of the sculptors' imagination: fancy presentiments of men as they might be, rather than of any who actually existed," commented one anonymous writer in *The Strand Magazine*. "But here we have a…man who lives and breathes at this very moment…and comes favourably out of a comparison with any of them."[42] Sandow's body fused beauty and strength in a way which commentators believed to be impossible in the decadent and degenerate final decade of the 19th century. He embodied the physical perfection of classical antiquity, and the perfectibility of white Caucasian manhood – and both women and men found him extremely sexy.

- 4 -

BETWEEN TITILLATION AND RESPECTABILITY - SANDOW'S SEX-APPEAL

At Christmas 1889, the writer John Addington Symonds took delivery of photographs of Sandow sent over by his friend the writer Edmund Gosse. Symonds was living in Davos in the Swiss Alps – at the time, not quite the Magic Mountain made famous by Thomas Mann, but still a paradise for this dilettante art historian and connoisseur of young male flesh. Symonds owned hundreds of pictures of naked men and boys: "I have quite a vast collection now — enough to paper a little room I think. They become monotonous, but one goes on seeking the supreme form & the perfect picture".[43] The images of Sandow were provocative rather than pornographic, at least in comparison to some of the hard-core images possessed by Symonds, for example the pictures of naked Italian boys taken by Guglielmo Plüschow. But the photographs, like the music hall performances, certainly packed a homoerotic punch and it is these and similar images that are flagged up as "gay int." on the Internet today. Gosse liked them so much that he took some of the pictures along with him to the funeral of Robert Browning in Westminster Abbey, distracting himself during the long service by contemplating the postcards of the near-naked man.

It was one of the paradoxes of Sandow's career that a man who quite literally embodied normative manliness, should have become a pin-up for a circle of homosexually-inclined intellectuals. Yet the classical body language deployed by Sandow could have been interpreted in an innocent light. As the historian Linda Dowling has argued, the "prestige of ancient Greece [and by extension the classical world in general] was…massive".[44] Sandow's poses were a way of capturing some of that prestige for his own account, of conferring legitimacy on an act that could have been judged indecent. In the era of Aubrey Beardsley and Oscar Wilde, the sight of a near-naked male body looking like a Greek statue was arguably more edifying than the aesthete in his lavender gloves and silk stockings. It represented an asexual, reassuringly normative vision of what a man should be – a real man, as it were, instead of a sexually indeterminate fop. In the last quarter of the century, sculptors such as Frederic Leighton, Henry Bates, Alfred Gilbert and Dorno Thorneycroft all produced "critically acclaimed nudes…as the epitome of the ideal form." The image of a naked man was less dangerous than the female body which with its "dangerous pleasures challenged public morals and sullied public space," argues the art historian Michael Hatt.[45] Sandow thus offered a populist complement to the so-called New Sculpture movement, a phrase coined by Edmund Gosse himself.[46]

At this time, London was full of thousands of prostitutes, yet it was only in 1895 that a woman's bare feet were seen on the West End stage for the first time, in the stage version of Du Maurier's *Trilby*. A few years later, it is said that a display of ankles led Queen Alexandra to require her ladies in waiting to avert their eyes at a Royal Variety Performance. Similar double standards were surely at work in the case of Sandow: the late Victorian public allowed itself to be convinced that his body was somehow wholesome and edifying, when of course many of both genders found his displays distinctly arousing. For all the fig leaf of respectability enveloping Sandow's act, there was little to conceal that a near-naked man was on display. By the time he got to the US, the leaf was often literal: for his photographic poses, this was all he wore, prompting to this day earnest academic speculation as to how this item might have been affixed to his body. "One method used a wire around Sandow's waist, which was later etched out of the photograph," writes Josh Buck of the University of Maryland. "The other common method was to either tie or glue the leaf directly to Sandow."[47]

The "tableau vivant," or living picture, such as performed by Sandow, had a salacious history: it was a form of entertainment first perfected by Emma Hart, Lady Hamilton, the notorious mistress of Lord Nelson. She got into the habit of dressing up and exhibiting her "attitudes" – poses modelled on classical pictures and sculptures – when she was living with her husband in Naples at the end of the 18th century. She later practised her art in south London drawing rooms where, after very little pleading, she would strip off behind a curtain, drape herself in muslin over which water was poured – the original of the wet T-shirt look – before striking her poses. Andrew Ducrow, the celebrated equestrian circus performer, further developed the form. In his 1828 season at Astley's, he was billed as "The Venetian Statue! Or Living Model of Antiquity". There were 19 poses in all, including "three of the celebrated Positions of the Dying Gladiator" and "Hercules struggling with the Nemean Lion" – both attitudes that Sandow himself would adopt on stage and for still photographs. Ducrow gave perfect renditions of other Greek statues, including the Farnese Hercules, Discobulus and the fighting and dying gladiator. "This man must be an admirable model for painters and sculptors: his form is faultless, and he can throw himself into any attitude with the utmost ease and grace."[48]

Sandow's *tableaux* can also be compared with the *poses plastiques* that inspired the wrath of the National Vigilance Association and the fearsome Mrs Ormiston Chant of the Britishwomen's Temperance Association. In October 1894, by which time Sandow had safely decamped to the other side of the Atlantic, the Association challenged the renewal of a licence to the Palace Theatre of Varieties in Shaftesbury Avenue, on the grounds of indecency, stirring up a frenzied media debate about the respectability of music halls in general. The immediate cause of what became known as the "Prudes" controversy was a set of three especially provocative poses: "Ariadne", which showed "a naked woman on the back of a lion"; "The Naiad," in which a naked woman displayed neck, stomach and thighs, barely concealed by a gauze drape, and thirdly the "Polar Star," in which a nearly naked woman stood on a pedestal, her arms above her head holding a lamp. Arthur Symons and George Bernard Shaw were amused by what they waggishly termed "the ideal form of indecency". Mrs Chant herself maintained "the issue of nudity on the stage would never have arisen if men had been involved, because 'men would refuse to exhibit their bodies nightly in this way'": she had obviously not witnessed one of Sandow's stage performances.[49] Nor, it seems, was she aware of the earlier scandal surrounding *poses plastiques* and a notorious homosexual brothel in the louche Fitzrovia district of London's West End.

In 1889, Henry Fitzroy, Earl of Euston, was walking along Piccadilly when a tout pressed into his hand a card promoting: "poses plastiques. C. Hammond, 19 Cleveland St." The nobleman took this to be advertising a display of female nudes, as many red-blooded heterosexual men of the period might have done too, and promptly repaired to Cleveland St where he handed over a sovereign to gain access to the building. Instead of finding naked women, as he had hoped, he encountered a rent boy who made an indecent proposal. Fitzroy left immediately when he realised the nature of his error (or at least, so he declared in the subsequent court hearing). Despite his protestations, the aristocrat's reputation was besmirched, and others were drawn into the scandal, including (it was rumoured at the time) Prince Albert Victor, the eldest son of the Prince of Wales. The government was accused of mounting a cover-up to protect this sprig of the Royal Family.

Homosexual practices in themselves were hardly new. After the trial of Oscar Wilde in 1895, the journalist W.T. Stead quipped that: "if all persons guilty of Oscar Wilde's offences were to be clapped into gaol, there would be a very surprising exodus from Eton and Harrow, Rugby and Winchester, to Pentonville and Holloway". But Sandow's rise to prominence in the 1890s coincided with the historical moment at which homosexuality emerged as a form of human identity, as has been argued by the influential French philosopher Michael Foucault and his followers.[50] In 1885, homosexual acts were criminalised (under the Criminal Law Amendment Act) and a decade later the law claimed its most spectacular victim in Oscar Wilde, who was ruined after his ill-judged libel case against the Marquess of Queensberry backfired. On 28 February 1895, the Marquess, father of Wilde's lover Lord Alfred Douglas, left a card for Wilde at his club, accusing him of "posing as a somdomite" (sic). Wilde unwisely sued the aristocrat for libel, and lost the case, thus exposing himself to a second, criminal trial on a charge of gross indecency. He was found guilty and sentenced to two years hard labour. The vengeful destruction of the playwright and his family that followed marked a vicious turning point: what had been playful and private, and ignored by society at large, became subject to public opprobrium and the retribution of the state. The dirty linen (in the case of the playwright's seamy sheets from the Savoy Hotel) was all too literally flaunted if not washed in front of the horrified public. "The love that dare not speak its name," as Wilde famously characterised gay relations at his trial, was driven further underground. Covert homosexuals such as Symonds and Havelock Ellis, known in those days as *Uranists*, developed a samizdat philosophy of male love. "Only one great race in past ages, the Greek race, to whom we owe the inheritance of our ideas, succeeded in raising [homosexual love] to the level of chivalrous enthusiasm," Symonds wrote in *A Problem in Greek Ethics*. "His old dreams of sailors disappeared," wrote Havelock Ellis in his description of the quickening of Symonds' sexuality. "But now he enjoyed visions of beautiful young men and exquisite Greek statues."[51] Images of Sandow look likely to have fuelled these *Uranian* fantasies.

As late as 1901, an anonymous British author felt compelled to defend Sandow against those individuals "who regard the cultivation of the body as a thing to be frowned upon, who are perfectly willing to hold up to our admiration the beautiful human forms of classical times, but regard any attempt to emulate these worthies as pernicious in the extreme".[52] Studiously avoiding any explicit erotic intent, Sandow himself steered a course between titillation and respectability.

- 5 -

SANDOW TRIUMPHS IN NEW YORK

Sandow sailed to the US for the first time in the summer of 1893, contracted to perform at the Casino Theatre, New York, a popular vaudeville venue located at the junction of Broadway and 39th Street. Personally curious to see the New World and its people, he wanted to try his luck in the commercially promising markets of North America, where the large German contingent among the population was expected to flock to his shows, and there was a lively interest in athletics. Indeed, in the wake of the failed revolution of 1848 many hundreds of thousands of Germans had migrated to America and had lost little time in establishing gymnasia modelled on those of their homeland: to this day, there is controversy over whether the first *Turnverein* in the US was established in 1848 in Cincinnati, Ohio, or in Louisville, Kentucky.

At the *Casino*, Sandow would come on stage at 10.30pm, immediately after a musical spoof entitled *Adonis*. This play, its author William Gillan and its lead actor Henry Dixey (then a matinee idol and a byword for male beauty) have all been forgotten, but the precise context of Sandow's North American debut is revealing. The piece was a playful inversion of the Pygmalion myth: in this case, a female sculptress creates a male statue so beautiful that she cannot bear to part with it. Adonis is brought to life and pursued so vigorously by a multitude of female admirers that he tires of life as a human being and reverts to being a statue. The play ends with him reassuming his pose as a perfect work of art.[53] The curtain would go down on Henry Dixey posing as Adonis, then rise to display Sandow in his stead, the strongman wearing nothing but a loincloth and Roman sandals. New York audiences found the contrast breathtaking, their notion of male physical perfection displaced in an instant. Sandow would launch into a series of poses designed to mimic famous classical statues and to demonstrate his control over his musculature. The second part of his act would concentrate on feats of strength and dexterity, culminating in the Roman display and the famous "Tomb of Hercules" act when he would support the weight of a team of horses on his chest. Martial music played throughout. The *New York Times* purred after his first performance at the theatre:

> Sandow is a wonderful creature. Such a development of biceps might not be unusual, but the man's back and chest have surely not been equalled since the golden prime of Samson. He is a broad-faced fellow, and looks something like Cinquevalli [Paul Cinquevalli, the German-born juggler and acrobat], whose strength and dexterity used to astonish us; but Cinquevalli was no match for Sandow in the matter of muscle. The man, blindfolded, with his legs pinioned together, holds a 56 pound dumbbell in each hand, and thus burdened turns a back somersault. He stands near the top of an iron column, his feet resting lightly on a cross-bar and his legs chained to the column, and bending over backwards lifts first one full-sized man and then another, holding them both, with his body in an almost horizontal position...Nothing like his wonderful feats of strength has ever before been seen here.[54]

Following his performances at the Casino, he first had himself sluiced down with cold water. Under normal circumstances he did not sweat, no matter how vigorous his exertions, but he complained that the heat of the theatre lights made him perspire. Then he gave private lectures in his dressing room that were attended by "many of the most notable people in America". Stripped to the waist, he would encourage his admirers to feel his muscles and experience how "when they were relaxed they were as soft as butter [but] when contracted they were hard as steel."[55] At a hotel on Broadway, meanwhile, he subjected himself to an anatomical examination at the hands of Prof. Dudley Sargent, Medical Examiner and Physical Adviser to Harvard University. This well-known physician performed a number of "anthropometric" tests to measure Sandow's strength, size and speed. He was weighed and measured: the strongman came in at 180lbs and the "length and girth of the ankles" demonstrated the ideal male proportion. His strength and speed of reaction were tested by a variety of machines.

"The first thing that struck me when I saw Sandow stripped was the extraordinary size of the muscles as compared with that of the bones," observed the Professor. "His skeleton is not large, as is seen in the girth of his wrist and ankles, but the bones are exceedingly fine. The muscles are also of very fine quality…his muscles in certain regions, notably on the upper arms and back, are developed to an extraordinary degree. The trapezius and extensors and flexors of the legs and thighs are also tremendous…another distinguishing characteristic is his voluntary control of his muscles. He can relax and contract them at will…"

This quality of being able to deploy only the set of muscles required for a specific task was most unusual, the professor noted. Normally big, strong men are rendered ponderous in their movements as one set of muscles worked against another – as had been the case, for example, with Thomas Topham, the famous English strongman who was a lumbering brute, or the paunchy but deadly American boxer John L. Sullivan. But Sandow had developed his muscles to such a pitch that he was able to disengage the so-called antagonistic muscles (when the use of one muscle impedes the use of another) and produce tremendous expansions and contractions in his individual muscles. Never, adjudged the professor, had he seen a man capable of exercising such control over the muscles in his body. Sandow could relax or flex them at will, a skill now highly prized by body-builders who take pride in flaunting their highly defined, sculpted muscles. As Arnold Schwarzenegger has testified, acquiring mass and strength is the first and easy task of the body-builder: much harder is to give those muscles definition. "I had come to London with a big, muscular body," Schwarzenegger recalled in his *Autobiography*, "[but] that was mere foundation". Thereafter he "started work on separating out the muscles … [looking for exercises] to burn every ounce of fat from between the muscles."[56] The result was the trademark "ripped" look of the modern body-builder. Sandow was quite explicitly Schwarzenegger's early role model, and prior to entering politics the self-fashioned Austrian-born body-builder turned movie star and Governor of California was considering making a biopic of Sandow's life.

As always with Sandow, science was commingled with showmanship: he encouraged the professor to stand on his corrugated abdominal muscles and, in flexing them, propelled the doctor into the air. He then picked up the professor with one hand and placed him on a table. Sandow also made his muscles "dance and jump" and with a twist of his wrist or neck was able to demonstrate muscles that "an ordinary man does not know he possesses". This session was a way of legitimising his performance, cloaking his near-naked body in medico-scientific language, and drawing the sting from any suggestion that he might be seeking merely to titillate his audiences.

"Altogether Sandow is the most wonderful specimen of man I

have ever seen," Prof. Sargent concluded. "He is strong, active and graceful, combining the characteristics of Apollo, Hercules and the ideal athlete. There is not the slightest evidence of sham about him." "The old authority who laid it down that an athlete, to be any use, should have a comely head, brawny arms and legs, a good wind and considerable strength, would have more than these requisites in Sandow," commented a reporter for the New York *Herald* on 5 October 1890. "[Sandow is] about middle height, but full-breasted and broad-shouldered beyond all ordinary men, and with thighs and lower limbs of wonderful balance and power. Withal, the young German carries himself gracefully, and might rival in statuesque beauty the Farnese Hercules."[57]

Sandow was not alone on his US tour – he had sailed over with his friend Martinus Sieveking (1867-1950), a Dutch pianist and composer, and together they shared an apartment during Sandow's time in New York. As Sandow recollected:

Sieveking…was a brilliant pianist…but as a man he was exceedingly weak and delicate. Indeed, his powers of endurance were of the slenderest, and he even found it difficult to remain at the piano long at a time. "If I only had your strength,' he used to say, regretfully, "I might become almost the greatest player in the world."…I suggested that he should accompany me as my guest to America, guaranteeing that in nine months or a year, under my personal supervision and training, he would grow so strong that his best friend would scarcely be able to recognise him…he travelled with me all through America. Weak as he was at the start, within twelve months he became one of the strongest and healthiest of my pupils and the most redoubtable amateur I have ever met, whilst he was able to continue as he wished his professional career as a pianist.[58]

Journalists visited them at 210 West 38th Street and found Sieveking stripped to the waist and thundering through his repertoire at the piano, while Sandow worked at his own exercises in time to the music.

Sieveking left a deep impression on those who met him, so much so that he has a cameo role in James Hilton's novel *Lost Horizon*, where he gives a recital on an ocean liner. Strengthened up under Sandow's personal tutelage, the fingers of each hand spanning nearly two octaves, Sieveking was said to have "the largest, most muscular and perfectly developed among piano hands" – as well as a beautiful tone and complete command of pianistic technique. He invented his own system for teaching virtuoso piano playing based on his trademark Dead-Weight Principle, a musical version of the Sandow system, involving much repetition in order to build finger strength and accuracy.[59] He later composed various entirely forgotten marches and waltzes and wrote and performed for piano-roll companies. He married an Englishwoman in 1899 and migrated finally to the US in 1918, establishing a piano-playing academy in New York – a pianistic version of Sandow's Institute of Physical Culture. He outlived his bosom friend by several decades, dying in Pasadena, California, in 1950.

At around this time, Sandow supposedly rebuffed the advances of Caroline "La Belle" Otéro, the voluptuous courtesan to Kings and Emperors, when she attempted to seduce him. "I should have taken the cue when Herr Sandow refused to drink my champagne and asked for milk," she said after failing in her objective. "He must have had a bad hour or two with me before I sent him back to the young man he was living with…"[60] It has been suggested on the evidence of this, and the fact that Sandow and Sieveking were inseparable for a while, that they were gay lovers. But the fact they shared an apartment is no more evidence of Sandow's bisexuality than deeming Sherlock Holmes homosexual because he cohabited with Dr Watson in Baker Street. Like the heroes of *Wirtshaus in Spessart*, Sandow and Sieveking were two young men seeking fame and fortune, in the New World rather than the forests of Bavaria.

A posse of reporters met Sandow on his arrival and, for the two months that he was in the city, he was hardly out of the headlines. Not all the reporting was respectful, however, especially when late in his stay in New York he was assaulted in the street by Sarah E. White, alias Lurline, the Water Queen, a Boston-born music hall artiste who had built a career for herself in Europe as a specialist in underwater displays. Several of the larger London halls, including most obviously the Aquarium where Sandow first made his name, boasted glass-walled tanks in which maidens in various stages of undress would wallow among the fishes, holding their breaths for an apparent eternity. On stage and underwater, Mrs White (neé Swift) was by all accounts a delectable creature, but Sandow was to discover that hell hath no fury like a water queen scorned.

On the night of 1 July 1893, having attended the performance with her friend Mr Dare, a clown, Lurline waited outside the theatre for Sandow to emerge, then accosted the strongman on the sidewalk. "I want to speak to you," she declared, incandescent with rage. One would have thought the encounter between a delicate mermaid and the strongest man in the world would have been uneven, but she got the better of him on that evening. As he tried to push past, whispering a warning to her to keep away, she pulled a whip out from under her wrap and lashed him three times about the face. Later in court, Sandow was asked whether he had actually threatened to crush her hand as she went for him. This he denied, but: "I did say that I hoped that she would not try to strike me, for if I should catch hold of her wrist

she might not be able to use that wrist again." As three members of
the crowd restrained Sandow, who for once lost control of himself,
Lurline was arrested on the spot and charged with assault.

She had travelled from Europe to accuse Sandow of inveigling
money from her under false pretences and cheating in his fateful contest
with Sampson. Equally worrying were various allegations concerning
his early life. At a court hearing in mid-July, her lawyers alleged that
long ago in Brussels Sandow had (somewhat preposterously) claimed
that he was a Count, thus beguiling the innocent Lurline into parting
with her money. "It would be shown that Sandow was an hostler [ie
a groom, paid to look after horses], and not a Count, when Attila,
[Sandow's by now estranged mentor] befriended him and Lurline lent
him the money." The amount concerned was relatively small – a matter
of £11 or so – but having expropriated it from the gullible Lurline,
Sandow is supposed to have scarpered to Italy with an accomplice and
never paid it back. Sandow insisted under oath that he had repaid the
money – and maintained that he would prove that he was an aristocrat
– the first and only time he would publicly make such a bizarre claim.

Lurline alleged further that he had frequently turned up at her home
in London without money, clothes or food, little better than a pauper.
Then later, in an unexplained reversal of sentiment, she claimed to
have advanced Sandow and Attila a much larger amount of capital in
order to finance the ultimately successful challenge to Sampson. Ahead
of the contest, she said, "we paid a man named Schlag £20 to make
chains and coins of brittle material." She knew all this because she had
plotted it all with Attila and Sandow and on the fateful night had sat in
the audience and had been the one who substituted these props for the
original, full-strength materials. The court session ended inconclusively,
but not before Lurline's attorney had rebutted any suggestion that she

was engaged in blackmail and revealed – to Sandow's evident dismay – that Attila himself would come across from Europe to testify on her behalf. He would confirm that Lurline had financed their London venture and moreover "could tell many things about Sandow's career equally unpalatable to the young man." The implication was clearly that not so long ago Sandow had led a desperate and disreputable existence.[61]

Later that summer, Attila did indeed pitch up in the US, complete with a new protégé, a young lad called Milo who claimed to be as strong as Sandow and for a while added his public voice to that of Lurline in denouncing the Prussian. Attila accused Sandow of being a "blackguard" and a "clog of quicksilver" and "other choice epithets that would burn a hole through this paper," prompting another lawsuit from Sandow. "If looks could kill, if scowls were clubs, Sandow and Attila would today be corpses," noted a New York newspaper, rather gleefully, when the two former friends and business partners faced each other in court later that summer, "dead with a thousand stabs or battered beyond recognition." Attila publicly declared that he would like to tear Sandow into three pieces, like a pack of cards; more damaging was his declaration that Sandow's career was based on deceit. "The chain Sandow broke [in the famous contest with Sampson], and so won £500, was a fabrication," he alleged. "One link just hung by a thread. Lord Clifford and the Marquess of Queensberry…took my word as Sandow's mentor that the feat had been correctly performed. That made Sandow's reputation. It is founded on a lie."

To add to Sandow's woes, his erstwhile opponent Sampson also arrived in New York, adding his own denunciations to those of Attila and Lurline, and then followed Sandow on to Chicago. "He [Sandow] broke chains to be sure," Sampson told the *Chicago Tribune* on 27 August

1893, "but he insisted on furnishing his own chains, and as for those chains, well – but I don't want to be personal. I left the stage when I saw that I could not obtain fair play." He could lift 18 men where Sandow could heft but three horses, Sampson claimed, maintaining that he and only he had the right to be called the strongest man in the world until Sandow agreed to submit to another public contest of strength, a challenge which Sandow was of course sensible enough to avoid. But by the autumn, the court cases appear to have been settled and the three partners in crime were reconciled. Lurline disappeared from the scene altogether, while Attila found that he liked America so much that he opened a gym in New York, and remained there for the rest of his long and happy life, proudly advertising himself as "The Tutor and Trainer of the Great Sandow". He married, became a proponent of physical culture for women and fitness coach to celebrities such as Gentleman Jim Corbett, the boxer.

Do these murky revelations imply that Sandow was a cheat? In an interview, the Prussian hinted that he had occasionally bent the rules as well as iron bars. "You don't go in for chain-breaking and wire-rope-snapping feats do you?" he was asked, a pointed reference to the critical moment in the original contest. "I don't care very much for them," he conceded. "They are more or less knacks, sometimes mere conjuring feats, indeed, but are, nevertheless, clever."[62] He thus drew a distinction between elements of his act that drew on his unchallengeable strength, fitness and suppleness, and those that had more in common with conjuring tricks.

Some lesser rivals practised unsubtle tricks when it came to lifting weights: Sampson himself was notorious for filling his set of hollow bar-bells with sand and inviting members of the audience to try and heft them. Naturally, this proved impossible. Then a few minutes would pass while the sand was allowed to trickle out of a hole in the bells. He would then lift up and juggle the by now much lighter weights. Or sometimes the bar-bells were bolted to the stage floor with the help of an assistant – of course, they could not be budged – and then they would be unscrewed when it came to the strongman's act. Another ruse was to lift a horse with the aid of a halter mounted in a frame: it was an impressive effort for Sampson to hoist the creature skywards. Typically, he would lower it back down to the ground with a grunt, feigning exhaustion. On one occasion, the horse and halter stayed aloft as Sampson came down for a rest, thereby exposing the fraud. Harry Houdini, no stranger to chicanery himself, investigated the claims of many strongmen and the occasional strongwoman and exposed them as bogus. He demonstrated how, for example, the American Lulu Hurst – making her name for herself at the same time as Sandow – deftly exploited the "elementary principles of the laws of mechanics, chapter of equilibrium," to lift up and knock over several men with a combined weight a multiple of her own. She claimed to be demonstrating the mystical powers of the as yet improperly understood force of electricity, but in fact she was manipulating the laws of leverage so that the strength and weight of her victims would unknowingly be turned against themselves. Such jiggery-pokery was part and parcel of the music hall scene, and one must take off one's hat to this lady's clever manipulation of her audience. "It is a phenomenon of stupidity," adjudged Houdini, "and it only goes to show how willingly people will be fooled, and with what cheerful asininity they will help on their deceivers."

Although Houdini deemed Sandow's feats to be genuine, a circus-trained performer such as Sandow of course knew plenty of tricks. When the occasion required it, he was capable of outwitting as well as out-lifting a charlatan such as Sampson: it seems certain that Prof. Attila and Lurline the Water Queen helped him substitute the crucial armlet for one that he knew he would be able to break. But that is not to imply that his act was fundamentally fraudulent: the essence of Sandow's performance was genuine, predicated on his physical prowess and the perfection of his body. "The feats are wonderful," gushed one interviewer. "Nor is there much doubt about their genuineness. The iron weights and dumb-bells are at the termination of each act, allowed to fall with a very real and solid sound on the stage, and, moreover, anyone among the audience is at perfect liberty to touch – and if he can – lift them." Another noted: "there may be some sort of trick in his feat of balancing [a pair of] see-sawing horses on his chest, but there is none in his other feats."[63] He performed his act with little appearance of effort and indeed insisted that the feats he performed were in fact easy for him to carry out and if he had to strain himself there was a risk of injury. He always denied undertaking any special training for these shows, saying that the performance alone provided the necessary amount of daily exercise. "I eat, drink, smoke and sleep quite in the ordinary way," he insisted. "I only practice, in order that grace and perfection may be attained when some new feat is introduced." The best time for a performance was some three hours after a meal, he maintained with exaggerated insouciance.

- 6 -

SEX AND THE CITY OF CHICAGO

I n July 1893, Sandow secured a short and successful engagement at the Tremont Theatre in Boston but by this time he was en route to fame and fortune as a protégé of Florenz Ziegfeld, a young, second-generation German immigrant who was himself on the brink of a legendary show business career. Through a succession of lavish musicals and ultimately his eponymous *Follies*, Ziegfeld is known today as the glorifier of American womanhood. But as Ziegfeld's daughter explained: "Sandow was [in fact] Daddy's first experiment in the fine art of glorification." Ziegfeld had come to New York in search of an act to rescue his father's failing business venture at the Trocadero, a substantial theatre in downtown Chicago. Despite the presence in the city of hundreds of thousands of visitors to the Chicago World's Fair (otherwise known as the World's Columbian Exposition) the theatre was not filling its complement of 6,000 seats. Ziegfeld had hired the Von Bulow symphony orchestra and the Russian Mirsky band, shipping them across from Europe and then putting them on a train from New York to Chicago at great expense "in a style befitting high class vaudeville," but classical music was simply too highbrow for the sensation-seekers who flocked to the Fair.

The exhibition, designed to celebrate the 400th anniversary of Columbus' discovery of North America, was set up with the aim of

surpassing other great national extravaganzas, notably the 1851 Great
Exhibition in London and the Exposition Universelle in Paris in 1889;
a recent best-selling book is testament to the grip that the Chicago
event still exercises on American popular imagination.[64] The fair took
place in Jackson Park, some miles from the centre of Chicago, in a
city specially constructed along neo-classical lines. After an uncertain
start at the beginning of May, it is estimated that some 27.5 million
out of a total US population of 65 million came to visit the fair by the
time it closed on 31 October. They could ride on the Ferris Wheel,
Chicago's answer to the Eiffel Tower, the chief innovation of the 1889
Paris Exposition, or edify themselves by visiting the Manufactures and
Liberal Arts Building or the Court of Honor, massive edifices clad in
white plaster of Paris to give the impression of marble. They could
seek a different kind of thrill by attending the performances of Little
Egypt, a louche belly dancer clad in harem pantaloons and little else.
Other attractions included a tribe of genuine pygmies imported from
Africa and "Buffalo Bill's Wild West and Congress of Rough Riders of
the World" – an equestrian extravaganza which included a display of
marksmanship by Annie "get your gun" Oakley and a re-enactment of
Custer's Last Stand at the Battle of Little Big Horn. Ziegfeld's father
was musical director to the fair, but until his son discovered Sandow
his theatre was half-empty.

Ziegfeld attended Sandow's show at the Casino and is said to
have burst into the strongman's changing room afterwards, so keen
was he to sign him up. After conferring with his business manager,
Sandow demanded $1,100 a week, a large amount of money that
shows the strongman's sense of his commercial worth to have been as
well-developed as his muscles. But as Ziegfeld had all but run out of
cash, he offered a ten per cent share of gross billings instead – which

Sandow shrewdly accepted. Stockholders in the Trocadero theatre later denounced Ziegfeld for entering into a ruinously one-sided contract. "Sandow proved a great 'card' and increased attendance enough [to earn his extravagant salary]," they grumbled when the company later went bust, "the equivalent to the Trocadero of losing $3,000 a month for the three months he remained in Chicago."

Ahead of the strongman's first performance on 1 August, Ziegfeld launched a publicity campaign, billing Sandow hyperbolically as "The Perfect Man" – "The Unprecedented Sensation of the Century" – "The Strongest Man on Earth". He deployed the techniques of modern public relations a century before the world had heard of Max Clifford or Alastair Campbell: he planted stories with a credulous press, devised absurd photo opportunities (as when he had the strongman pushed about the city in a wheelbarrow, as if he were too muscular to move about by himself) and disseminated invariably fabricated details of his client's love life. All of which helped ensure the success of his protégé's performances, but there was one further ingredient that Ziegfeld promoted most shamelessly: Sandow's sex appeal.

As we have seen, it was part of the curious double standards of Victorian London that a near-naked man was not considered dangerously sexy, while the mere exposure of an actress's ankle was a scandal. In North America, such squeamishness did not universally apply and accordingly Ziegfeld encouraged Sandow to make his performances racier than in New York or Victorian London. The Prussian exchanged a blue top and discreet pink body suit for a pair of skimpy silk briefs. He covered himself with white powder and performed his classical poses against a black velvet backdrop. Over-sized copies of Greek statuary were displayed prominently throughout the World's Fair campus and those who attended Sandow's performances often commented that he seemed to be bringing the statues to life. From the opening night onwards, the theatre was packed and weekly grosses jumped from $2,000 to $28,000. Barely weeks after Lurline had so rudely reminded him of his impoverished past, Sandow found himself on the road to genuine riches, hauling in a handsome $2,800 a week.

With an instinct for the public relations gesture, Ziegfeld lured Mrs Potter Palmer and Mrs George Pullman, wives of local plutocrats and two of the more prominent *grandes dames* in Chicago society, to a private interview with Sandow in his dressing room after his premier at the Trocadero. Ziegfeld offered this opportunity to anyone who was prepared to donate $300 to charity. Once in the dressing room, the ladies – like the soldiers of Woolwich – were given the opportunity to run their hands over Sandow's musculature. Mrs Potter declared that she was thrilled to the spine after running her hands over Sandow's chest. "You were no-one, really no-one, my dear, unless you felt Sandow's muscles," commented another society lady. Amy Leslie, the drama critic for the *Chicago Daily News*, attended one of these intimate sessions, enumerating for the delectation of her readers Sandow's "blue eyes and wealth of golden, close-cut curls," his velvety, pinky-white skin, his attractively modest, even girlish, facial expression. "He walked over to me and threw out a stack of corded muscles under the white smooth skin of his chest in a sort of mechanical way that rather stunned me," she panted. "A dangerously handsome young man."

While in London and, indeed, in New York, Sandow's near-naked form had been displayed predominantly to other men and it had been possible to hide any erotic suggestiveness under a cloak of quasi-scientific respectability. In the US, goaded on by Florenz Ziegfeld's none-too-subtle PR stunts, his act became downright sexy and was directed as much at women who wanted to feel his body, as at men who wanted a body like his.

"Wherever he went," noted a newspaper columnist many years later, "mobs paid dollars to see, and after the mobs had looked their fill, there were private séances to which nice people went, first in secret, then in brazen bravado. Always ladies were present, and always their private amazement was recorded in the despatches. But though amazed, they tarried and though coyly fearful for a time, they managed to repress their terror for a time and test the great muscles with a delicately gloved forefinger..."[65]

In Chicago, and in the two years he spent in the US thereafter, the private viewing would become a staple part of his routine. For example, Mrs Jack Gardiner, leader of Boston's social elite, got up a private party for her female friends, as did a (coyly anonymous) senator's wife in Washington DC, who invited all her friends (also senators' wives) and their daughters. "There was nothing wrong in it all," she insisted. "The Senator has agreed with me that there's no harm." As the *Washington Post* reported on 9 January 1896:

> The ladies had prepared veils and other facial disguises against the too ardent stare of the men below [during the public performance], but still they were glad when the play ended, and it was time to go behind the scenes...The supreme hour had come. Sandow having rested and bathed, appeared in front of the expectant group. His colossal figure, nude to the waist line, stood out in bold relief, and about him gathered the visitors, most of them nervous and trembling. Sandow at once laboured to put the feminine contingent at their ease. He invited them after grouping them in horseshoe style around him to come up one at a time and examine his muscles. This at first they were loathe to do, touching the giant gingerly with gloved hands. Gradually they became more confident, and off came the gloves.

In January 1893, the *National Police Gazette*, an early and immensely popular lads' magazine, put an image of his near-naked form on the front-page, with the headline "The Ladies Idolize Sandow". "I want you to feel how hard these muscles are," he told the ladies. "As I stop before you I want each of you to pass the palm of your hand across my chest." The first woman he approached was too overwhelmed by the sight of him to touch him. "Oh please," she gasped, in a language that would not be out of place in an overtly pornographic narrative. "These muscles, madam, are as hard as iron itself, I want you to convince yourself of the fact." Gently insistent, Sandow took the woman's hand and applied it to his flesh. "It's unbelievable," she is supposed to have said, before passing out and needing a dose of smelling salts to be revived. Even when Sandow lectured at the respectable Yale University, it was noted that the tremendous crowd consisted "largely of ladies" fascinated by his muscular displays as much as by what he had to say.[66]

Sexy he may have been in the eyes of his female admirers, but there is little evidence that Sandow himself showed much interest in sex. It is one of the ironies of his early career that a man clearly able to send women into frenzies of erotic excitement, never seemed to reciprocate this passion. For a man whose stage act celebrated strength and conquest, he erred on the side of self-restraint when it came to women. Perhaps this was out of exaggerated desire to maintain the respectability of his public reputation, which at the time deemed it acceptable for a man to strip off in the interests of science, but not so if he were actively trying to titillate women. Or was it the self-obsession of a man so besotted with his own beauty, that he could not be moved to take an interest in others? This interpretation seems uncharitable, for Sandow – while no doubt egotistical – was not a narcissist: indeed, his whole artistic and commercial career was designed to share the secrets of his fitness and beauty with as many people as possible.

But there were no stories of romantic interest in the various articles and books about his early life, beyond being named in passing in the scandalous divorce case of Bale vs Bale and O'Gorman. In February 1897, George Bale, professional juggler, sued his wife Jessica Bale (also a music hall artiste, a performer on the slack wire) for divorce by virtue of her alleged misconduct with Joseph O'Gorman, a comedian. It was a scandalous case, in which "Beautiful Jessica" was revealed to have had many admirers – including Sandow. "Did Sandow the strongman make [Beautiful Jessica] innumerable presents of jewellery?" prosecuting counsel asked. The judge ruled immediately that the question had nothing to do with the case in question, so we will never know the extent of Sandow's infatuation with the lovely Miss Bale.

The passion that impelled Lurline across the Atlantic in search of revenge was evidently not romantic in nature. Rather than chase after his many female admirers, he was much keener to spend time with his friend Martinus Sieveking, or even with a boar hound called Sultan, a giant of a dog, which was allegedly presented to the strongman by Prince Bismarck and was known as Sandow's particular pet. The dog stood 34 inches high at the shoulders and weighed some 200lbs. It used to carry Sandow's baggage and guard his bedroom. Sandow insisted that the dog had a gentle temperament, belied only by it getting into a tremendous fight with a St Bernard called Lion at the corner of 13th Street and Pennsylvania Avenue in Washington. Sandow stopped the fight by grabbing his dog by the neck, shaking it loose from the other, and holding him out at arm's length - with one hand, of course. Sandow preferred its company to that of his female fans. After being separated from this beer-drinking hound on one occasion, Sandow "hugged the brute with a dozen endearing caresses, and for a minute forgot the presence of a group of admiring spectators…"

Ziegfeld identified a public relations deficit with respect to his protégé's romantic life and set about manufacturing a "love interest" to garner still more publicity. He put it about, by the simple expedient of briefing gossip columnists who were unconcerned about the factual basis of the stories they published, that Sandow was romantically linked with – even engaged to be married to – Lillian Russell, a great female sex symbol of the era. The stories retailed tittle-tattle about how he and the actress met, when they were to marry and so forth. In early January 1894, on arrival in New York, he was asked whether the rumours of marriage were true. "You must excuse me," Sandow answered in what looks like a coyly scripted reply, "You know there are some things we can't talk of. Still," he added pensively, "strange things sometimes happen, you know." When Miss Russell was asked the same question she said: "watch me for the next five years".[67] In fact, it seems that he and the actress met but once and Russell was distinctly unimpressed by the Prussian. Her biographers suggest that she found him to have a weak personality and viewed him cordially but without any great passion. Is this evidence of Sandow's asexuality, or even bisexuality? More likely he was lukewarm because he was secretly engaged, news of which was soon made public.

When not titillating his female admirers, there were other distractions for the young Prussian at the fair. Somewhat improbably, Ziegfeld arranged for him to have a minor part in a production of Shakespeare's *As You Like It*. The play was put on in late-August in a bid to add highbrow respectability to the cornucopia of merely popular entertainment. Sandow, playing Charles the wrestler, was given prominent billing in a role designed to showcase his musculature, rather than his command of Elizabethan English.

As one of the star attractions of the fair, he had the opportunity to meet many of the celebrity visitors; certainly, Ignacy Jan Paderewski, the pianist and future Prime Minister of Poland, was present and would subsequently become a customer of Sandow's Institute of Physical Culture in London, contributing an enthusiastic article to *Sandow's Magazine*.[68] Theodore Roosevelt, the future President of the US and a proponent of energetic physical exercise, also attended and certainly met Sandow during his 1903 tour of North America. Edgar Rice Burroughs spent the month of June at the fair and must have seen Sandow perform and possibly remembered his form when he created Tarzan as one of enduring symbols of modern manhood. Bernarr Macfadden, a less exalted personage, was working at the fair as a demonstrator of athletic equipment and on witnessing Sandow's performance determined there and then to emulate him, which he did, with considerable success, building an American physical culture empire to rival that of Sandow himself. Macfadden, who lived from 1868 to 1955, held the first American body-building contest in New York's Madison Gardens. He had a predilection for raw carrots as well as energetic exercise. With none of Sandow's subtlety, he was frequently arrested for promoting indecency, which was no bar to his accumulating a fortune.

There is no record of Sandow encountering Mark Twain, Scott Joplin, Houdini or the Archduke Franz Ferdinand of Austria – among the many celebrities who visited the fair – but it seems probable that he met Buffalo Bill, hero of the Wild West turned vaudeville star. Their business managers calculated that the two men appealed to the same audiences and Sandow's Gym Equipment was advertised on the back of Buffalo Bill Cody's programme for a European tour in the same year.[69] Certainly, they represented complementary versions of ideal

manhood at the end of the 19th century. Buffalo Bill gave his audience
a nostalgic glimpse of what it had been like to be a frontiersman,
battling with Red Indians on the Wild West frontier. That life and
death contest had been won and the frontier no longer existed, as the
historian Frederick Turner famously declared in a speech given at the
Exposition. He argued compellingly that the defining characteristic of
American history was the existence of an "area of free land…and the
continuous expansion westwards"– and that this process was now over.
The man who had shot and scalped the Cheyenne leader Yellow Hand
in revenge for General Custer's death, and had played a prominent role
in the taming of the frontier, was reduced to performing on stage to
earn a living. It has to be said he adapted extremely well to the world of
show business – the highpoint of this part of his career being a private
performance for Queen Victoria on the lawns of Windsor Castle in
1892. Sandow appealed to classical notions of ideal beauty and strength,
but his message was forward-looking rather than nostalgic: even if
you lived in a city and had never had to scalp an Indian in earnest, or
even slay a buffalo or build a log cabin, you could turn yourself into a
real man – by following the principles of Physical Culture. For Sandow,
the music hall stage was no refuge, it was the medium that created him
and provided the platform for his later successes.

Following his Chicago triumph, Sandow carried out engagements in
a number of American cities, before returning to New York in January
to perform at Koster & Bial's Music Hall on 34th Street, New York, near
Broadway. A programme for the opening night, on 1 January 1894,
shows that Sandow was the fifteenth and last in a series of acts which
included: Professor Carlisle and His School of Performing Dogs, the
Zanetto Troupe (Japanese Jugglers), the Frères Crescendoes (Electrical
Clowns), the Hungarian Elite Orchestra and a trapeze artiste, and a

troupe of sand-dancers and jumpers. In New York, he came to the attention of Napoleon Sarony, the eccentric society photographer who took portraits of celebrities such as Oscar Wilde, Sarah Bernhardt and Mark Twain in a studio with a stuffed crocodile hanging from the ceiling. Sarony pioneered Sandow's trademark poses with animal skins, clubs, sandals and other paraphernalia.

Sandow, ever alert to the potential of new technology to promote his business interests, was also the subject of one of the earliest motion pictures: on 10 March 1894 he shook the hand of Thomas Edison after performing for the kinetoscope, the prototype cine-camera invented by Edison's assistant William K.L. Dickinson. Sandow was filmed at the Edison Corporation's studio in West Orange, New Jersey, and the resulting 50 feet of film were shown in thousands of peepshows and special theatres across America. Other subjects chosen for the very earliest motion pictures included a cock-fight, a prize fight, a busy time in a blacksmith's forge, and a serpentine dance: contemporaries were deeply impressed with the life-like flickering of the flames in the blacksmith's forge, as well as the dilation and construction of Sandow's muscles.[70] Thereafter he starred in a production by American Mutoscope, a rival film company, whose Biograph projector made its debut in Pittsburgh in a show featuring Sandow in September 1896.

One can view a short film from this era on the Internet, which shows Sandow posing in a long shot against a black background, wearing only tight trunks and laced sandals. "He begins with his arms folded against his chest, looking off screen left, then strikes a variety of poses that accentuate his muscular development," notes the original programme. "These…include flexing his right arm with the first to the head and face to shoulder; turning his back to the camera while flexing his upper arms and shoulder muscles…and stretching out and up with one arm at a time." The 24 feet of film conclude with a trademark standing back flip from a standing start – which is executed with impressive speed and agility.

Convinced by Ziegfeld of the commercial benefits of publicity, the young athlete – still only 26 years old – commissioned his first "authorised" biography. "Sandow on Physical Training: A Study in the Perfect Type of the Human Form" was first published in 1894. Written by G. Mercer Adam, a former Captain in the British Army, the book contained a sanitised version of his life and triumphs to date, complete with abundant photographs and illustrations, as well as Sandow's "views on the physiology of gymnastics, the functions of muscles etc…[and] the great athlete's simple method of physical education for the home". The book is in part an attempt to counter the allegations of Lurline, Sampson and others about his origins and career, but it is also a surprisingly coherent statement of a set of beliefs about the benefits of exercise, together with the first outline of a practical system designed to deliver those benefits (we will consider this agenda more fully in a later chapter). However much of an opportunist he might have been in building his show-business career, he was consistent in these beliefs and the system outlined here would become the basis of his physical culture empire when he eventually returned to settle in the UK. For now, his career as a fledgling social reformer was secondary to his willingness to do anything it took to create headlines and remain in the public eye.

On 22 February 1894, Sandow attended the College of Surgeons and Physicians in New York, and allowed himself to be hypnotised:

> Sandow came into the room and threw himself onto a couch. One of
> the gas jets was lighted and Sandow was told to fix his eyes on it. The
> doctor explained that this was merely to hold his attention and help him

concentrate on the idea that he was going to sleep. The physician sat on the couch, facing Sandow. 'Keep your eyes on the light,' he said, 'and think only of going to sleep.' Sandow obeyed…'Draw deep breaths, deep breaths. Your eyelids are beginning to flutter. You – are – going – to – sleep. Don't resist me. Breathe deeper: so. Now – you – are – asleep.'

And it was true that the mighty Sandow had in the space of 30 seconds been reduced to utter powerlessness. When the doctor pushed his arms up in the air, they would remain there until they were pushed down again. The doctor then made sport with Sandow, telling him that a three pound dumb-bell was so heavy that he would not be able to lift it. "Sandow tugged and struggled, straining every muscle in his body in a vain effort to lift it." Having thus demonstrated that not merely weak and hysterical people were subject to hypnotism, the doctor awakened the strongman, who was bright and cheerful after his ordeal.[71]

A more preposterous publicity stunt came three months later when, on 22 May 1894, Sandow entered a wrestling contest with a lion: a high-point in terms of his willingness to cater to his audience's desire for spectacle, a low-water mark however in terms of his credibility as a serious artiste. The encounter in San Francisco provoked controversy, even mockery, as the lion appeared to have been drugged by the time the contest took place. Sandow maintained that the lion was an especially aggressive beast, which had recently eaten his keeper, and for that reason it had to be muzzled and wear boxing gloves on its claws. The strongman claimed the lion showed its true mettle in a practice bout:

No sooner had I stepped inside the cage [in which the contest was to be held, in order to protect the audience] than he crouched preparatory to springing on me. His eyes ablaze with fury, he hurled himself through the air, but missed, for I had stepped aside, and before he had time to recover I caught him around the throat with my left arm and round the middle with my right, and though his weight was five hundred and thirty pounds, I lifted him as high as my shoulder, gave him a huge hug to instil into his mind that he must respect me, and tossed him to floor. Roaring with rage, the beast rushed fiercely towards me, raising his huge claw to strike a heavy blow at my head. As his paw cut through space I felt the air fairly whistle…as I ducked my head to miss the blow I succeeded in getting a good grip round the lion's body, with my chest touching his and his feet over my shoulders, and hugged him with all my strength. The more he scratched and tore the harder I hugged him, but although his feet were protected by mittens his claws tore through my tights and parts of my skin. But I had him as in a vice; his mighty efforts to get away were to no avail.[72]

Come the actual performance in front of the 20,000-strong crowd, the lion bathetically refused to fight any further, even when Sandow tried to goad it into action by tweaking its tail. Sandow walked around the arena with the beast on his shoulders "quiet as a lamb". As one report suggests, the contest turned out to be a fiasco:

When Sandow entered the cage the lion crouched in a corner moaning and trembling. The lash was vigorously applied and the brute was stirred up with poles and to no purpose. He would not wrestle, and Sandow did what he liked with him. The spectators were disappointed, and greeted this ridiculous exhibition with hisses.[73]

Sandow claimed that the lion was tired out after the practice bout. "Most beasts are cowards at heart, and this beast having met his match at the rehearsal refused to budge…The lion, recognising that I was stronger than he, would fight no more…that lion was clearly conquered."[74]

Sandow ducked out of another contest, with James J. Corbett, the boxer known as Gentleman Jack. Sandow and Corbett bumped into each other at the Mount Vincent Hotel in New York: Sandow was at a table with his manager when the pugilistic champion came in and ordered a bottle of wine. Sandow gazed at Corbett from afar and then whispered to his manager. The latter came over to Corbett and said:

> Mr Corbett, Mr Sandow would like you to understand that he is in no way responsible for the statement made in many newspapers that he claims to be able to defeat any pugilist by entering the ring and breaking the prize-fighter's arms or crushing his ribs. He knows such stories are ridiculous, and trusts you do not believe they emanated from him.

Corbett turned round and, throwing a contemptuous glance towards the strongman, said in quite a loud tone of voice: "You tell Mr Sandow that not only do I believe the story came from him, but I know it to be a positive fact. And also tell him that my offer made to wager him $2,500 that he dare not step into a ring with me and stay one three minute round still holds good. And," he continued belligerently, "while you are telling him all this just add that his head will be a good deal bigger than it is when I get through with him. Now, that's all. My money is ready now or at any time." One cannot feel surprised that the strongman's manager returned to his table with a discomfited and, withal, indignant face. The bystanders waited with breathless expectation to see what the strongman would say to such strong language. They were destined to a great disappointment. Sandow and his manager went out and took the air.[75]

Later that summer, Sandow returned to Europe and, to the surprise and no doubt consternation of his many female admirers, married Blanche Brookes, the daughter of Warwick Brookes, the Manchester photographer who had taken his picture several years before during his tour of the English provinces. The official publicity suggested they had first met in 1891 and that they had secretly been engaged for some time. Blanche was a raven-haired beauty, described thus by an admiring reporter from the *Chicago Times*:

> She is tall, slender, and exquisitely beautiful. Her eyes are large and soft, black as night, and very sensitive. Her hair is just as black, and curls naturally about her oval face. She is one of the prettiest women of the season, and well dressed in a scarlet and white striped silk, with black shirt, and wore a heavy combed lamb's wool cloak and broad screening hat.[76]

Despite her evident attractions, she was an unusual choice for an international celebrity. Could he not have chosen a famous beauty or a fellow star? The absence of such calculation suggests a love match. One story described their alleged first meeting during a much earlier performance at Crystal Palace in south London. Sandow had been midway through his act when a fatal accident was narrowly averted. "The platform on which he was supporting horses on his breast broke and it was only his presence of mind that saved him from being crushed to death," the *Chicago Tribune* reported on 27 January 1894. "As it was he escaped unhurt and crowds of people pushed forward to shake hands with him and congratulate him. In the midst of this excitement a lady, who was sitting in a box, threw him a bunch of violets." Then, fairy-tale like, Sandow happened to be passing a few months later when a runaway truck horse came near to rushing into a carriage occupied by a lady. "Sandow…saw the danger, and by his great strength succeeded in diverting the course of the runaway horse, and so saved the life of the young lady." By remarkable coincidence, the lady rescued by Sandow turned out to be Blanche, who was of course the woman who had thrown the violets at Crystal Palace.

Even if the fanciful story captures the essence of their feelings for one another, it seems more likely that the first meeting took place when Sandow posed at Warwick Brookes' photographic studio in the heart of Manchester. Brookes was a person of consequence in the grimy, energetic city of Manchester of the second half of the 19th century and had a considerable and hitherto unacknowledged influence on his muscular son-in-law. An older, avuncular man, and a successful businessman with excellent show-business connections, Brookes was a father figure and mentor to Sandow. By the time of his marriage, Sandow had no living relatives that he cared to acknowledge and had badly fallen out with Prof. Attila, the man who had most been a father to him since he left Prussia. Brookes befriended him early in his career and took him into the bosom of his family: one senses that Sandow was entering into a business partnership with the family as well as marrying Blanche. Born in 1844, the photographer had the same name as an uncle who had enjoyed the patronage of Queen Victoria as artist and lithograph maker. All first-born males were named Warwick, in honour of some putative family connection with the Earls of Warwick, causing problems for genealogists: the photographer's son Warwick, born in 1875, became Sandow's business manager as well as brother-in-law.

The royal association – albeit at one generation's remove – conferred a prestige on the younger Warwick, helping him build a thriving business in an age when photography was almost as painful as dentistry. Those who wanted their portraits taken, when Brookes first opened his studio in 1864 at Cathedral Close in the heart of the city, had to have their heads fixed in a clamp for a minimum of 20 seconds while the image was recorded on a plate. There were no negatives in these pioneering days and each plate was prepared chemically while the customer waited. For a period of half a century, Brookes was one of the

leading professional photographers in Manchester, capturing images
of the public events of the great city in its heyday and taking portraits
of the industrialists and merchants who created its prosperity and of
their wives and children. Early in his career, he captured an image of
Elizabeth Gaskell, the novelist, who lived not far from Manchester in
Knutsford. Moreover, "it is said there is not a man in the country with
a better theatrical connection," noted the *Manchester Guardian* when this
patriarchal figure died in 1929, having thus outlived his more famous
son-in-law. Sir Henry Irving, the leading actor of the day, sat for him
at least three times. Irving himself refused to set a professional foot
on the music hall stage, but Brookes acknowledged no such distinction
between high and lowbrow culture and had regular business taking
photographs of visiting music hall performers such as Sandow.[77]

Sandow took a summer break from his vaudeville commitments,
crossed the Atlantic and the marriage took place in Manchester
Cathedral on Wednesday 8 August, with little of the fanfare associated
with a show-business wedding. But there was a hint of glamour, even
royal association at one remove, in that the ceremony was performed
by Archdeacon William Macdonald Sinclair of London, private
chaplain to Queen Victoria – there is no knowing how Sandow became
acquainted with him, but they remained in contact and Sinclair was
one of those who gave a character reference for the strongman when
he applied to become a British citizen many years later. The wedding
took place a few weeks after Blanche had returned from studying in
Germany, presumably all the better to converse with her husband-to-be.
There is no record of a honeymoon as such, but, in October 1894, Mrs
Sandow joined her husband and the Sandow Trocadero Vaudevilles on
a gruelling seven-and-a-half month tour of the US. Under Ziegfeld's
direction, they criss-crossed the continent, from Philadelphia to

Washington DC and Baltimore, to Pittsburgh, Cincinnati, Kansas City, Sioux City, Omaha, St Paul, Chicago, and back to New York. It was an exhausting schedule, but not without moments of good-natured fun.

In Washington, very early in this tour, the couple visited a Soldiers' Home on the outskirts of the city. Ziegfeld encouraged Sandow to try riding a bicycle. Sandow gamely accepted this challenge, though despite being photographed near-naked on a bicycle much earlier in his career, he had not tried this particular and increasingly fashionable form of exercise before.

"When the suburbs were reached, Ziegfeld turned the wheel over to Sandow, and the wheel at once proceeded to turn Sandow down. He succeeded in mounting it, grasped the handlebars with a determined air, and started down the road. But alas, with all his might he had not yet learned the secret of cycling, and was soon making a ludicrous endeavour to extricate his trousers from the front wheel. Before succeeding in this, however, the fibre of his trouserings let loose and when Sandow picked himself up he was trying to keep his muscular leg inside a badly ripped "pant" leg. Not disheartened, he climbed pluckily on the wheel again, but this time fared worse than on the first trip. The wheel commenced to wobble. Sandow brought all his strength to bear on the handle bars, twisted them out of shape, fell off the wheel in a heap, and succeeded in breaking the seat and one peddle. By this time, a large crowd of spectators had gathered, thinking someone was intent on committing suicide."[78]

Sandow took his misadventures in good heart. His wife and friends roared with laughter, while he surveyed the wreckage of the bike and his silk hat ("which looked as if it had been to a political jollification"), vowing never to try cycling again.

The power of photography ensured instant recognition and he

received a hero's welcome wherever he went. But there is no hiding that this was a workmanlike kind of celebrity compared to that he had enjoyed in New York and Chicago. This was the secondary vaudeville circuit – they visited anywhere that boasted an opera house or theatre. Typically, Mr and Mrs Sandow and the artistes stayed no more than two or three nights in each place. In deference to Sandow's new and wholesome status as a married man, the private viewings that he would invariably give on arrival were less revealing than in the past, with more emphasis on science than sex. Moreover, Sandow had banished his boon companion Sieveking. By the autumn of 1895, when he gave the first of several farewell performances in Chicago, he had parted company with Ziegfeld as well. The only reminder of the bachelor phase of his existence was the boarhound Sultan, who performed sterling service as a guard dog, surprising a stagehand in the act of stealing valuables from Sandow's dressing room. Despite the dog and indeed his own reputation, Sandow was frequently a target for thieves: his valet Albert Chapman ran off with $3,000 worth of diamonds and jewellery and on a later trip he had his trunk stolen in Washington.

More than happy to take his clothes off at the slightest opportunity, Sandow was unrevealing when it came to details of his personal life. So we just don't know what Sandow and his new wife talked about, or what they were feeling or hoping, on this peripatetic beginning to their married life. There are neither diaries, nor letters or interviews with Mrs Sandow and, however frustrating for the biographer, there is nothing surprising in that. In contrast to figures of highbrow Victorian culture, who preserved letters and other memorabilia in the full expectation that their lives would be embalmed in a three volume life and letters, music hall stars typically lived for the moment and had no thought of posterity. Sandow's friend Vesta Tilley was an exception: she retired from her career as a male impersonator in 1920 and, following her marriage to a rich businessman, became Lady de Frece – a vertiginous journey which took her from entertaining the mill-hands and factory girls of Lancashire to a title, presentation at court and genteel retirement in Monaco. Her autobiography seems designed to demonstrate that there was nothing untoward about dressing up as a man for a living. But there are few memoirs from this group of unstuffy, unself-important and energetic Victorians.

Sandow wanted to convey that he was a respectable gentleman living an irreproachably uxorious existence – an image for now aligned with the reality.

Despite the pressures of travel and a punishing schedule of performances, Sandow had at last found stability, personal happiness – and wealth. At the age of 29, the former shoeless and coatless fairground acrobat had accumulated more than $250,000 in cash earnings, a fortune that he would use to capitalise his future business ventures. It is difficult to translate directly to modern money but by any measure it was a significant sum, equivalent to several millions today. He had married a beautiful woman and had been taken into the bosom of a family who not only loved him as a son, but also could be helpful to him in his career as entertainer and businessman. In this spirit of optimism and contentment, Sandow and his wife conceived their first child early in 1896, when Sandow had returned to New York and was creating an "enormous sensation" during a ten week engagement at Proctor's Pleasure Palace.

This New York show was a worthy swansong to his spectacularly successful American adventure, the highlight being a series of tableaux illustrating mythical episodes in the life of the Farnese Hercules. In the first of these living pictures, a beautiful maiden and her betrothed were reaping in a vineyard, when along came Hercules and snatched the fair one, flying away upon horseback. In a scene his New York audiences found thrilling and original, the aggrieved lover chased after them, intercepted Hercules and the maiden, and then cut a bridge crossing a ravine, thus preventing their escape. At which point Sandow picked up the lover and threw him into the ravine, leaving only one problem: there was no way across. Hercules knelt down beneath the broken bridge, sustained it on his chest, while the horse (a real horse) and the maiden (who has fainted) crossed in safety. "The bridge alone weighs nearly 1,200lbs," it was noted, "and the maiden is no featherweight".

Sandow later claimed that after New York he collapsed from nervous exhaustion. "My enthusiasm took wings and outsped my physical strength," he recalled, "and though I never had a day's illness or contracted an illness in my life, I had at last a very serious nervous collapse – my weight sank from 190lbs to 100lbs and my muscles seemed almost to fade away. My skin simply covered my bones. I restored myself after a hard battle…" The breakdown conveniently allowed Sandow to renege on his contractual obligations and return to England, where he quickly returned to the music hall stage and set about building a business empire.

- 7 -
BACK IN THE UK

S andow took the steamer back to Liverpool in the summer of 1896 and spent the following few months with the Brookes family at their home at 350 Oxford Road in central Manchester. It was a time of respite from the demands of the stage, a rare interval of stable, domestic life spent in the company of his wife and new family. His daughter Helen was born at home on 6 October 1896 and one imagines him a solicitous husband and proud father. But at the same time, he was energetically plotting the next phase of his career. A wealthy and famous man, he had no desire to retire to provincial obscurity. Together with Warwick, his commercially savvy father-in-law, and his brother-in-law of the same name, he drew up what we would call a business plan. The objective was to capitalise on the brand recognition associated with his name and tap vast international markets. But first, he needed to reaffirm his popularity with the British public. Accordingly, he signed up to a lucrative Christmas season at the London Pavilion Theatre (now the tawdry London Trocadero centre, on Piccadilly Circus). He was booked in to start on 23 November and run right through the Christmas period to the end of the year. All was set for a glittering comeback.

The first performances went exceedingly well. After an absence of four years, he was hailed by the London press as "the brilliant young gladiator, who preserves in his performance something of the traditions of ancient Rome." It was said that Sandow was the only strongman who could give "life, variety and attractiveness" to exhibitions of strength. The highpoint of the routine was a modification of the human bridge act he had performed in New York earlier in the year. *The Era* reported:

> He formed a table of his body, his arms and legs being the legs thereof. Across this table lay a wood platform, in the form of a seesaw. One end being lowered, the platform became an inclined plane, up which a horse and chariot were driven. While this cargo stood in its centre, the platform balanced. The horse moved onward, and then an incline was formed on the opposite side that brought the chariot safely to the ground again.

The successful execution of this act depended not merely on Sandow's strength, but on the sure-footedness of the animal. As the strongman was obliged to admit, he took no great care in the selection of his four-legged accomplice. Alas, it turned out that the horse had no great experience of public performance and was quite nervous and frisky. As Sandow explained, "a troupe of acrobats working together are always on the alert to save and ease each other, but the horse is quite 'on its own account'..." On the night of 6 December 1896, towards the end of the scene and quite early in the run, the animal slipped as it was making its way up the ramp. As the horse tried to regain its footing, it brought its full weight down onto Sandow's arms. Unable to maintain his balance, Sandow "with a stupendous effort" resisted the force of the platform and tore two muscles in his forearm, the first halfway serious injury he had sustained in his entire career. He tried to laugh it off, promised that it was a mere nothing and that he would be back on stage within a day or two, but the injury proved more serious. He could not return to the *Pavilion* at all that year, thus missing the busiest and most lucrative nights of the season. "In future," he declared, "the preparation and examination of [my] mechanical and other apparatus shall be so careful that, humanly speaking, [I] can rely on them as implicitly as he is able to rely on them."

He spent his convalescence mulling over his plans to develop an entirely new vocation, as (one newspaper described it) a "consulting physicalician," a cross between a physician and a physical culture instructor. As he explained in an interview early in the New Year:

> For a long time…[his] correspondence with people wishing to know the secret of his strength has been very heavy. He accordingly elected to make a business of what would have been an intolerable burden on goodwill, and he has set apart a few hours daily, during which he receives patients for a fee. The idea is not to instruct pupils in the way of becoming professional strong men. Sandow has the belief that judicious exercise will prevent most diseases and cure many – in particular indigestion.[79]

He went on to describe how he was in the practice of holding consultations with as many as ten patients a day, for a fee. He would ask a long series of questions and take a set of measurements, before prescribing a specific set of exercises designed to address a particular ailment and restore the patient to general health and strength. Sandow's rhetorical method would become as familiar to the late-Victorian and Edwardian public as the elements of his regime: he made extravagant promises that hinted at the arresting and even the reversibility of the ageing process. This grandiose proposition went hand in hand with extremely specific recommendations for improving exercise and diet, buttressed by scientific method. Then, to prove his point, he used himself as an example. Even those who recoiled at his braggadocio could not fail to be impressed by his spectacular body, which went on getting stronger and more beautiful every year. He was, he declared, much stronger at the age of nearly 30, than when he first arrived in London seven years ago. He gave the measurements to prove it: height, 5' 9"; chest 48' when "normal", expanding to 62"; his biceps measure 19.5"; deltoid 22"; forearm, 16.25" thigh 27"; calf, 18"; neck, 18"; waist, 29". "It never occurred to him to fix an age at which he might begin to wane, or retire from the pursuit of a profession which was forced on him by his own strength rather than chosen with deliberation."

Later in the month, Sandow and his wife attended the farewell dinner held in honour of Marie Lloyd, the most popular of all music hall stars, who was setting off for a tour of South Africa. The event at the Trocadero was for the flower of the variety profession and it was testament to Sandow's prestige that he was not merely invited but identified as one of the guests of honour in the subsequent enumeration of those who attended, along with Little Tich, Dan Leno and Alec Hurley. His slip-up at the Pavilion had damaged his muscles, but not his reputation. He and Blanche enjoyed the celebrity high-life. Joe Lyons of teashop fame laid on the catering; Marie Lloyd recited a poem and Dan Leno gave a speech entrusting her to her new manager (the menu carried a picture of a Matabele chief in native habit, carrying assegai and shield, "and kissing his hand to a capital portrait of Miss Lloyd"). After the speeches, the tables were cleared away, the Tivoli band struck up and dancing kept up until the early hours of Monday morning. At about two in the morning, Marie Lloyd had to be rescued from an imaginary watery grave by "a number of the sterner sex, who had to wave their arms and hop on one leg". One of those legs, hopping up and down on the finely-polished parquet floor, was more muscular than most.

SANDOW'S SCHOOL

OF

PHYSICAL CULTURE,

ST. JAMES'S STREET, PICCADILLY,

LONDON, W.

'TO young men in ordinary health I guarantee the following minimum developments in three months' training in light weight exercises at my of Physical Culture, viz. :—

Neck	...	1 inch.		Forearm	...	1 inch.
Chest	...	3 inches.		Thigh	...	1½ inches.
Upper-arm	2	,,		Calf	...	1 inch.

Waist ... Proportionate Reduction.

If these minimum developments are not attained—and in the majority of cases, no doubt, they will be much greater—I will return the pupil's fees for the three months' course.

Ladies have no need to develop their muscles to this extent, but in their case I promise that three months' training at my School will give them increased health and strength, the size of the waist being also reduced to its natural proportions.

Photographs of the pupils will be taken free of charge before and after training.

Heavy weight lifting will be taught at my School by skilled Instructors.

Terms for the Three Months, Two Lessons Weekly :—

TEN GUINEAS.

PRIVATE LESSONS BY ARRANGEMENT.

EUGEN SANDOW.

Advertisement for Sandow's School of Physical Culture, c1897

Sandow's School of Physical Culture at 32a St James's Street opened in the summer of 1897 and became the heart of a business empire that expanded as rapidly and impressively as his trapezius muscle. From this establishment, formerly a fencing school, Sandow offered one-on-one tuition and guaranteed results: over a three-month period, with two lessons a week, one could expect a three inch improvement in chest measurements, two inches in the upper arm, four-and-a-half inches in the thigh, and a corresponding decrease in waist size. The personalised tuition cost a great deal of money – some ten guineas for three months' tuition, compared to the working man's weekly wage of around one pound. The high prices were to be expected from an establishment located on the eastern side of St James's Street between White's and Boodle's – those most aristocratic of gentlemen's clubs – and a little up the hill from Berry Brothers and Rudd, wine merchants to the gentry, and the royal St James's Palace. No trace of the Institute remains, but contemporary accounts suggest that the fixtures and fittings were in keeping with the refined neighbourhood: one entered a wood-panelled hall, fitted out with heavy furniture, antiques, medallions and a full-sized statue of the great Sandow, as well as the oil painting of him as a gladiator that had previously hung on the wall of his flat in Pimlico. Sandow himself provided personal consultations in his private office. There were none of the usual trappings of a gym: no parallel bars, trapeze poles, or vaulting horses: just dumb-bells. One early visitor was the future King George V, whose diaries testify that on 29 April 1898, he "went to see Sandow's gymnasium." The future monarch was not known as a great adherent of exercise of any kind, but like his father before him was fascinated by Sandow and would honour the Prussian with his royal favour.

At a lower price, and for a lower class of clientele, Sandow offered training sessions for groups at 115a Ebury Street, London SW (a "popular branch at popular prices" is how he billed this secondary establishment, where the three-month course cost a comparatively modest three pounds and ten shillings), and other slightly less salubrious locations, for example, Tottenham Court Road in the heart of the West End, Walbrook in the City and Crystal Palace in the suburbs. The target here was the "average young man of today" who played sports at school, then got a job in an office. "Now," Sandow explained, "his time is fully occupied, and he has no time for pleasure…He gets flabby, and it is for such a person that my school is chiefly intended. He will be able to undergo a thorough course of exercise, to bring every muscle of the body into play, each evening." Even the Tottenham Court Road establishment had features of a gentleman's club: in addition to three spacious exercise halls, there were 40 well-appointed bedrooms and pupils were encouraged to take up residence during the course of instruction. There was also a restaurant serving special Sandow dishes.

He also opened up two Institutes in the provinces, one in Liverpool and the other at Manchester. "I am established at Manchester," his advertisements declared as he announced the opening of his consulting rooms at Exchange Chambers, St Mary's Gate. "My pledge to you," he promised, "is that provided your illness is not an incurable one, I GUARANTEE TO PASS YOU AS A FIRST-CLASS LIFE, that is to bring you to such a pitch of physical perfection and health and strength, that you will pass unrestricted the severest physical test possible." He expansively urged all to write to him, especially businessmen, those seeking health in order to get insurance cover, women who look after children and also "all who suffer in any way," and promised that he would PERSONALLY plan their course of treatment.

Sensing that he had an immense market, encompassing virtually all living human beings, men and women, from the very young to the old, he softened some of his declared opposition to recreational exercise and took pains to convey to his potential customers that his regime did not require anything as strenuous as actual weight-lifting. It was fun for all the family, as *The Times* makes clear in describing the opening of the Crystal Palace establishment in November 1899:

> The most recent addition to the attractions of the Crystal Palace is a School of Physical Culture, under the direction of Mr Eugen Sandow. The rooms set apart for the school...are admirably suited for the purpose, and they have been arranged and fitted to carry out efficiently the system of physical development which is associated with Mr. Sandow's name. There are separate departments for ladies and gentlemen, the equipment in each being suited to classes and also to individual instruction. Every branch of athletic endeavour and physical culture receives attention, but weight-lifting does not form a part of the course, and only the very lightest dumb-bells are used. The object of the instruction...is to develop the physical system as a whole by exercises founded on scientific principles and adapted to both sexes and all ages. It is claimed that the instruction is beneficial to nervous cases and to those who suffer from indigestion and weak heart. Children have physical culture imparted to them by means of Maypole dances, tip-toe marching to music, and many other entertaining expedients...[80]

Sandow's commercial ingenuity knew no bounds: in July 1898, he launched his own publication, *Sandow's Magazine*, on sale for six pence per issue or eight shillings for a year's subscription. This was an era of tremendous innovation and vitality in the newspaper and publishing industry. The advent of universal education, following the 1870 Education Act, had created a literate, mass audience. New technologies and expanded markets created opportunities for what we would call niche-publishing. Hundreds of new periodicals came into being in this decade, from the decadent *Yellow Book* and *Savoy Magazine* to Sandow's own offering. Sandow rightly sensed that there would be an appetite for a new publication catering to the public's growing interest in physical exercise. Known for the first few issues as *Physical Culture*, his *Magazine* had a breezy, populist tone, each issue with a foreword from Sandow himself and articles on subjects as various as Rational Riding for Women, Stray Dogs, Self-Defence, Something about Criminals – and Athletic Queens, which was about the crowned heads of Europe rather than his closet gay clientele. "The production of a perfectly sound body, that is Physical Culture," he explained in his foreword to the first issue, of July 1898, "to undo what civilisation has been responsible for, in making man regard his body lightly – that is the aim of Physical Culture." He outlined a practical agenda for promoting "positive" eugenics: his objective was to "raise the average standard of the race as a whole".

Just as modern television seeks to engage its audience as directly as possible, chiefly through the mechanism of the phone vote (which dictates the outcome of shows from *Strictly Come Dancing* to *Big Brother*), Sandow dreamt up ruses to ensure the active participation of the readership. The fiction that he answered each and every letter from his mail-order clients was one: in fact he devised an elaborate system for categorising questions and employed clerks to sort through post and despatch prepared answers. This method was exposed in April 1899 when Sandow dismissed a clerk by the name of James Charles Carpenter from the Ebury Street establishment, paying him a week's salary in lieu of notice. Incensed, the chief clerk of Sandow's 2s 6d mail-order instruction scheme walked out with a parcel under his arm containing a stolen set of five code books in which all questions and their possible answers were contained. Sandow took Carpenter to court in a bid to recover these valuable documents.

Sandow also launched a rolling competition to find the best-developed men in the country. Not the men with the biggest muscles, he insisted, but the best, the heats to be held at various regional centres and the winners to be awarded statuettes of Sandow in gold, silver and bronze. The gold statue was supposedly worth the substantial sum of 500 guineas. The publicity surrounding the early rounds of this competition was enough to attract not merely thousands of entrants, but also burglars, who broke their way into the establishment in Ebury St in the hope of finding the valuable trophies. The thieves were themselves adherents of Sandow's system. "It would seem they were not deficient either in general culture or physical development," noted a laconic newspaper account. "For after waving about a 150lb bar-bell and unrolling a huge piece of coconut matting, they took off the flannels they had borrowed for those exercises and calmly enjoyed the luxury of a bath, followed by cigarettes from the manager's box". They were no doubt disappointed to learn that the statuettes they managed to appropriate were in fact bronze replicas, rather than solid silver or gold. Sandow said the valuable statuettes were locked up elsewhere at the time, but it seems more than possible the prizes were not as advertised and were merely gold-plated after all.[81]

At first, Sandow was not certain of the pulling-power of his own name and he adopted what we would call a co-branding strategy, co-opting the name of a famous department store to ensure the appeal of his products to the wider public. One of his earliest inventions was thus the Sandow-Whitely pulling machine, which, as readers of James Joyce's *Ulysses* will note, is the contraption that Leopold Bloom used in his pursuit of repristination, keeping measurements of his vital muscles before, during and after three months' consecutive daily use of the device. In time, however, Sandow developed a sophisticated marketing and branding strategy. He saw how retailers and food and drinks manufacturers promoted products that bespoke quality and reliability, competing for customers in the new mass markets. This was the first great era of branded goods: Woodbine cigarettes, Grape Nuts breakfast cereal, Oxo, Germolene, Bisto and Pears soap all date from this period. Bovril was frequently promoted in Sandow's publications ("Personal Strength is one of the greatest benefits arising from a constant use of Bovril...") and Quaker Oats were launched at the Columbian Exposition. These products were advertised in the newspapers, in bright and prosperous posters that were illuminated at night, catching the eye of the casual consumer. "Advertisement has revolutionised trade and industry," says a character in H.G.Wells's *Tono-Bungay.* "It is going to revolutionise the world." By adopting the aggressive marketing strategies of the early consumer goods companies, Sandow's name and bodily image soon became as powerful a brand as many other mass-market products introduced at the *fin de siècle.*

Like any modern corporation, Sandow fought hard to defend this brand, quashing those who sought to appropriate his name and image. As early as 1892, he had fought a court case against one William Blumefeld, who was alleged to have obtained one shilling at the Corn Exchange in Lincoln by pretending to be the strongman Herr Sandow.[82] Now, the stakes were higher and he did not hesitate to sue a printer who had allegedly misused an image of him lifting a horse with one hand. "In his moments of recreation Mr Sandow used to juggle with a cart-horse," counsel explained. "While he poised one in the air, an artist sketched the tableau, and Mr Sandow had the sketch transferred to posters, as an advertisement." The problem arose when

Sandow discovered that the printer had held back some of the stock of posters. "Strong as [Sandow] is, [he] was overcome with emotion when he learned that the printer had enabled some of those posters to be adapted to the purposes of an Irish brewer [Arthur Guinness & Co] who was advertising his stout. The suggestion was that, by the sole use of this article of diet, and without any fatiguing exercise of the muscles, the purchaser would be able to lift horses with the greatest of ease." Impossible, Sandow claimed, an outrageous slur on his own unique powers of strength!

Guinness had not meant the claim literally and, in any case, always had a defence: if a tippler tried and failed to lift a dray-horse after a pint or two of stout, it could always be argued that he had failed to drink enough beer. The court urged the brewer and strongman to come to an accommodation over the use of the poster. "Stout of this virtue might be served out to the police engaged in the regulation of the traffic," noted the leader writer of the *Daily News*, his tongue firmly pressed into his cheek as he reflected on the power of brands. "It would sometimes greatly facilitate their labours if they were enabled to lift horses out of the way. The weight of the vehicle, however, would have to be taken into account, but this difficultly might be met by the additional use of the right sort of meat essence, and the right sort of cocoa. The idea is well worth the attention of the Home Secretary...A policeman who breakfasted, lunched, and dined wisely, and took the right sort of pills, might in time be able to snap up an unruly omnibus, and gently drop it in a side street, without turning a hair."[83]

In taking this apparently trivial case to the law, Sandow garnered publicity that more than compensated for the alleged pecuniary loss. The press coverage and the multiple representations of his body in many different media served to maintain consumer awareness of the corporeal perfection to which customers could aspire by buying his products and following his System. A versatile self-promoter and ingenious entrepreneur, Sandow was thus a beneficiary as well as exponent of the commoditisation of leisure in the last decade of the 19th century. There was only one Sandow – the unique body that could be viewed on stage or fondled backstage by the lucky few. But his image was replicated and disseminated through still photographs, press reports, scientific "anthropometric" measurements and anatomy lectures, films and magazines. He was supremely skilled in marrying showmanship with seriousness of purpose, deftly exploiting the mutually self-reinforcing opportunities opened up by the new techniques and technologies of the mass leisure industry of the day. To appropriate the title of Walter Benjamin's celebrated essay, his body was a "work of art in the age of mechanical reproduction".

In his heyday, Sandow operated scores of franchise establishments around the world, in the US, Australia, New Zealand, and India, backed up by a range of mail-order products which allowed one to follow his courses in the comfort of one's own home, wherever one lived. "There is not a portion of the world with which I do not treat," he would later claim.[84] "Tens on tens of thousands immediately flocked to [my] standard", igniting a "veritable furore in favour of physical culture".[85] In October 1898, his company went public:

> Sandow, the famous strong man, has turned himself into a limited liability company. He has capitalised himself at $125,000 in shares of $5 each. His assets are his school of physical culture, a monthly magazine called Physical Culture and his muscle. The public was invited today to subscribe to the stock of the company. Many jokes are being made about the strength of the company.[86]

Thus the somewhat sceptical US media greeted the news of Sandow's latest transfiguration, from vaudeville star to entrepreneur and evangelist for the cause of physical fitness for all.

- 8 -
SANDOW'S SYSTEM – BODILY PERFECTION FOR ALL

"Sandow…was the personification of the transcendental muscular aesthetic," one admirer wrote. "It booted little how much he could lift, or whether he could lift anything at all; one attended his exhibitions to look and be exalted by pure beauty."[87] Yet, unlike "art for art's sake," a phenomenon celebrated by decadent contemporary figures such as Oscar Wilde or James Whistler, Sandow's cultivation of beauty was allied to a clear social purpose. As early as 1894, he had documented and published a fully worked-out system for the physical regeneration of the race. In *Sandow and Physical Training,* Sandow argued that late-Victorian society had "neglected the consummate beauty of physical form for which the Greek, especially the Athenian, athlete was famed. Greek and Roman alike knew, in a high degree, the value of bodily exercise, and in their competitive games, as well as their training for war, adopted a system of physical education which produced wonderful results." In the spirit of Max Nordau, he argued that in the absence of rational exercise, the human body is ill-equipped for the "jar and fret of business life." Sandow cited approvingly the following passage from Archibald Maclaren, the founder of the Oxford Gymnasium: "We see around us every day of our lives masses of our race of imperfect growth and unsound constitution, and almost daily the lesson comes home to us of the breakdown of some friend or acquaintance, whose weakness of body could not withstand the mental and bodily strain in the struggle for life." By virtue of disciplined exercise and will-power, he had created himself, called himself into being from the unshaped raw material that was his boyhood body. When he appeared on stage as a Greek or Roman statue, his audience would understand that he was both artist and work of art, both sculptor and sculpture. Just as for Arnold Schwarzenegger, Sandow's chest was more than a body part: it was the realisation of a thought: "it is a concept that has been transferred by love and will-power from his consciousness into external reality," the body-builder and writer Sven Lindqvist has observed, "a reality that has been shaped to correspond exactly to his idea."[88]

The message was the more powerful because Sandow did not try to hide the secret of his success. On the contrary, in taking his clothes off and displaying his incontrovertible physical perfection, he flaunted it for all to see. In keeping with the democratic spirit of the age, he sought to disseminate his credo as broadly as possible, giving his adherents the chance to sculpt their own bodies. He published the details in *Physical Training*, in his best-selling *Strength and How to Obtain It* – which appeared in 1897 – and in numerous books, pamphlets, articles and lectures thereafter. As Sandow later explained (in remarkably good English, it was noted) to a crowded audience of students at Oxford Town Hall:

Physical culture was the education of the body just as mental culture was the education of the mind. It did not aim at making its students strong men so much as making them swift of movement, and capable of great endurance. If they wanted to bring their bodies to the highest state of physical perfection they must know how to exercise. Everyone, the middle-aged man, the woman and the child must endeavour to possess themselves of good health and strength as their first aim in life…If a man wanted to bring his body to the highest state of physical perfection, he must practice self-control, cleanliness and perseverance. They must also acquire the power of concentration. The last was the most important point of all. While they were exercising, they must forget everything else in the world but their muscles; and they should endeavour to concentrate themselves solely on the individual muscle they were using… [March 1900]

After Sandow had posed in front of the Oxford students, three of his pupils went through their exercises: a young Hercules aged around 25, a boy of 15 and a young woman. "Both the former were wonderfully developed and their exercises with the dumb-bells were calculated to strengthen the individual muscles of the body and legs, as well as invigorate the whole frame." Then volunteers were asked up onto the stage. The captain of the Oxford University Athletics Club and an international rugby player were obliged to change into Sandow's regulation tights before being put through a particularly exhaustive sequence of drills. The show concluded with more displays from Sandow and the obligatory tearing apart of three packs of cards.

His system relied on multiple replications of individual exercises with relatively low weights. "Before Sandow," Arnold Schwarzenegger has explained, "no one did more than two [lifting] repetitions of anything. The idea of developing strength was to take the heaviest weight you can lift, lift it one time, put it down, wait three or four minutes until you get your breath back. Sandow was the first one to do 50 repetitions. He would use a lighter weight. He was the first one that shaped his body with muscles." The regime laid great emphasis on gentle, repetitive exercise, using at first dumb-bells so small that athletes would laugh at them.

Take the ordinary dumb-bell antics – how they jerk and strain at the muscles, Sandow explained. He [on the contrary] would begin to teach a child at two years age with half-pound dumb-bells, gradually increasing the weight to five pounds – and there fix an absolute limit. With such light apparatus Sandow professes his ability to develop every muscle in the body at no cost to any other muscle. How many so-called strong men have developed biceps to the degree of rendering it impossible for them to straighten their arms? They are muscle bound, and in fact deformed ... Weight-lifting...is not recommended by Sandow as a popular recreation. If, by judicious exercise one has attained so remarkable a degree of strength that feats with heavy weights cause one no inconvenience, well and good; but as a means of muscular development they would partake of that very violence which Sandow so strongly deprecates.[89]

It was a rational form of exercise, Sandow argued, because it was based on a scientific understanding of the way the body works. Sandow had a detailed knowledge of anatomy and repeatedly impressed his contemporaries with his ability to name and display individual muscles. The diagrams and charts he used to describe his exercise routine remain admirably clear to this day. Sandow thus laid bare the secrets of muscular development. Through the application of rational exercise came power for the individual, in the form of a fitter and more effective body, and for the nation, comprised as it was of millions of individuals. This, Sandow never tires of reminding his readers, is a benefit of his System that is not available to those who pursue mere sport. *Sandow's Magazine* would contain articles on cycling, rowing, hurling, football, golf, cricket, rock-climbing, and numerous other sports, but Sandow was contemptuous of the benefits of such "recreative" exercise. "Physical Culture is the scientific building up of the body to supply the strength which has to be applied to recreative exercise," he argued.[90]

Sandow noted that women also tended to participate in strenuous

FIRST SERIES.

Exercises for the Treatment of Lateral Curvature, for both sexes, with or without apparatus.

Exercise 1.

Ex. 1a.—Repeat with right hand.

Exercise 2.

Ready Position.

Have a hook securely fastened in the floor and attach one end of the rubber thereto. Stand a full arm's length from the hook, turning the body to left side; the right leg about 12 inches from the left.

Movement.

Left arm outstretched, press slowly upwards from the shoulder above the head, and recover to ready position.

Ready Position.

Stand erect, feet wide apart, bells by sides.

Movement.

Reach down with left hand to ankle, bending right knee, but keeping left leg absolutely straight, at the same time drawing right hand under arm-pit. Reverse. The face should follow the movement of the descending hand.

A page from Sandow's Body-Building

games "far more than is good for them," particularly town-bred
women who were not brought up amid healthy surroundings and thus
able to undergo less bodily strain than their suburban sisters. He was
adamant that Physical Culture was "admirably suited to the purpose of
producing in a woman the symmetry of form that cannot be obtained
by any other means, and surely there is no woman on the face of the
planet who does not but desire to possess a perfect figure". Although
to the modern reader his chivalry comes across as patronising and
sexist, he was on the side of those women who wanted to enjoy new
freedoms, in what they did with their bodies as much as what they
wore. He supported rational exercise and rational dress. He rejected
the accusation from some conservative critics that exercise made the
modern woman muscular and unfeminine – even "self-assertive and
hybridistic," unfitting her for any useful role in life and taking from
her "the grace and charm of womanhood". "If I thought that was
so, I would be the first to decry Physical Culture for women, for I
utterly abhor the idea of a woman without feminine grace, which is her
distinctive charm, and if I thought for a moment that in advocating
Physical Culture I was militating against these, I would never have
proceeded with the subject." He claimed that his system could help
women take weight off, or put it on, as required, and as with his male
customer base, all the exercises could be fitted into a busy life in twenty
minutes a day, without any need to adopt a special diet. In among the
articles on hog-hunting or cycling in winter, his magazine regularly
carried features designed to appeal to women, often about clothes or
beauty but sometimes touching the more exotic, for example, a piece
on ju-jitsu for women. "It is marvellous to note that a girl, slight and
lissom, can throw a large man over her shoulder across her hips with
perfect ease, and with the grace inseparable from power."[5]

By the time *Strength* was published, Sandow had distilled his System down to 18 simple exercises. "The body, like a child, wants to be educated, and only through a series of exercises can this education be given," he says. The exercises are set out in detail, together with an anatomical chart and tabular details of the number of repetitions that are required according to age, height and other variables, and a summary of expected improvements in terms of weight-loss, waistline and other vital statistics if the regime is adhered to. The first set of exercises were for the muscles in and around the abdomen and contributed to the reduction of obesity, or helped relieve constipation and indigestion, and generally strengthened the liver and kidneys; the second were designed to develop the lungs and the chest and thereby stimulate the circulation of blood about the body; the third group were intended to strengthen the spine. The fourth group of exercises was arranged for the general development of the whole of the muscular and nervous systems.

"For chest development," the pupil is told, "stand erect, arms extended in front of the body…bring the arms slowly forward in a line with the shoulders, inhaling steadily all the time the hands are travelling. Make a momentary pause, brace up the chest, and bring the arms forward again, exhaling to the utmost all the time that the hands are travelling. Breathing movement slow."

Having thus worked on the deltoid, pectorals, rhomboid and trapezius, one could tackle the serratus, latissimus dorsi and quads by standing with the left toe pointing to the left, and right foot to the front, the left arm flexed, forearm horizontal, elbows close to sides, eyes front…and then lunge three feet to the front with the right foot. Or if you happened to be suffering from constipation, bend the body to the right side as much as possible, at the same time as bringing the

100 Netherwood Road
West Kensington Park
Jan. 25th 1897

Dear Sir

I write to give you my measurements as requested. I am 22 years
of age, and I bought Sandow's book
on Physical Training 18 months ago, since
when I have been an ardent admirer &
follower. If Mr. Sandow knew what a
good thing he has done for the young
fellows of England by inspiring them to
dignify their physical powers. I think he
would be more than pleased. My measurements when I started training were as.
follows. — (I had done work on Gymnastic
apparatus previous to that)

Present Measurements.

Chest	36 inches		Chest	40 inches	
Waist	29	"	Waist	29	"
Biceps flexed	12¾	"	Biceps flexed	13½	"
Forearm	10	"	Forearm	10½	"
Thigh	19	"	Thigh	20	"
Calf	13	"	Calf	13½	"

Height 5 feet 8 inches.

A letter to Sandow from a grateful pupil

left hand under the left armpit, stretching the right arm down as far past the knee as possible.

The book contains facsimile copies of letters from satisfied customers, drawn from all parts of the British Empire and from all classes of men (and, to a lesser extent, women.) It is significant, perhaps, in terms of contemporary concerns over London's urban poor, that the first testimony comes from a five foot high, 19-year-old man from 23 Church Row, located in Limehouse in the dreaded East End; this adherent declared himself transformed by the regular pursuit of his exercises. Sandow's message was that by improving the physique of the individual, it would lead to an improvement in the race overall. "The prime lesson for all, is to seek to raise the individual strength, which is much lower for the race than it ought to be," he wrote in *Physical Training*. "By raising the physical standard in the unit, time and training will accomplish like results for the race." By 1897, his immodest aim was to "permanently raise the standard of physique for the whole race."

Some aspects of Sandow's System could not have been entirely appealing to his audience. He recommended taking a cold bath twice a day and suggested that it was particularly restorative to jump straight out of the bath into one's clothes, without taking the trouble to towel oneself down first. Otherwise, the regime was less than Spartan: Sandow said that he himself adopted a philosophy of "everything in moderation". "I eat, drink, smoke and sleep quite in the ordinary way," he said. He recommended eating frequent light meals rather than two heavy meals, as was the custom at the time. He recommended a great deal of sleep: "he needed nine hours in bed, unconscious and motionless, and declines to yield a minute of this habit". He drank weak tea for breakfast, abominated coffee and champagne. Red and white wine, lager beer and up to six small cigars were permissible during the course of the day (he conceded however that tobacco was "absolutely pernicious" to some people and they should avoid it altogether). When working on stage he ate a large supper, but all other times he avoided a late meal.

To his middle-aged followers, he offered the optimistic assertion that one's physical fitness and strength could keep on improving to the age of 45. On arriving back in London, he boasted that he could perform with ease feats that as a younger man he would have found impossible. To the commuter and the office-bound, he made it clear that the exercises could be carried out in a matter of 15 minutes a day and in the privacy of one's bath- or bedroom. His system was tailored to the exigencies of modern living. One famous (albeit fictional) middle-aged man who took up the exercises was Leopold Bloom, hero of James Joyce's *Ulysses*. "The indoor exercises…prescribed in Eugen Sandow's *Physical Strength and How to Obtain It*…designed particularly for commercial men engaged in sedentary occupation, were to be made with mental concentration in front of a mirror so as to bring into play the various families of muscles." Bloom had in youth excelled "at the half lever movement on the parallel bars," but in middle age he was unfit and running to fat. Like many real-life practitioners no doubt, he started the Sandow regime enthusiastically, but soon relapsed. The exercises were at first "intermittently practised [and] subsequently abandoned."[92] James Joyce himself might have seen Sandow's performance in Dublin in April 1898 (when Sandow performed for a week at the Empire Theatre), and he may even have signed up to Sandow's correspondence course from his exile in Trieste. His countryman William Butler Yeats did follow the system, making sure to carry out twenty of Sandow's exercises a day when he was staying with his muse, Lady Gregory at

Coole Park, working out between writing poetry, reading Chaucer and going fishing.

P.G. Wodehouse was also an adherent, contributing articles to Sandow's *Physical Culture* magazine while working for the Hong Kong & Shanghai Bank in the City of London in the early 1900s (for example, a piece on how boxers train, or on physical culture at Dulwich College, both somehow lacking the wit of the Psmith stories). Paderewski, who needed to stay in tip-top shape, "used light twelve-ounce dumb-bells," records his biographer. "His gymnastic exercises he takes in the morning on rising, and anyone overhearing him from an adjoining room at that hour might think that he was counting piano scales, 'one-two, one-two one, two, three.'" His strict adherence to the regime kept him so fit and healthy that, despite the demands of running a country and playing the piano for upwards of seventeen hours a day, he was able to perform Sandowesque feats of strength, for example, lifting a man perched on his calf muscles.

Edward Carpenter, the militant gay activist who inspired E.M. Forster, and the man who introduced sandals to British socialism, took to the pages of the strongman's magazine to extol the benefits of open-air gymnasia. "There should be a large open swimming bath," he wrote, "and round the ground a running track, while horizontal bars and other apparatus could be placed in convenient locations." Thus these neo-Greek gymnasia would supplant the stuffy, dingy and dusty gyms of the town. The plea is suffused with the fantasy of healthy outdoors living. "I am assuming that clothing (if it is necessary) is of the slightest," Carpenter says. "I think this is important because, as any doctor will tell you, the action of the sun and air on the skin is a great item of health or strength. I believe that 'catching cold' is greatly due to our everlastingly covering the skin and checking the action of the sweat glands. At any rate occasional exposure for an hour together would greatly strengthen this most important organ, and with it the general health." *Honi soit qui mal y pense…*

George Bernard Shaw – although wanting to create a race of Nietzschean Supermen as an answer to the ailments of modern society – was not impressed. "I never wanted to stand my piano on my chest," he told Sandow when they met. "Nor did I consider it the proper place for three elephants…" Shaw's scepticism notwithstanding, there are abundant literary examples of Sandow's influence – for example the opening scenes of George Du Maurier's immensely popular *Trilby*, in which the heroine's bohemian admirers sit around carrying out their exercises in their Parisian garret – Baron Corvo's *Hadrian VII*, where the would-be Pope possesses a set of dumb-bells and exercises in front of a mirror as Sandow recommends – and E.M. Forster's *Longest Journey*, where one of the characters sits awkwardly on his horse "as if Sandow-exercising". In Frances Hodgson Burnett's children's classic *The Secret Garden* (1910), Sandow's influence can be detected in the regime pursued by the ailing Colin, the invalid scion of an aristocratic family who finds regeneration through fresh air and exercises:

> Dickon [the fit and healthy peasant boy from the moors] stood up on the grass and slowly went through a carefully practical but simple series of muscle exercises. Colin watched them with widening eyes. He could do a few while he was sitting down. Presently he did a few gently while he stood upon his already steady feet…

Pretty soon, Colin and the other children have muscles "standing out like lumps…"

Quite apart from these literary endorsements, contemporary newspapers show the extraordinary extent to which Sandow and his

SANDOW'S
SPRING-GRIP
DUMB-BELL.

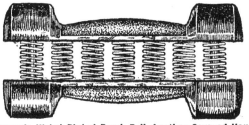

Gentlemen's Nickel Plated Dumb-Bell, Leather Covered Handles.

The Dumb-Bells are made in different sizes for Gentlemen, Ladies, Youths, Boys, Girls and Children, and are packed in elegant cases.

This appliance is very simple and cannot go out of order. It consists of a Dumb-bell made in two halves, separated about 1 inch from one another, the intervening space being occupied by small steel springs, which may be of any strength.

When exercising, the springs are compressed by gripping the Bells, and bringing the two halves close together, in which position they are kept until the exercise is over.

The pupil who possesses these Bells will find that instead of having to be continually buying heavier Dumb-bells, one pair will suffice him for all time. All that it will be necessary for him to do will be to purchase, at a small expense, new springs from time to time. All pupils are advised to use the "GRIP" DUMB-BELL, upon the merits of which I need not enlarge.

I have always taught that muscle is developed BY WILL-POWER, not by mechanical movement, and the simple principle of this latest invention is, by calling forth a continual exercise of will-power, to obtain results impossible with any previous Dumb-bell.

Yours faithfully,

EUGEN SANDOW.

The Dumb-bells can be had from ATHLETIC OUTFITTERS, SPORTING GOODS DEALERS, and OUR AGENTS throughout the World, as well as direct from ourselves.

Sandow's Grip Dumb-Bell Co.,
SANDOW HALL, SAVOY STREET,
LONDON, W.C.

An advert for Sandow's spring-grip dumb-bell, c1905

system were embedded in the culture of everyday English life. One can read about the muscular lady cyclist (a follower of Sandow's) who was attacked by what we would call a mugger. "He asked for money, watch, trinkets and everything." When she rode on, she left him "prone in the dust, with a ruddy nose, and nothing else". There was the annual concert and gymnastic display given by the pupils of the Royal Normal College and Academy of Music for the Blind (later, the Royal National College for the Blind), where boys and girls demonstrated their facility with the Sandow developer, expander and grip dumb-bell. A lady correspondent for the *Bristol Mercury and Daily Post* recommended the developer as the perfect Christmas present for a boy ("I can recommend [it] with the certainty that it will be pleasing to him, she wrote on 20 December 1899). At Shrubland Park, near Ipswich, 150 cadets from the training ship the *H.M.S. Ganges* were to demonstrate a programme of Sandow's exercises, but could not go through with it due to an unseasonal deluge (despite this failure, their physique was very much admired). A woman was arrested for obtaining scores of Sandow's dumb-bells "on appro," and selling them on without ever paying for them. On the music hall stage, Sandow continued to spawn many imitators, notably Mlle Zitka, who arrived in Britain in November 1900 and billed herself as the Female Sandow, the Perfect Woman, and the greatest teeth-lifter experts had ever known. There were Sandow girls aplenty, including a pair of comely if bulky Australian ladies whose image I have on a postcard. And there was Kate Sandwina, neé Brumbach, a maid of German extraction who had 17.5" biceps, 26.5" calves and a good claim to be the strongest woman in the world. Born in Vienna in 1884, she died in 1952 after a long and successful circus career.

Sandow made it clear that his exercise system could be followed without purchasing too much in the way of special equipment. The minimum requirement was a set of dumb-bells or hand-grips, ideally the patented Sandow grip dumb-bell which consisted of "two halves, longitudinally separated about 1.5 inches from one another, the intervening space being occupied by a small steel spring". There was a whole hierarchy of such dumb-bells, from the expensive to the cheap, for men and for women, reflecting the stratifications of late Victorian society. I managed to acquire a pair of gentleman's dumb-bells on eBay midway through writing this book: they are immaculately preserved, made of shiny, nickel-plated steel with six springs apiece and have worn red leather handles. They are more than a hundred years old, giving off a faint musty smell evocative of ancient exertions. They weigh three pounds each and, in handling them for the first time, I felt not unlike the poet W.B. Yeats, who experienced a frisson when picking up an ancient Samurai sword. I was conscious of all the other people who must have lifted these beautiful objects in the century since they were first manufactured and all the hopes and energies expended in their use. These well-crafted (and now distressingly expensive) objects are housed in a rusted tin box – like an old-fashioned biscuit tin – which boasts that they are supplied to King Edward VII. They also came with a detailed and well-preserved manual of instruction.

Like Leopold Bloom, I took them up in pursuit of repristination. The first time I went through the entire routine of 19 different exercises, I underestimated the amount of physical effort that I was undertaking and blithely performed twenty or so repetitions of each exercise. After 20 minutes, I had finished and felt pleasantly energised, not conscious of having had an especially strenuous workout. The next morning I could hardly walk: there were aches and pains in strange parts of my anatomy, suggesting that Sandow had helped me exercise muscles that

SANDOW'S GRIP DUMB-BELL.

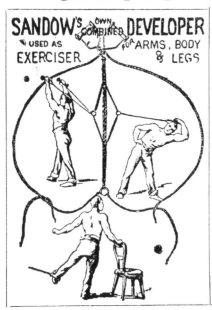
An advert from Sandow's Body Building

I was but dimly aware existed. The next time I tried them, a day or two later, I was much more circumspect and went through eight to ten repetitions only. I still hurt all over the next day, but realised that I was getting the kind of concentrated burst of exercise that a visit to the gym has never quite delivered. I have kept going with the full workout daily for several months now and it has definitely got easier and I am fitter. It is a form of exercise that is easy to squeeze in around all the obstacles likely to come between an author and his fitness regime: taking the kids to school, going to work, opening a bottle of wine, watching a DVD or taking the dog for a walk. It would be going too far to say that my muscles now twist like lianas or coil sinuously like a serpent, but my wife and children have noticed there is a spring in my step and have noticed a new definition in my musculature. I only wish I had made the before and after measurements, as great-uncle Eugen advised. I do find that listening to music helps, as Sandow recommended. While exercising, you have to compress the two halves of the bell, holding them tightly together throughout the entire workout and, as Sandow intimates, this extra effort has the effect of concentrating the mind wonderfully on the precise task at hand.

For babies and children, Sandow recommended wooden equipment. He offered the opportunity to purchase the Sandow patented Combined Developer, which combines dumb-bells with rubber exercises. This device came with a Special Photographic Chart and patented detachable handles; it could be affixed to the back of a door and used by all the family – for only 12s 6d. I narrowly missed acquiring one of these objects in an online auction, but I have taken possession of a slightly battered Sandow chest expander where one of the four springs has gone missing, perhaps explaining why there has been so little expansion in my own chest, despite regular usage.

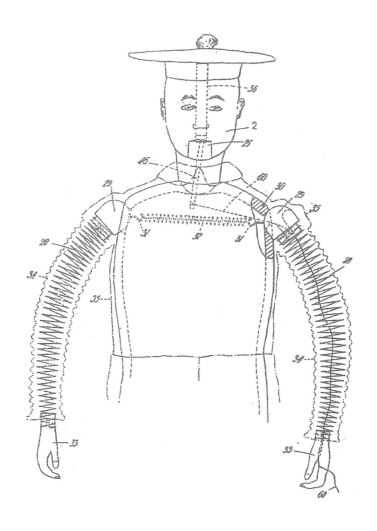

A drawing of Sandow's exercise doll for children

Later, from the offices of the Sandow Developer Company at 17-18 Basinghall Street in the City of London, Sandow patented numerous contraptions, including: a portable shower bath (which could be used in the bedroom "at any time in connection with an ordinary sponge bath...without danger of splashing or wetting the carpet"); an electric muscular exerciser, and a version of the developer dubbed the Symmetrion, specially designed for the fair sex "who are able by its use to produce the perfect symmetry of form which is the charm of women, and the ideal aimed at by all..." This device gave rise to the Symmetrion Girls, a music hall act, who were just like the posters, "soft, sleek and supple," according to a review of their performance at the Apollo in April 1906. There was even an exercise doll for children, where the child was encouraged to train its muscles by pulling the elasticated limbs of the doll. The reward came in the form of a sweet dispensed from the doll's mouth on completion of the exercises. Later, as we will see, the products became even more bizarre and the connection with Sandow himself tenuous, but the exercise equipment proved enduringly popular and there was a company selling Sandow dumb-bells and other paraphernalia until well after the Second World War. Over the next few decades, more than 500,000 of his branded dumb-bells were sold.

Sandow was not the first to develop a system of physical training as a way of improving racial stock. Pioneers include the Swedes Per Hendrik Ling (1776-1839) and his son Hjalmar (1820-1886), who earlier in the 19th century devised a system of exercises part modelled on martial arts, part on military drill. The "Swedish system," as it became known,

became very popular and Sandow would do his utmost to combat
its influence. He could not stop a version of it being introduced into
English schools. Indeed, Ling's system proliferated to populations even
more numerous than Great Britain and its Empire: Chairman Mao took
a liking to the Swede's exercises and promoted them in China. Sandow's
own model was his fellow Prussian Friedrich Ludwig Jahn (1778-
1855), a war hero and schoolmaster who in 1811, during Napoleon's
occupation of Prussia, organised group athletics on the Hasenheide,
an area of heathland outside Berlin. Jahn's efforts led to the creation
of the *Deutsche Turnverein*, the German Gymnastics Association, which
became closely associated with liberal politics, firstly in opposition to
Napoleon and later in support of the pro-democracy movement in the
mid-century. After the crushing of the 1848 Revolution, many German
athletes immigrated to the US and it was this legacy that contributed to
Sandow's popularity in North America. In Germany, Jahn is revered
to this day as the *Turnvater*, or father of gymnastics and many German
towns and cities have a *Turnhalle* or gymnasium. Sandow, who trained
at the Königsberg Turnhalle, credited Jahn with the "regeneration of
Germany, which assisted in no small measure towards the overthrow
of the Corsican".[93] According to George Mosse, Jahn saw gymnastics
and physical fitness as "the lifeline of the German people", creating
a community of Germans without regard to caste, religion or region.
"As the nineteenth century progressed, gymnastics became a social
hygiene that might even serve to transform feckless proletarians into
virtuous citizens and eventually keep socialism, internationalism, and
nihilism at bay."[94] Viewed as a liberal during his lifetime, Jahn's more
sinister legacy was a brand of anti-semitic nationalism adopted by a
later generation of outdoor- and exercise-loving German patriots, in
the 1930s.

While Jahn developed his system in response to French invasion and occupation, the French responded in a similar fashion following their defeat at the hands of the Germans in the 1870-71 Franco-Prussian War. In 1888, Pierre de Coubertin established the Ligue Nationale d'Education Physique in an attempt to promote athleticism in French schools, before going on to set up the International Olympic Committee in 1895, the precursor of the revived Olympic Games. Less well-known is the life and work of his countryman Professor Edmond Desbonnet, the proponent of a system of rational physical culture which is very similar to that of his friend Sandow. His agenda, as documented in the seminal but exceedingly obscure *L'Art de Créer le Pur-Sang Humain*, was quite literally to create a nation of "human thoroughbreds":[95]

> The aim of physical culture is noble above all. It allows one to become beautiful and enjoy excellent health, and to breed beautiful children to whom one will transmit the qualities acquired by virtue of one's own hard work.

Desbonnet cites English expertise in breeding racehorses as a model for this program of positive eugenics, explaining his mission as a way of rebuilding the strength of the French nation following the humiliations of 1870-1871. However confused he was about the principles of heredity, his thinking was not untypical for his age and was shared by Sandow:

> Healthier and more perfect men and women will beget children with better constitutions and more free from hereditary taint. They in turn [having imbued the principles of Physical Culture] will grow up more perfect types of men and women than were their mothers and fathers. So the happy progression will go on until, who knows, if in the days to

come there will not be a race of mortals walking this earth of ours even surpassing those who…were the offspring of the union of the sons of Gods with the daughters of men.

"Surely what has been done for the horse and the dog cannot be impossible of accomplishment in the case of man," Sandow exhorted in his first article as Editor of *Sandow's Magazine*. "At all events it is worth trying."[96]

- 9 -
JEKYLL AND HYDE

At night, Sandow was to be seen more or less naked or in the garb of a gladiator on the music hall stage; by day, he donned the uniform of the prosperous professional gentleman, wearing well-fitting frock-coat, dark trousers, shirt with starched winged collar and neatly arranged satin cravat, and patent leather boots. This daily transformation took place around midday when Sandow bestirred himself after a long, lazy morning recovering from the exertions of the previous night. His afternoon attire was of unobtrusive correctness. He looked like a Harley Street medical consultant, or perhaps a retired soldier, his thick, short, curly hair and fixed moustache adding a military suggestion to his professional appearance. Still only in his early 30s, he dressed as a figure of authority, a man with money and influence and solutions to the ailments that afflicted *fin-de-siècle* society.

From now on, Sandow took trouble to circulate images of himself as frock-coated professional gentleman, typically sitting at a desk in his well-appointed office – a foil to the racier pictures of him dressed in little more than loin-cloth or leotard. There was thus something of the Jekyll and Hyde in Sandow's existence as the 19th century drew to a close. Robert Louis Stevenson's famous novella dates from 1886 and describes precisely the London that Sandow would have known: the city of hackney cabs and greasy cobbles and tenebrous gaslight and fog, the large houses and the innumerable dark alleys, of double standards and dark secrets. Sandow affected to dismiss his show-business origins, as if Jekyll the respectable businessman wanted nothing to do with Hyde the showman. He maintained that "his exhibitions [were] a very minor though onerous function, in comparison with the interest he feels in athletics in their relation to bodily health and the physical equipment of the race". Towards the end of his tortured life, Dr Jekyll himself could only preserve his respectable form with a "great effort, as of gymnastics".

A series of incidents suggest that Sandow was losing a modicum of his strength as well as his appetite for such showmanship. In early January 1898, Sandow was four nights into an eight-week run at the Empire Theatre, Liverpool, when his act went badly wrong. His show typically concluded with a display of raw power, in this case picking up a grand piano from an elevated platform, together with a fully-grown pianist in mid-recital, then marching off-stage in time to the music. In full evening dress he affected to listen with delight to the pianist's performance but then be horrified when the latter started singing. This was the cue to carry him off stage. The trick was to reach round the piano to a handle, invisible to the audience, which allowed Sandow to shift the weight of piano and performer onto his shoulders, while giving the impression that he was lifting the weight with just one arm.

On this occasion, Mr Harry Leigh, professional pianist and Paderewski impersonator, noticed that Sandow had been struggling with some of the earlier feats in his act and seemed quite exhausted. Leigh asked Sandow whether he was up to the trick that evening, receiving an abrupt retort from the strongman that this was one of the easiest feats in his repertoire. Did he want to spoil the show, Sandow asked? "Thereupon," according to a laconic account of the subsequent court case, "[Sandow] gave [the pianist] a push on to the stage and attempted to do the feat as usual, but instead of carrying the piano and the plaintiff off the stage, shot both off the stage, smashing up the former and partly smashing up the latter." The smash for the pianist proved quite serious: having damaged his head and hands, he spent several months in hospital and lost his livelihood, ending up in the workhouse.

At first, Sandow acted generously, paying for a doctor to attend his stage accomplice. However, before too long, Sandow abandoned him to his fate. By the time of the court case, heard before Mr Justice Darling of the Queen's Bench in late November of the following year, Sandow argued that the accident had happened because he tripped over a crease in the carpet and, as it had been the pianist's responsibility to prepare the stage for the performance, the pianist was negligent and not he. (The judge was unsympathetic, remarking that the action would not have been heard in vain, if only for a single piece of hard evidence. The press found the episode highly entertaining.) Unfortunately for the strongman, several other witnesses testified that he had been out of shape on that night and the jury determined against him, awarding Harry Leigh damages of £125.[97] Sandow appealed against this ruling and was triumphantly vindicated in the Court of Appeal a few months later when Lord Justice Smith ruled that "he was unable to find a rag of evidence that Sandow had been negligent." The earlier judgement was overturned and the unlucky pianist did not receive a penny.

One month after the incident in Liverpool, Sandow suffered another stage reversal after he was goaded into accepting a challenge from Arthur Saxon, one of a trio of German strongmen who had come to England in the hope of emulating their more famous countryman's commercial success. Just as Sandow had made his career by taking on Sampson, the Saxons sought to throw down the gauntlet to Sandow, stating that: "Arthur Saxon challenges Sandow or any other man in the world for any amount...man and money ready." As business magnate and would-be social reformer, Sandow now ought to have seen himself as above such music hall shenanigans, but perhaps an atavistic competitive spirit drove him on, or more likely he was worried about the commercial implications of letting a bare-faced challenge go unanswered. He defended his own personal brand as indefatigably as a modern multinational.

On the evening of Saturday, 26 February, both Sandow and the Saxon trio happened to be performing in Sheffield, at separate theatres. As the finale to their act at the Grand Theatre, Arno Saxon announced that Arthur would heft a bar-bell that even the mighty Sandow would be unable to shift. Not for nothing was Arthur known as the world's leading exponent of the bent press; effortlessly he jerked and lifted a 264lb weight above his head. As he replaced it on the floor, a cry came from the audience. "Stop!", yelled a figure in evening dress. "I dare you, sir, to repeat that remark about Sandow being unable to raise that bell". Arno reiterated the calumny, at which point Sandow identified himself and jumped on the stage. The ensuing contest caused a sensation reminiscent of Sandow's trial of strength with Sampson, but in this case with a less gratifying outcome for our subject. Sandow found that he could lift the weights nominated by the Saxons, but only as far as his shoulders: thereafter, he could either not lift them further or, if he did, they started wobbling uncontrollably and he was forced to let the weights drop to the floor. On one attempt, he managed to raise the weights above his head, but without standing fully erect, as was required under the terms of the contest. When the curtain finally went down, it was apparent to most in the audience that Sandow had been bested. Arthur Saxon and his colleagues began to advertise their success as the men who had defeated Sandow. "The World's Strongest Men, and only Conquerors of Sandow," they bragged. "Their strength is more than exceptional, it is marvellous…Arthur Saxon supports fourteen men with his legs, whilst three other men seated on a barbell are lifted at the same time."[98]

This produced a typically pugnacious response from Sandow, who sued the trio for criminal libel. In the resulting trial, Sandow won on a technicality, not before stripping off to the waist in front of the judge and jury to flaunt his peerless muscles. It was also alleged that the dumb-bells on the night in question had been filled with mercury, thus making them inherently unstable for anyone but Arthur Saxon (this allegation was supported by Arno Saxon, one of the trio who had fallen out with the others and somehow been induced to side with Sandow). The judge ruled that, as Sandow had "handled" the bell in exactly the same bodily attitude as Arthur Saxon, "the Saxons were not justified in stating that Sandow had failed to 'lift' the weight under discussion". They were prohibited from making any further such claims in their marketing literature, but for the cognoscenti at least, Sandow's victory was pyrrhic: there is little doubt that Arthur was the stronger man.

By now, Sandow would have loved to have hung up his fig leaf and exchanged treading the boards for a career in the boardroom. Indeed, in early February 1899, he made a quite emphatic declaration of his intention to retire from the music hall stage. He was performing in Cardiff where, sitting in his room at the Park Hotel, he granted a rare interview to a reporter from the *Western Mail*. The article is worth printing at length, as it offers a vivid picture of Sandow at the height of his popularity, and indeed pomposity:

Those who wish to see Eugene [sic] Sandow's remarkable performance on the stage had better visit the Cardiff Empire this week, for this is probably the last time that the prince of strong men will be seen in a place of amusement in Cardiff. Sandow is now in the height of his popularity. He does feats which excel everything he has hitherto attempted, he is in the pink of health and condition and he is earning from the musichalls alone an income which is considerably over £10,000 a year. And with all this, Sandow is going to retire! Why? That was a question to which one of our reporters went in search of an answer on Tuesday morning.

In company with Mr W. Lea, the manager of the Empire, he found the strong man at the Park Hotel. Sandow was busy dictating letters to two of his private secretaries, and before him was a big pile of documents, numbering anywhere between 800 and 1,000. Sandow spared a few minutes while his secretaries went on transcribing.

"Yes," he said, in answer to a question, "it is quite true that I contemplate retiring from the stage. I thought I should have been finished before now, but I had so many contracts to fulfil, and managers refused to let me off, so that I had to keep before the public some weeks longer. Still, I have succeeded in making arrangements with several managers, many of my contracts have been cancelled, and in a few short weeks I shall have left the boards for good."

"But, why, Mr. Sandow?"

"Well, there are several reasons for coming to the decision I have. The principal reason is that I have not the time to continue on the boards. When I started my school of physical culture in London some eighteen months ago I had about 35 scholars. Now I have other schools…and I am receiving hundreds of letters from all parts of the country requesting that I should open more schools. This I intend doing. In the course of time I hope to have a school in every large town or centre in England and Wales. In the meantime, I have started a scheme by which anyone desirous of doing so can undergo a special course of instruction by communicating direct with me. This takes up my time in correspondence. It is no uncommon thing for me to receive 800 or 900 letters a day, and you see this heap here – they all arrived this morning. The students in my schools have increased from 35 to over 5,000. My correspondents number at the very least 150,000 per annum, and then I have to edit my monthly magazine, "Physical Culture," as well as consider the next edition of my book on the subject, of which, by the bye, over 300,000 copies have already been sold.

"All this takes up a lot of time – a vast amount of time – for I superintend everything myself. Therefore, I am bound to give up something. I am sorry to leave the stage, but I feel that I can do more good in my schools than I can on the stage, and that is why I am leaving. The rapidity with which my schools have grown, and the success which has been achieved in them, convinced me that my mode of treatment is the right one. It has been adopted by the Army, doctors recommend it, and my students rank from royalty downwards. Only this morning I received a letter from a well-known peer asking for advice."

"So are you going to make the whole country strong?"

"I am going to improve the condition of all those who seek my advice. I am, as you know, a professor of anatomy, and I work on scientific principles…the secret of my system is the connecting of brain with muscle. I use no medicine, and I trust to nothing but exercise – and, I think I may say, I never fail…"

"When will your school in Cardiff be opened?"

"That I cannot say. I shall want to get money first. Each school costs £10,000 to furnish alone, and that is a big expenditure. Still, Cardiff is already in my county competitions, and anyone living here is entitled to compete for my gold statue prize, value 500 guineas, as well as the gold medals which I issue."

In conclusion, Mr Sandow explained that it was improbable that he would be seen in Cardiff again unless it was on the lecture platform. Therefore, it behoves everyone of the local public who would care to see his sensational performance to hurry to the Empire this week.[99]

Sandow did not disappoint: he gave two performances that Monday night, both to packed houses, and he met with the usual enthusiastic response. However, he never did open an Institute of Physical Culture in Wales.

In early March, Sandow was performing in Glasgow where he paid a visit to his friend Auguste van Biene, the virtuoso cellist, who was appearing at the local Empire. Sandow brought with him Sultan the boarhound, who accompanied him on tour and went to sleep in the corner of the cellist's dressing room. "Sandow then went round to the front of the house to hear van Biene play one of his cello solos. In due course Mr van Biene's cue was given and his valet went to his dressing room to call him." But the 15 stone animal had planted itself across the door and refused to let the performer leave the room. The result was a long stage wait. It suddenly dawned on Sandow what had happened and he sped backstage to release van Biene from his captivity. The animal, though entirely docile, had been trained not to allow anyone to leave the room during his master's absence.

Far from retiring, a few weeks later, on Easter Sunday, 1899, Sandow was the opening act at the launch of the New Empire Theatre, a large and luxurious variety theatre in Broadway, Stratford, in the East End of London. "In the presence of the Mayor and Corporation of the town, and of numerous gentlemen distinguished in the variety world, an orderly and superior-class audience, cramming every available nook and cranny, broke out into hearty and sustained cheers and exclamations of satisfaction at the beautiful establishment with which they had been provided."[100] Edward Moss and Oswald Stoll, the prominent music hall entrepreneurs, sought to create a palace of pleasure in the East End. The new theatre had one of the largest auditoriums in London and was equipped with all mod cons. It was evidence of Sandow's popularity – and hence his commercial pulling-power – that he was chosen to be the headliner on the opening night. On this occasion, the strongman opened his act with a "tableau" – a formalised display of his body carried out from inside a velour-lined "posing box," a large cabinet lined with black velvet, with spotlights trained on his body to accentuate the muscles. He started off by showing muscular repose, with all his muscles relaxed. Then he flexed the muscles so that they were as firm as steel. He went on to flaunt "the action and uses of the different muscles", starting with the abdomen, then the biceps, triceps, the deltoid, the trapezino and the muscles of the back. He finished off with a terrific display of chest expansion, from 48" in his normal state to 62". After this exhibition, the curtains were raised to display a classical arena in which he carried out his feats of strength.

"Expressions of wonder are everywhere heard during the exposition of the athlete's marvellous physical development," noted a review of the first night's performance. "In a scene representing a Roman amphitheatre, Sandow then takes hold of bar-bells and dumb-bells of extraordinary weight, one of which he balances on his knees while another stalwart attendant is swung to and fro. Other astounding feats are performed by this modern Hercules, who, later, seated on the haunches of a horse, bends backwards, lifts a man from the ground up over his head, and seats him astride on the horse's back. As a specimen of finger strength Sandow tears in halves one and two packs of playing cards, his last effort being to separate no less than 154 cards. Sandow is encored again and again, and his performance is discussed with eager astonishment long after he has left the stage."[101]

As with Dr Jekyll and Mr Hyde, it is apparent that the two sides of Sandow's personality – showman and physical culturist-cum-business mogul – were indivisible parts of the whole. He could not quite bring himself to retire from the stage and maintained his music hall performances for years to come. At the turn of the century, he remained one of the highest paid stars on the music hall stage: according to a study carried out by *The Era*, he earned £150 a week, an amount exceeded by just three others stars: Leopoldo Fregoli, the Italian quick-change artist (who earned twice as much, but only for a short period); Albert Chevalier, the comedian, who commanded £250 a week, and Vesta Tilley, the cross-dresser, who earned £200. Sandow earned as much as Dan Leno.

Sandow did indeed find himself mocked by the cultural elite. *Punch* purported to describe (in entirely deadpan tones) the sensation caused when Sandow acquired the *Spectator* for £1 million, complete with commendatory remarks from Fleet Street proprietors: a gentle prod at both the strongman's wealth and his self-important desire to be a publisher. Taking the joke in good heart, Sandow wrote back saying that neither his youth, nor his ability to lift 40 men and a grand piano, positively disqualified him from being the publisher of a weekly magazine. But for all the snootiness of the establishment towards his sheer popularity, and his own professed ambivalence towards the medium that made him, Sandow's celebrity status continued to give him the pulpit from which to preach his message.

- 10 -
FIT TO RULE?

In 1900, Sandow performed for two months at the Casino de Paris in the French capital (the big line of the bill, ahead of the Nishihama-Matzui Imperial Troupe of Japanese human jugglers and the Charmion Quartet of comely dancers), then undertook a long stint as the headline attraction at the London Hippodrome. The year ended with a tour of northern England and Scotland. He continued to enthral the crowd, but by this time there was an undertone of deadly seriousness in his act. The British Empire was at war in South Africa. A private obsession with physical fitness had become first a craze and now a matter of vital public policy: was Great Britain fit to rule?

As Sandow knew from his own direct experience, the young men of the Empire on which the sun never set were a puny bunch. Their poor health and scrawny bodies had at first presented themselves as a business opportunity: now they were the cause of a national scandal. When the South African War broke out in October 1899, the British were surprised by the speed and effectiveness of the Boer offensive. In a matter of weeks, the Boers invaded northern Natal and Cape Colony, laying siege to Ladysmith, Kimberley and Mafeking. For a period, the conflict looked set to turn into a fully-fledged disaster. In the "Black Week" of 10-15 December 1899, the British lost three major battles in a row (Stormberg, Magorsfontein and Tugela). The mighty British

Empire was on the receiving end of a humiliating drubbing "by a handful of farmers amidst the jeering contempt of the whole world," as H.G. Wells put it.[102]

Cometh the hour, cometh the strongman. The crisis provided the perfect opportunity for Sandow to make the case for the applicability of his system, not merely as a way of promoting the health and fitness of the office-bound commuter, but to defend the vital interests of Empire. "The serious war in South Africa in which Great Britain is now involved, and which is taxing the resources of the Empire and testing the moral qualities of its people, make it an urgent duty to appeal for the training of the body for the highest consideration of all," he exhorted from the pulpit of his eponymous magazine, "the consideration of patriotism!" The Empire bestirred itself, and, by early 1900, thousands of Reservists were despatched to the Cape to boost the army, and tens of thousands more volunteered. "It has been thrilling reading, these last few weeks, that our eager volunteers have made for us," urged Sandow, "and those whom duty compels to stay at home more than half envy the chance these young fellows have of proving that England's sons are ready at her call to give up everything – even life – for her sake."

Despite the upsurge of patriotic sentiment, it was notable that a high proportion of those who volunteered for death or glory in the veldt, were turned down on the grounds of one physical defect or another. In Manchester, for example, 8,000 out of 11,000 would-be volunteers were rejected outright and only 1,200 were declared fit in all respects. Nearly a third of all volunteers across Great Britain were rejected in 1899, 28 per cent in 1900 and 29 per cent in 1901. British troops had to be augmented by battalions of volunteers from other parts of the Empire, chiefly Canada, Australia and New Zealand, which served to highlight just how healthy these outdoors-living colonial subjects were when compared to the urban underclass from which domestic recruits were drawn. Far in advance of the inevitable official enquiries, Sandow provided an instant explanation as to what was wrong with the physical stock of the nation: "the contraction of the lungs, the weak, irregular action of the heart, the irregular liver, are all defects due...to unnatural conditions of life and diet...and the absence of any counteracting influence in the shape of proper exercise." Even those volunteers who passed muster, could not really be classified as fit: "with chests that have cramped over desks, shoulders that have stooped in standing at counters, and digestions enfeebled by studious habits, many brave fellows are going out to South Africa to encounter rigours of climate, exhausting marches, and conditions of life which only the strongest can survive." Without wishing to seem unpatriotic, he thought that most of them would end up in hospital – or worse. Sandow did not say it himself, but many felt the Boer farmers were, by comparison, paragons of manliness: fit, lean and flexible, and uncorrupted by the pressures of office or factory existence. Cecil Rhodes told W.T. Stead that he never walked along Piccadilly, "without being appalled by the number of flat-breasted women, chicken-chested, pallid-faced men, with stooping shoulders. Especially when I contrast them with the Boer on the Veldt..."

In the dog days of early 1900, newspapers suggested that the quality of recruits would be much improved if they deployed Sandow's exercise machines on the long sea voyage to South Africa. Like other merchants keen to combine patriotism with commercial advantage, Sandow offered to equip the transports conveying the City of London reservists to the front with his Health Exerciser devices – free of charge, of course. He also offered to train up a number of men on board so that they could act as instructors. The offer was not in vain and Sandow's methods were used in earnest: in February 1900, with all the world on tenterhooks as the Imperial forces held off the Boers at the sieges of Ladysmith and Mafeking, it was reported that British prisoners at Pretoria followed his keep-fit routine. "During the morning the officers go through Sandow's developing exercises, in the afternoon they play rounders."[103] Under the far from uncivilised conditions of captivity, it was reported that the prisoners were generally developing wonderful muscles. Later, Sandow's exercises were also taken up by Boer prisoners-of-war held at the Diyatalawa prison camp in Ceylon – or at least so Sandow claimed in the pages of his magazine, which displayed pictures of healthy English jailors and Boer inmates, asserting that "our Tommies" and "our friends the enemy" were exponents of the Sandow system. A soldier of the 2nd Coldstream Guards, stationed at Graaff Reinet in South Africa, even found a picture of Sandow on the veldt, "evidently dropped by a Boer admirer," and sent it in to the magazine, where it was published to demonstrate the universal appeal of his method.

At home, meanwhile, Sandow offered to "fatten up" volunteers who had failed to pass muster with the recruiting sergeant and it was from this time that he began his training of young men in organisations, such as the Church Lads' Brigades. He exhorted every man to look upon it as his highest duty to become as healthy as his physique allowed, "for England's sake!" This was the best answer to the poet's question, "What can I do for thee, England, my England?" His magazine earnestly discussed the physical fitness qualifications required for English officers. "The measurements taken are height, weight and chest," he mused. "The chest measurement is generally a correct enough guide to the physical capacity of a man, for in it are contained the vital organs.

But the army measurement of the chest is taken below the shoulder blade and above or across the breast. The present system of measuring merely means that the candidate possesses the necessary number of inches a certain distance above the waist. Whether these inches represent fatty accumulation, hydrothorax, enlargement of the heart, or rickety deformity is not taken into account." It was at around this time that Sandow's court case over the dropped piano was resolved; displaying a weariness with the essential triviality of the case, the Judge praised Sandow's role as a "fattener" of young men and joined him in expressing scepticism about the requirements of the War Office. Lord Wolseley, Lord Roberts, or even the Duke of Wellington and Napoleon, would have failed to pass muster under the then prevailing rules.

Sandow's medico-jingoistic tone, while odd in a man who was still a German citizen, was in keeping with the flood tide of patriotic sentiment that swept through his adoptive homeland in the early and most critical months of the war. By the spring of 1900, when General Field Marshall Lord Roberts had reasserted imperial authority, and the sieges were raised, the prospect of outright defeat receded. Despite some dissenting voices, popular support for the war remained extraordinarily enthusiastic and was expressed feverishly in London. The entertainment industry both reflected and reinforced this "khaki fever", responding with customary inventiveness to the demands of war. In Portobello Gardens you could enjoy the spectacle of bush-savages imported from South Africa "every night exhibiting the habits and customs of their native country, tracking and killing the lion, leopard, buffalo etc and their superstitious bush dance." In August 1900, Earl's Court (home of an exhibition centre then as now) contained Boerland, a shooting gallery where visitors were encouraged to "wipe something off the slate" and take potshots at the enemy; while a full replica of a goldmine was operated to remind Londoners of the economic incentives for prevailing in South Africa. "By 1900 exhibitions and spectacles consciously designed to combine entertainment and tuition in the benefits of empire had become a staple of London life," notes the historian Jonathan Schneer, and "most London musichalls broadcast a clarion imperial and militarist call."[104]

The tycoons of the media and leisure industries, the music hall artistes and their audiences all threw themselves behind the patriotic cause. Rudyard Kipling wrote a poem to raise money for the families of British soldiers: *The Absent-Minded Beggar* generated £250,000-£300,000 (equivalent to £14-17 million in today's money) and is thus (it is said) the most practically effective poem ever written in the English or any other language. It was subsequently set to music by Arthur Sullivan and turned into a stage play. At the Alhambra (scene of Sandow's early triumphs), the highlight in the early months of 1900 was a ballet called *Soldiers of the Queen*, which attracted regiments of soldiers as well as the Colonial Secretary Joseph Chamberlain. The same bioscope technology that some years previously had captured Sandow in motion was deployed to transmit documentary footage of the war to music hall audiences. Meanwhile, the numerous war correspondents sent to cover the war had the effect of turning the conflict into pure spectacle. Robert Baden-Powell's exploits at Mafeking were magnified in the popular imagination. "B-P had always a somewhat childish liking for amateur dramatics," writes G.R. Searle, "and his fame owed much to his instinctive recognition that the Boer War was a spectacle, played out on a global stage before an audience of millions."[105]

Seeing a bandwagon, Sandow knew he had to leap onto it, and he thus adapted his stage act to the mood of the time. In the autumn of 1900, at the London Hippodrome, he went through his routine of poses, manipulations and feats of strength (including the grand piano trick and supporting on his chest the whole of the apparatus used in the show, plus attendants). Then, in a patriotic finale, he came back on as Tommy Atkins, a British soldier who was being chased by a battalion of Boers. Sandow's trademark leopard-skin briefs were replaced by regulation army khaki. To the tune of Rule Britannia, he turned his body into a bridge over which the British soldiers were able to escape to safety. *The Era* reported:

> Sandow completes his performance with an extraordinary exploit. The scene represents the successful defence of a bridge by a detachment of British troops in South Africa; but, just as the enemy withdrew, the commanding officer received despatches stating that all the bridges along the route have all been undermined. He immediately gives orders to have the wires cut, but it is too late. An explosion occurs, and the bridge is demolished. A passage must be found, and the officers are in a dilemma until Private Sandow volunteers to hold the bridge in position until the mounted officers and staff have passed...[106]

Following the accident that had nearly ended his career, Sandow now ensured that the horse was guided across the bridge, rather than left to its own devices. But one night in September 1900, the man supposed to be leading the animal was peering excitedly at the audience. His concentration lapsed and the horse stumbled and fell off the bridge. This time, Sandow was unhurt, but the horse landed on top of his star-struck assistant, who ended up in Charing Cross Hospital with a fractured thigh.

To highlight the contest between Lord Salisbury (Prime Minister after the Khaki election of October 1900) and Paul Kruger, leader of the Boers, the press depicted Salisbury as a ferocious Sandow-like figure wearing an animal-skin, while Kruger was portrayed exercising on a chest expander. Even as the tide turned in Britain's favour, the conflict had the flavour of a national humiliation. Hopes of a quick victory proved illusory and the war dragged on as the Boers adopted guerrilla tactics. The British responded brutally, introducing the first concentration camps, into which thousands of women and children were driven and would eventually die. Britain was winning the war, but it was evident that 500,000 imperial soldiers could barely contain a total population less than one fifth of that size. This was as disconcerting to the national psyche as the reversals in the Crimea nearly half a century before and it gave rise to a desperate search for explanations and remedies. Before he was elected, Lord Salisbury issued a warning: "Remember what has happened to the great maritime Powers of the past – to Holland, to Spain, to Venice, and if I might go into ancient times, to Carthage and to Tyre," he declaimed. "In every one case the great maritime power has been paralysed and killed, not by the disasters it may have suffered in its provinces or its outlying dependencies, but in every case it has suffered by the blow directed at the heart. That is a lesson which a Power like England should not neglect…if our heart is struck, there is at once an end to the history of England." In January 1902, General Sir Frederick Maurice blamed the debacle on the physical condition of the English working class: in an article in the *Contemporary Review*, he argued that a terrifying 60 per cent of Englishmen were physically unfit for service.[107] The notion of degeneracy thus acquired an alarming literalness: the civilian population was "too enfeebled to carry the burdens of Empire"[108] and Great Britain was correspondingly unfit to rule.

The Conservative-Unionist government was stirred into action. It launched first a Royal Commission into Physical Training in Scotland

(March 1902), and then formed the Intergovernmental Committee on Physical Deterioration, charged with making a "preliminary enquiry into the allegations concerning the deterioration of certain classes of the population, as shown by the large percentage of rejections for physical causes of recruits for the Army..."[109] In its report, published in 1904, the committee traced the problems to poor hygiene and diet, combined with a near-total absence of physical education for the working class. Its recommendations would ultimately include the provision of school meals, measures to reduce pollution and to improve working conditions, together with a programme of compulsory physical training. But that is to look ahead. Even before the first of the two Commissions started to gather evidence, Sandow advertised his own flamboyant solutions to improving the nation's fitness.

- 11 -
THE GREAT COMPETITION OF 1901

London, Saturday 14 September 1901

At eight o'clock sharp, the band of the Irish Guards started to toll out the sombre chords of Chopin's Funeral March. The audience of 15,000 people, gathered that night in the Albert Hall, rose to their feet, paying a solemn tribute to President McKinley, slain a week before by an assassin's bullet. The music came to a halt and the lights went down. Suddenly, the darkness was penetrated by the beams of 20 searchlights that picked out row after row of young athletes who marched in time to the sound of Sandow's own "March of the Athletes" (this was a lively composition reportedly almost as stirring as Chopin's and probably written by Sieveking: the sheet music for the piece was distributed inside *Sandow's Magazine*, along with wallcharts, to encourage rhythmic exercising). As they made their way to the stage of this massive auditorium, they performed displays of gymnastics and wrestling, flexing their well-developed muscles to roars of approval from the crowd. There was a pause in the music and the three respected judges of Great Britain's first nationwide bodybuilding contest ascended the stage. They were Sandow himself, Arthur Conan Doyle, and Charles Lawes, a sculptor. As Conan Doyle recounted:

There were eighty competitors, each of whom had to stand on a pedestal, arrayed only in a leopard's skin. [The judges] put them up ten at a time, chose one here and there, and so gradually reduced the number until we only had six left. Then it became excessively difficult, for they were all perfectly developed athletes. Finally the matter was simplified by three extra prizes, and then we got down to the three winners, but still had to name their order, which was all important since the value of the three prizes was so different [they were three statuettes of Sandow, the first prize in gold, the runner up in silver and third in bronze]. The three men were all wonderful specimens, but one was a little clumsy and another a little short, so we gave the valuable gold statue [a naked image of Sandow] to the middle one, whose name was Murray, and who came from Lancashire. The vast audience was very patient during our long judgement, and showed that it was in general agreement.

The fact that Murray, like all the contestants, was dressed in black tights and a leopard-skin leotard did nothing to diminish the audience's enthusiasm for the victor, or to temper the admiration of the reporter from *The Times* who celebrated the "novel and interesting display." Francis Galton, the father of eugenics, was in the audience and also found the competition highly instructive, but with reservations. He told Karl Pearson:

I did not think these best specimens of the British race to be ideally well-made men. They did not bear comparison with Greek statues of Hercules and other athletes, being somewhat ill-proportioned and too heavily built. I must say that I was disappointed with them from an aesthetic point of view, though in respect to muscular power they seemed prodigies. Sandow afterwards exhibited himself in a pose that brought out his chest and arms to full advantage, and in that statuesque position I placed him as far superior to all the competitors.[110]

Meanwhile, that night, Sandow invited the winners and judges to a sumptuous champagne supper, after which Conan Doyle encountered

Murray in the street:

As I left the place of the banquet [early in the morning] I saw in front of me the winning athlete going forth into the London night with the big golden statue under his arm. I had seen that he was a very simple countryman, unused to London ways, so I overtook him and asked him what his plans were. He confided to me that he had no money, but he had a return ticket to Bolton or Blackburn, and his idea was to walk the streets until a train started for the North. It seemed to me a monstrous thing to allow him to wander about with his treasure at the mercy of any murderous gang, so I suggested that he should come back with me to Morley's Hotel, where I was residing. We could not get a cab, and it seemed to me more grotesque than anything of Stevenson's London imaginings, that I should be wandering around London at three in the morning in the company of a stranger who bore a great golden statue of a nude figure in his arms. When we at last reached the hotel I told the night porter to get him a room, saying at the same time, "Mind you are civil to him, for he has just been declared to be the strongest man in England." This went round the hotel, and I found that in the morning he held quite a reception, all the maids and waiters paying homage while he lay in bed with his statue beside him. He asked my advice as to selling it, for it was of considerable value and seemed a white elephant to a poor man. I told him he should open a gymnasium in his native town and have the statue exhibited as an advertisement. This he did, and I believe he has been very successful...[111]

In fact, as David Chapman has discovered, Murray lived to the age of 79. After the competition, he established a strongman act of his own which thrived until he joined up and was gassed in Flanders. Despite debilitating injuries, he subsequently became manager of a successful theatre in Newcastle. It will not surprise the reader to learn that, when his nephew came to sell the coveted golden statue, it turned out to be made of bronze after all.

The Great Competition was the begetter of modern body-building events such as the Mr Olympia contest, where oiled many-muscled strongmen pose and flaunt their freakish physiques and, since 1977, the winner has been awarded a copy of the statuette claimed by Murray. A century before shows like *Britain's Got Talent* or *The X-Factor*, but based on the same principle of audience participation, the contest captured the imagination of men the length and breadth of the country – and even further afield. Caroline Daley tells the story of how a bronze statuette, possibly awarded as the third prize in the competition, created headlines as late as 1955 when it turned up in a New Zealand farmhouse. "Sandow Statue in Nelson Home: Gift to Star Pupil," recorded the New Zealand *Herald*. It had belonged to Harold Robinson, originally from Lancashire, who had been born with a deformity of the leg and was a "hopeless cripple" until he took up Sandow's exercises and became an ardent exponent of physical culture. Somewhere along the way, he had acquired the statue of the naked strongman plus bar-bell, and had taken it with him as a prized possession when he and his family emigrated to the other side of the world.[112]

Sandow gave all the proceeds of the competition to a charity supporting the widows and orphans of those killed in the Boer War, which would not be concluded until May of the following year.

Sandow and his friend Conan Doyle found themselves together not merely on the stage at the Albert Hall, but also in the pages of the *Strand Magazine*, where Conan Doyle, having capitulated to popular demand for the resurrection of Sherlock Holmes, was spinning his immortal tale *The Hound of the Baskervilles*. The October 1901 issue carried a long article about Sandow's appearance in another part of South Kensington – this time, not in the flesh but as a plaster cast statue displayed at the National History Museum, as the Natural History Museum was then known. Together with its neighbour the Victoria and Albert, this august institution had been erected with the proceeds of the 1851 Great Exhibition, and constituted hallowed imperial ground. Here one could see the scientific equivalent of: "the stoutly-earned results of a wide-spread domination…the fruits of British pluck, endurance and industry." There was likely to be some sniffiness on the part of the British establishment that someone such as Sandow, unclothed or otherwise, should have won a place here, as the anonymous author acknowledged:

My friend the Superior Person had been to the South Kensington branch of the British Museum, and he came back in high dudgeon. When I met him, indeed, he was literally spluttering with wrath. Evidently his very superior susceptibilities had suffered cruel outrage. "Great Scot!" he ejaculated, in replying to my look of inquiry, "what will the Museum be coming to next? A penny show with marionettes and performing dogs, I suppose. They've actually got a cast of Sandow the Strong Man – music hall people in the British Museum, faugh!" And the S.P., having delivered himself of this outburst, turned on his heel and tempestuously took himself off.

Sandow insinuated himself into the museum at the initiative of Professor Ray Lankester, the mollusc expert and Curator of what was then the Natural History Department of the National Museum, who presided over a bizarre and ultimately ineffectual attempt to create a life-size model of Sandow's exemplary body. Lankester maintained that Sandow was "the perfect type of the European man," and sought to preserve his body in a form that would "hand down to future

generations the most perfect specimen of physical culture of our day
– perhaps of any age". This was to be the first in a series of statues
illustrating the physical types of different races. It was an easy jump
from eugenics to what we today would call abject racism.[113] However
repellent to our sensibility, this way of thinking was commonplace in
the early years of the 20th century. It was Rudyard Kipling who coined
the phrase "White Man's Burden" to describe the obligations of the
Aryan ruling classes, positing a moral, economic also technological
superiority to what he dubbed "the lesser breeds without the law".
Statesmen such as the keep-fit fanatic Theodore Roosevelt, US
president from 1901-1909, gave such notions broad political currency.
Prof. Lankester's commission was part of what he and many of his
contemporaries viewed as a civilising mission.

Lankester himself dismissed the notion that Sandow's statue
would dilute the earnestness of the museum's imperial mission with a
tincture of music hall levity. On the contrary: "he is fully alive to the
educational value that the cast may pose to the public…probably the
last man in the world who would be moved by mere considerations
of what is likely merely to amuse and gratify the idle curiosity of a
certain section of the public." The professor commissioned Messrs
Brucciani, a well-known firm of cast-makers of 40 Russell Street,
Covent Garden, to fashion a model of the great Sandow. The firm had
experience of delicate assignments involving statues of naked men;
earlier in the century, when the Grand Duke of Tuscany had presented
Queen Victoria with a replica of Michelangelo's David, they had been
commissioned to cast a half-metre high plaster fig leaf to cover the
statue's offending manhood. This time, there were fewer scruples, as
it was the professor's plan to present Sandow's form fully naked, but
it turned out to be a painstaking and indeed painful process in which

sections of the strongman's body were successively daubed in liquid plaster of Paris:

> A mould roughly corresponding in shape but somewhat larger than the object of which the cast is to be taken is made…This is placed round the object and the intervening space filled in with plaster of Paris in a semi-fluid condition, and this, of course, moulds itself to the exact shape of the object it covers…when the plaster is set it is carefully removed in sections, and these, when pieced together, form a perfect mould. Into this plaster is again poured; when this hardens the mould is broken off and the cast itself remains…

As a procedure for taking a cast of an inanimate object, or even a body in a state of repose, this was straightforward. However, it was a different proposition altogether when the subject was a living, breathing mountain of muscle. Sandow had to keep his body flexed for 15 minutes at a time in order to allow the plaster to set, without mechanical support and without moving so much as a hair's breadth, and he had to keep this up, day-in, day-out, for a full month. Sandow lamented afterwards:

> This is what had to be done, and whether it was the arm, or the neck and shoulders, or the legs that were being operated on, the whole pose had to be struck, all the muscles contracted, as otherwise the pieces would never have fitted properly when they came to be joined. I regard it as the greatest feat of endurance I have ever performed. Good heavens, time and time again I thought I'd have to give up, the strain was awful. I used to finish after each piece was done fairly 'blown,' perspiring and winded much more than after the most arduous weight-lifting competition I have ever accomplished…really, when my chest and abdomen were being moulded, what with the peculiar 'biting' feeling of the plaster as it dried on the skin, and the difficulty in regulating the breathing, I thought I should burst…[114]

Casting the face, hair and moustache had proved especially difficult:
they could not apply the plaster directly, "otherwise the consequences
would have been very disastrous to the victim", and had to wrap him
up with linen before making the cast. After all this effort, the finished
work could not hope to emulate the perfection of the original. For all
Sandow's determination to stay still, he could not avoid involuntary
movements, thus introducing tiny flaws into the reproduction. The
resulting statue was the butt of much jesting in those elements of
the press who were not prepared to acknowledge the seriousness
of the professor's eugenicist intent. "The dead plaster does not and
cannot represent in its full perfection a form the charm of which to
no small extent depends upon the fine gradations and mobile finish of
its development," acknowledged even the otherwise adulatory *Strand
Magazine*.

Despite all the effort and the discomfort of the preparation, and
the £55 cost to the Museum, the statue was withdrawn from public
view after less than three months on display, as it was deemed obscene
by the museum's trustees, even after the application of a Brucciani-
crafted plaster-cast fig leaf. Delivered on 18 July, the statue was removed
on 26 October at the insistence of Lord Walsingham, who considered
the work to be too offensive to be displayed in any way. There was
clearly a struggle between the reactionary and the more enlightened
trustees as by the end of November, following a motion put down by
the Bishop of Winchester, Lankaster ordered that the statue should
indeed be accessible to those who had scientific grounds for seeing it.
Following this reversal, Lankester abandoned his plan to make casts
of types of all the races. However, copies were sent as far afield as the
Harvard gymnasium and the museum of the Gaekwar of Baroda, an
Indian potentate who developed an interest in physical culture; and

much later Arnold Schwarzenegger had a new cast made so that he could procure a replica of the statue.

The original was damaged during the Blitz and it lies neglected and armless (the limbs having become detached from the torso, head and legs) in the basement of the Natural History Museum. Getting to see the statue today is a considerable challenge, if only because Sandow now rests among a collection of ancient human remains which elicit sensitivities far greater than those provoked by this ideal Aryan. Amid the boxes of Neolithic skulls and femurs, the armless statue hangs from the ceiling, bound for its own security by a length of frayed climbing rope, its arms resting on the floor. It is the closest one will ever come today to Sandow's body as seen by his contemporaries and, despite the chipped plaster and other imperfections, one cannot but be impressed by the ochre-coloured form. He is neither tall, nor over-developed in the freakish manner of the modern body-builder. The waist is trim and the muscles of the legs and chest are exceptionally well-defined and one gets a decided impression of the power if not the beauty that made such an impact on his contemporaries. The head turns insouciantly to one side and one is struck by the immaculately preserved moustache and by his shocking nakedness.

- 12 -
IMPERIAL PROGRESS

Within weeks of the Great Competition, Sandow returned to the US and stayed there for the best part of six months, performing in New York and Boston and embarking on a typically frenetic tour of the continent. He and his wife returned from North America in April 1902 and, after less than a month in England, shipped out via Marseilles, together with a troupe of sketch artistes, character comediennes, mimics and dancers, on what would prove to be a year-long tour to Australasia and the Far East, with another visit to the US tacked on at the end. Sandow left his business affairs in the hands of his brother-in-law Warwick Brookes – a vigorous and ambitious young man who ran Sandow's Institute in St James's, took on the dumb-bell company and ultimately supervised Sandow's further disastrous diversifications. He left his daughter Helen with his in-laws in Manchester and kept in touch with his followers through his monthly magazine editorials, which over this period were filed from all parts of the globe. From New Zealand, Sandow travelled on to the US, while his newly-pregnant wife returned to the UK. In May 1903, after a two-month sojourn in Boston, he rejoined his wife and daughter in England. His second daughter Fanny Lorraine was born a few months later on 20 August, like her sister, at the family home in Oxford Road, Manchester. He tarried in the UK until May

1904, when he (and his wife) set off for a brief tour of South Africa; then they went on together to India. At some point, Blanche returned home and Sandow travelled on alone to Java, Hong Kong and China – he is strangely silent about this leg of his mammoth tour. It was only in mid-September 1905 that Sandow returned home for good.

This restlessness betrays mixed motivations, some worldly, others more exalted. As a businessman, Sandow was scoping out the enormous commercial opportunities of turning himself into a truly global brand. Like a colonial explorer, he sought to plant the flag of his exercise system in the virgin markets of Britain's imperial colonies and in America he sought to replicate the success of his magazine and training schools. He would claim at this time that he had established 120 Sandow schools around the world – not including the numerous gyms and other establishments that adopted his system as part of their ordinary curriculum. As usual, he cloaked such prosaic motivations in high-falutin' language, presenting himself as an apostle if not the absolute Messiah of physical culture. The Mayor of Brisbane told an assemblage of distinguished guests on Sandow's arrival in that city, he had found that Sandow was "on a crusade, which he was pursuing with enthusiasm, all round the world, for the purpose of carrying out his gospel of physical strength. He came with the gospel in acceptable form because he mixed brains with physical work."

Unlike John Lennon, Sandow never said that he was more popular than Jesus Christ, but he did claim, quite regularly, that he could cure the sick, dying and even the insane. He would pull out "before and after" pictures of pupils apparently cured of tuberculosis by his regime and declared proudly that physical culture had helped cure the lunatics at the Coney Island Asylum in New York. Off-stage, he hectored civic leaders, journalists and doctors, explaining that his system offered a "rational, scientific program for reform." He told whoever would listen that men trained under his method had served in South Africa and proved themselves loyal citizens of the Empire. He claimed to have "sent more men to South Africa than any man alive". As usual, he derided the mere entertainment value of his act, insisting that he intended to pose to the inhabitants of Western Australia not as a strongman, but as a "pioneer of health".

For all his declared mission, he was goaded on by an unacknowledged desire for adulation: having repeatedly said he was going to retire from the stage, he just couldn't bring himself to withdraw from the limelight and went in search of fresh and uncritical audiences who would worship him and his body. This craving for applause was almost wholly gratified: nearly everywhere he went, he was greeted with the frenzy that we associate today with the arrival of a boy band or Hollywood star. Late at night on 20 March 1902, for example, several hundred patient youngsters were inside the East Side Boy's Club at the intersection of 10th Street and Avenue A in downtown New York, waiting for Sandow to come and tell them how he obtained his great strength. Sandow was finally spotted, just before 11 o'clock. "He's come in a cab, fellers!" yelled those keeping watch on the sidewalk. "Huh, why doesn't he carry the cab?" shouted those inside. When the strongman appeared on the stage, "a great yell went up from hundreds of boyish throats, and cries of admiration punctuated his every pose." The show went on until well after midnight, as Sandow went through his poses, delivered his standard lecture about how he had conquered his youthful weediness, and then wrestled in the club gymnasium with some of the strong East Side boys.[115]

On his subsequent trip to the US, he had an audience with President Theodore Roosevelt, when they must have discussed how physical culture could make the white man's burden more tolerable. (Sandow hailed Roosevelt as "the strenuous President" and later drew his readers' attention approvingly to the statesman's exertions in running a quarter of a mile to meet his recently married daughter on her return from Europe.) He was reunited with Thomas Edison, on a more equal footing than a few years previously when Sandow had been filmed doing somersaults in his leopard-skin loincloth. A photograph published in *Sandow's Magazine* underlines this new status by showing Edison and the strongman standing side by side, both fully clothed in frock-coats, under the caption: "Genius and Strength".

Following several dozen acts including a piano overture, German dialect comedians and a pair of clever female duettists, "the World Famous Athlete in his Spectacular Exhibition of Superhuman Strength" took top billing at the B.F. Keith Theatre in Boston. At the Empire Theatre in Washington, "the physically perfect man, and his own vaudeville company, consisting of an unusually well-balanced bill of players, make an especially strong card," reported the *Washington Post* on 25 March 1902. But despite this acclaim, his Institute of Physical Culture established in Boston closed after a few months and an attempt to get an American version of his magazine off the ground was likewise a failure. There was intense competition in the US – former disciples such as Macfadden had already occupied this commercial ground – and in any case some American audiences were becoming jaundiced. His shows at this time were divided into two parts: the first, a display of his muscles from within his velvet-lined posing box and then, in the second half, the stage was set in the form of a Roman amphitheatre, around which Sandow postured wearing toga and loin-cloth. He went through his lifting routine, culminating in those staples from the earliest stages of his career: the Roman column exercises and the piling of men, animals, dumb-bells and other accessories onto this chest. The Americans had seen variations on this theme before and some began (fatally for Sandow's commercial success) to find his act funny rather than impressive. "Even when he was with us the last time," one commentator wrote, "the strongman was prone to pose. Now he handles his hands as though he were a soubrette with a new diamond ring and shoots them out like a western congressman at a Presidential reception wearing his first pair of cuffs. [The posing] injects therein a brand of comedy that is better than any premeditated humor." "The absurd array of petrified persons in togas and things make the Roman arena scene almost ridiculous," carped another.[116]

In the distant colonies of the British Empire, there was no such cynicism – on the contrary, Sandow's brand of messianic eugenic imperialism was embraced with unqualified enthusiasm. His celebrity preceded him. When, in July 1902, the *S.S. Oriziba* approached the city of Fremantle in Western Australia, a band of reporters boarded the ship at the same time as the pilot. By the time he gave his first performance at the Theatre Royal in Perth, he attracted one of the biggest audiences this establishment had ever seen.[117] "The audience went absolutely frantic at Sandow's Marvellous Performance, and recalled him no less than fifteen times," raved the Perth *Morning Herald*.

From Perth, Sandow travelled to Kalgoorie, Coolgardie and Boulder City, rough-and-ready gold-mining towns where there were no metalled roads or gas-lights and the hotel beds were shared with chickens. One wonders what Mrs Sandow thought of these primitive conditions. It's probable that, like her husband, she was adventurous and took it in her stride. She often features in articles about her husband and she seems game and happy, not a hint of the infidelities imputed to Sandow in some accounts of their marriage. The theatre at Kalgoorie was made of tin, but the miners manifested "their appreciation in their vociferous and whole-hearted manner". Then the party returned to Fremantle and sailed round to Adelaide, where the triumphal reception continued. At the Tivoli Theatre, he gave a private display to "many hundreds" of the city's medical professionals, journalists, businessmen, legislators, soldiers and other leading citizens and was accorded a hearty reception. "Stripped to the waist, and wearing a leopard skin on his loins, the mighty man brought into play the various muscles of his body. He let his interested audience feel the muscles, both in the relaxed and contracted states, and everyone was amazed at the wonderful physical development. Sandow answered many questions…"

He was clearly enjoying himself but he did not let himself forget the didactic or business objectives of his visit, betaking himself to police and fire stations in the city to expound the virtues of his system and entering into contract with a syndicate of businessmen wanting to open a Sandow Institute in Western Australia. Here, there was no hint of the irreverence shown by his North American audiences, nor indeed the overt sexiness encouraged by Ziegfeld. Antipodean audiences, it transpired, were rather prim compared to their American counterparts so Sandow and his managers focused on the scientific lessons to be derived from contemplation of his body and went to greater lengths than usual to find doctors and other professionals who could reassure the general public that there was nothing illicit or smutty about his show. With Blanche in tow, there was in any case no question of private viewings for the matrons and maidens of Adelaide, Bendigo or Melbourne. In Melbourne, he was granted a mayoral reception at the Town Hall, invited to garden parties and even the opera, where he heard Dame Nellie Melba sing. He gave a long private display (what the journalists called a "séance") where he took his clothes off in front of a "large muster of public men of all grades" and delivered a lecture on the muscles of the body. At the Melbourne Opera House, he inspired awe and adulation:

> The famous athlete came upon the stage amid a round of applause from the assemblage, which was drawn up in a semi-circle facing the purple flush curtains, which were draped at the back of the scenery. Over him was thrown a long fur-lined dressing-gown, and at first sight there was little remarkable about him save his quick spring motion and the poise of his classic-looking head, with its regular features, clear grey eyes and curly hair. After bowing his acknowledgments, Sandow made a little speech, informing his viewers that his object was to show how they could get their bodies into perfect condition, if they so desired. He did not wish to talk about himself, but would gladly ask questions afterwards. No doubt they had been struck with his appearance, but he would remind them that it was not the "quantity" of a man which made him wonderful, but the quality. (Loud laughter.) Quickly stripping off his dressing gown, Sandow revealed his form to his listeners, and as he did so a murmur of amazement and admiration rose from them. His arms, chest and shoulders and magnificent torso – like that of one of Canova's "Boxers" were bare. Round his loins was a leopard skin; his legs were sheathed in skin-tights and his feet in modern sandals. As the eye ran over his superb figure one noted the almost perfect proportions which above all athletes distinguished this great exponent of physical culture. Nothing was awkward, clumsy or distorted. The skin, with the grand muscles 'rippling' – that is the only term applicable – beneath it, shone like satin; every movement was graceful. The hands and feet were small and well-shaped, and the contour of the whole body such as is only seen in the glorious marbles of Canova and Michael Angelo. Sandow, standing there, for a moment brought back to earth the vanished heroes of Greece and Troy…
>
> The throngs which crowded the Opera House on Saturday evening in every part of the house jostled for every foot of standing room and peered out from every corner, were hushed in expectancy as the attendants removed the placards announcing the names of the previous

performers and revealed that of the man of mighty muscle. As a moment later, the curtain curled upwards, the audience burst into one reverberant round of enthusiastic cheering. Upon a small red pedestal stood Sandow himself. His pink and glossy flesh, bared to the waist, looked even more pink against a background of purple velvet. Once more the people were silent. Slowly the red pedestal began to revolve, and the living statue with it. For one moment the strong man stood with all his muscles relaxed, the suspicion of a smile haunting the corners of his clear blue eyes as his closely-cropped, regularly-shaped head turned to take a survey of the tiers of spectators. His thick, well-developed limbs looked as if they were as soft and velvety as the rolls of fat and flesh upon a healthy baby. One twitch of the body effected a transformation. The muscles across his abdomen and chest swelled until they resembled ropes that were piercing his flesh. The chest muscles rose and fell in bulbous masses that appeared at one moment to be soft and flabby, and the next as hard and firm as steel. The right arm shot out from his shoulder, and the mounds and knots of muscle which covered it from wrist to biceps altogether obliterated its symmetry. As the pedestal turned to disclose Sandow's back and shoulders, an involuntary "oh!" escaped from the spectators. A network of muscles, each of which appeared to be in perfect control of the strongman's will, traversed the trunk from the neck to the comparatively narrow waist, and formed such tremendous ridges on either side of the spinal column that one might have put his two hands in the cavity between them. Then there was a sound as if somebody had just opened the valves of a small steam boiler. Sandow was inflating his chest. Two deep, long-drawn breaths puffed out the body until above the belt there was an escarpment like that below the ribs of a skeleton, and the breasts stood as convex as the sides of a barrel. By this effort Sandow had increased his chest measurement from 48 to 62 inches. As the curtain went down men cheered and cheered again. Women were as enthusiastic.[118]

Intriguingly, although Sandow had lived the life of the English professional gentleman for years, on this visit he made a very public display of his German origins; when a reporter visited him in his characteristically ostentatious suite of apartments at the Menzies

Hotel, Sandow displayed on his mantelpiece (alongside a picture of his daughter Helen) portraits of three generations of German Kaisers, each draped in Germany's national colours. In keeping with the German liking for impressive titles, he now called himself Professor Sandow, but otherwise (he insisted) "he considers himself an Englishman— [and] all his thoughts are English." Indeed, the reporter noted that "in all but speech idioms Eugen Sandow might well be taken for a 'Britisher'". For a moment, the growing rivalry between Germany and Great Britain was brushed aside amid Anglo-Saxon racial solidarity.

If there was any delicacy in addressing descendants of convicts – the colony was, of course, created as a way of disposing of the residuum of British society – it was unacknowledged. His message was that, by the judicious adherence to the Sandow system, the people of Australia could shape their own destiny and thus free themselves from the legacy of the past and conquer any genetic predisposition to degeneracy. Like many visitors since, he was overwhelmed by the sheer friendliness of the people. "I was greatly impressed with the hospitality extended to me, and the friendly bonhomie accorded everywhere I went," he recalled later. "In going to Australasia I did not go as a stranger to a strange land; for I found amongst the hundreds of the followers of my system a kindness and devotion that surprised me...I was at home everywhere. I fully realised the immense vitality of the Saxon race, and the splendid future that must be in store for such a people. Not the least factor in the evolution of this future will be their steady and undeviating adherence to the cult of the body."

From Melbourne, the quasi-Imperial progress continued, first to Warranabool, then to Geelong, Sydney, Newcastle and finally Brisbane and then on to New Zealand, where he began with Auckland, touring through Wanganui, Napier, Christchurch, Timaru and Dunedin. Once again, wherever he went, he was lionised: his theatre displays were "packed to suffocation" and he was invited by policemen, firemen and soldiers to put them through their paces. "Both Mr and Mrs Sandow have been pets of society, their social qualities being as powerful as Sandow's marvellous strength," gushed the *Wanganui Herald* on 24 November 1902. He was granted mayoral receptions and was mobbed at railway stations, although at least one female admirer waiting to see him at Wellington was disappointed at his appearance in the flesh. "A general impression prevailed everywhere that I was possessed of enormous bulk," Sandow recalled. "A young lady who had come to the station out of curiosity...remarked to her companion: 'Why, he's just a MAN!'" The Kiwis proved especially responsive to his message, however, and Caroline Daniel has explained how Sandow had an enduring impact on the culture of a colony that was situated thousands of miles from Great Britain and the heart of European "civilisation," but nevertheless suffered some of the anxieties identified by Max Nordau. "New Zealanders seem to have regarded modern society with the same worried eyes as the rest of the modern world," this historian writes. "Their solution – a desire to strengthen themselves morally and spiritually – was not unique. They looked overseas for role models and reassurance, and were pleased when their gaze fell on Sandow and the physical culture movement".[119]

New Zealand settlers were typically of hardy farming stock, often of Scottish and Irish descent, and thus unencumbered by the kind of disgraceful genetic legacy that was the unspoken burden of the Australian populace at large, if not the colonial elite. Working outdoors, they suffered little from the privations of industrialisation or the oppression of urbanisation. However at the time of Sandow's visit, Kiwis were rather in awe of the mother country and had yet to develop a strong independent identity. Sandow encouraged New Zealanders to feel confident in their skins, to be less stiffly Edwardian in their attitude to physical exercise (by taking some of their clothes off on the beach) and to channel some of what was beginning to be seen as native vigour into sport, especially the fledgling national game of Rugby Football. "New Zealand will bring forth men to enter the ranks of sport and fight the battle of life second to none in the universe," Sandow predicted, and he was right. The All Blacks won their first match against the mother country in 1905, after a triumphant tour of the UK. As *Sandow's Magazine* noted, the tour was "regarded with positive consternation as a last proof of national degeneracy". Thus New Zealand was first acknowledged as an international sporting superpower. Sandow does not appear to have met any of these rugby players in the flesh, but in one fictional account of the birth of New Zealand as a rugby nation (*The Book of Fame* by Lloyd James), he is depicted going to see the All Blacks in their communal bath after they have defeated the England team. In his magazine for November 1905, he praised the visiting side's "wonderful consistency of form" and "magnificent all-round fitness." "If I were asked what is the reason for the New Zealanders' triumph," he wrote, only a little self-servingly, "I should not have the slightest hesitation in saying that their success is due entirely to the conscientious attention the members of the team pay to rational Physical Culture."[120]

He returned to the UK in May 1903 and stayed there for a year, attending the birth of his second child in August and throwing himself into the broiling national debate over the physical education of the masses. Reading Sandow's various pamphlets from this time, one can sense deep frustration, especially after the adulation he had received in the colonies. He was adamant that his System held the answer to the nation's problems. "Given a system of physical culture, making it compulsory for every school to give a set amount of time every day for systematic physical training...we shall soon see a marked improvement in the physical standard of the nation," he argued in *Body-Building: Or Man in the Making*, published in 1904. "We all know that it is the masses upon whom largely depends the prosperity of the nation, by reason of its supplying the fighting strength of the nation, so that you can see how necessary it is that we should endeavour to maintain the standard of the supporters of the empire, in order to enable us to maintain our great prestige."

Yet to enforce change, state intervention was required: and that naturally touched on more complex and deeper-seated issues than the question of universal physical education. Great Britain had achieved its dominant position in the world by virtue of a *laisser-faire* political culture that discouraged state intervention under any circumstances. The country that seemed most to threaten Britain's political and commercial hegemony was Germany, which espoused an antithetical political philosophy. The legacy of Bismarck's rule was a powerful army, social insurance, a highly organised educational system, close links between science and industry – and a fit and healthy population. As H.G. Wells wrote in *The New Machiavelli*, Germany was "beating England in every matter upon which competition [was] possible".[121] Even as Germany was feared, studied and envied by Great Britain's ruling classes, the prospect of becoming more Germanic was understandably controversial, especially given growing public hysteria at the prospect of a German invasion. Anti-German sentiment was inflamed by popular novels such as Erskine Childers' *Riddle of the Sands* and William le Queux's *Invasion of 1910*, which created a sensation when serialised in the *Daily Mail* during 1906 and subsequently sold more than a million copies.

Lord Rosebery's campaign for "National Efficiency" proved short-lived, although the mantle of state intervention was taken over by the Fabians and post-1906 reforming Liberal governments. Sandow gave extensive evidence to the first of the two government enquiries and was rewarded with official recognition: the Scottish investigators spoke highly of his exercise system and the government went so far as to accept that an element of compulsory physical education should be introduced to the Board Schools. To Sandow's intense and lasting irritation, however, the system adopted was not his own but the rival one developed by P.H and Hjalmar Ling, the father-and-son founders of Swedish gymnastics. "From 1904 to 1914...the Swedish system with modifications was adopted, and the development of physical education in elementary schools went hand in hand with other welfare services such as school meals and the medical inspection of schoolchildren."[122] Sandow dismissed the "Swedish System" as little more than military drill in a civilian guise, but he was aggrieved at the government's outright refusal to endorse the use of dumb-bells in schools. Years later, Arthur Conan Doyle joined his friend Sandow in urging the state to "look after the health of its component parts". He saw the 1870 Education Act as the first step, the acknowledgement on the part of the government that it was responsible for the minds of its subjects, but lamented the fact that the state had not taken similar responsibility "for the body as well as the mind".[123]

►⟫·•‹‹◄

Putting his domestic exasperations behind him, Sandow's international peregrinations continued in May 1904 when he set off for South Africa and India. In Johannesburg, his appearance at the Empire Palace Theatre was hailed "as one of the greatest events since the arrival in the town of Earl Roberts", and from the English if not the Boer elements of the community he received a rapturous welcome, feted as an ambassador of British imperialism. It was a comparatively brisk tour: he visited the two main cities of Johannesburg and Cape Town.[124] He and his wife then set off to the port of Aden, where British soldiers threatened to wreck the theatre where he first performed, thinking him an impostor, and then mobbed him when they realised he was the real thing. And then it was on to India, where Sandow-mania proved if anything more intense than anywhere else on his travels. "I was astounded at my reception," he told the *Daily Mail* later, "and the fact that I was so well known."

As Sandow's monthly despatches to his magazine make clear, he was beguiled by India and the appreciation was fully reciprocated: from the first, he was embraced as one of the subcontinent's own – as a kind of fakir of physical culture. Like a holy man, he had wondrous powers, not merely over the 400 muscles in his own body (he claimed most improbably that he could stop his own heart from beating), but over other people too, holding out the promise of transformation if they only so much as followed his exercise system. He played down the rational aspect of his regime and presented it as a kind of meditation with muscles. "The essence of his system [is] to concentrate the mind upon the physical effort, so that mind and body may both work together to produce the muscular development," commented an approving editorial in the *Bengalee* newspaper. "It is the cooperation of the mind with the body that makes the system so unique and explains the great results which have been attained."

While his claims to be able to heal almost any ailment sounded preposterous in the cold light of northern Europe, in India they were not out of place at all: it was on this visit that he cured Dhunjibhoy Bomanji, a prominent Bombay shipping contractor who suffered from what was said to be elephantiasis, but was more likely a goitre or debilitating swelling. "When he first came to me he was suffering terribly...he was only about thirty-five, but had suffered from this dreadful disease for eighteen years. He had undergone an operation in London, and had consulted specialists in most European countries. After an examination, I undertook to cure him if he would follow my directions."[125] Christ-like, Sandow laid on his hands and Bomanji recovered, expressing his gratitude by paying Sandow a large sum of money and trying to entice him to stay in India with a further offer of £10,000 a year. The story is not fanciful: Bomanji (1862-1937) was an immensely wealthy Parsee businessman who was later knighted for his services to the British Empire and certainly had funds with which to express his gratitude. Sandow did not take up the offer, but when he finally settled in London, he named his house after this Indian benefactor and was a regular guest at Bomanji's estate near Windsor.[126] Sandow claimed that Bomanji, whom he revered as the "merchant prince," named a house after *him* and granted Sandow and his heirs the right to stay in Sandow Castle, Bombay: there was indeed a property of this name, set in 18 acres and overlooking the sea at a place called Pir Pau, which caused some controversy in 1947 when M.A. Jinnah, the founder of Pakistan, expressed an interest in buying it.

Sandow's arrival in Calcutta's magnificent Howrah Station was a momentous occasion. The crowds gathered at least an hour before his train was due, in the words of the *Indian Daily News*, an assembly of:

...an immense number of Europeans and natives of all castes and creeds, all of whom were bent on catching the first glimpse of the great man they had for the most part heard of, but only seen in books and pictures. There were some among the native folk who gave vent to their opinions and vied with each other in describing what the great Sandow would look like. Some were quite positive he would be as large as the huge posters depict him. Suddenly the toot of the whistle announces the arrival of the long expected train, and thither that vast assembly hastened with eager footsteps, and by the time the train stopped there was an impassable barrier of human beings round the compartment occupied by Sandow. The crowd was kept back by the police, and Sandow alighted, looking fresh as ever, though a little travel-stained. He was followed the whole length of the platform by an eager crowd of ladies and gentlemen. The ignorant native element seemed to be disappointed at his appearance, for some were heard to remark that he was like any other mortal, only with a fine muscular build and set up, and certainly not the giant the huge posters depicted him to be, while others of the more educated, strained their necks over the heads of the crowd and were satisfied with a glimpse of him, and spoke in eulogistic terms of his physique. The European element were thoroughly enthusiastic, and it is clear from their demeanour that Sandow will have a warm reception.

As proved to be the case:

The reception accorded Eugen Sandow at the Theatre Royal, Calcutta, was one absolutely unparalleled in the records of Calcutta...not only was the theatre full in all its departments, but in the upper circle, and also at all the door-ways and exits on both sides of the house, the crowds were standing ten and twelve deep, and hundreds had to be turned away...no entertainment that has ever come to the East has been such a big draw or aroused an audience to such a pitch of enthusiasm as that of Saturday night. It was a representative assemblage of every class of society, both European and native, and a number of the boxes were filled with native noblemen and gentlemen who had come down to Calcutta specially to see one of the modern wonders of the age...

Sandow was exceptionally popular with all elements of Indian society, from the European ruling class to their native subjects. The British, for their part, responded less to the mystical elements of his doctrine, than the practical, military applications: given the small number of Europeans compared to the vast native population, their hold on power in the sub-continent was something of a confidence trick and anything that made the officer class physically stronger could only help with the imperial mission. "Imperial rule can have no ultimate basis than adequate and organised physical force," urged Lord Esher, the quintessential Edwardian courtier and future Sandow ally. This was acknowledged explicitly by an editorial in London's *Evening Standard*:

> Whether the Indian government will hasten to avail itself now of Mr Sandow's services is not known but as we frequently hear of a lack of strong men in the administration there might be room for one of his unquestioned vigour. Personal strength has before this enabled English officials in India to maintain the prestige of empire even more than the alleged superiority of western intellect.

Native Indians regaled him with honour and favours. He toured the country with a tent capable of holding 6,000 persons and nightly had to turn away thousands. He was hailed as Sando Pahlwan – the honorific Pahlwan betokening physical prowess when applied to a wrestler or athlete. Gamun Baliwala Pahlwan, a champion Hindu wrestler, challenged him to a contest "so that all classes of people might see and appreciate our good points". Sandow ducked this confrontation, knowing that a champion of the calibre of Gamun would have been difficult to beat. He befriended Maharajahs such as the Gaekwar of Baroda (who commissioned a copy of the Sandow cast for his own private museum) and the unnamed prince who took him on a 40-mile drive from his palace. "We had not gone very far before I noticed that at regular intervals on the route various carriages and pairs were stationed," Sandow recalled. "At first I could not make out whether they were there by accident or by design, but later on I heard that for fear that the motor might, perhaps, break down, my host had ordered a carriage and pair to be waiting at every mile on the route."[127]

In Bombay, his new friend and benefactor Dhunjibhoy Bomanji used his influence to invite Sandow into one of his residences to give instruction to a group of high-class Parsee ladies. Normally, the zenana was out of bounds, but Sandow was given special dispensation to penetrate the inner recesses of the palace:

My pupils were separated from me by a beaded screen", he recalled, "and the apartment they were in darkened so that I could not see them. Some unlovely waiting women watched them very closely. On the other side of the screen where I stood all was bright, so that my mysterious pupils could easily see what I was doing. I faced the screen and commenced demonstrating the first simple exercises of my system. A quiet rustling from the other side of the screen told me that my unseen watchers were imitating my movements...

When the lesson was finished, the ladies behind the screen passed on the message that they would be very curious to feel the muscles of his arms.

"I approached the beaded screen and raised my biceps; and through the screen half a dozen small hands stretched out and touched them nervously."

Exotic this experience might have been, but perhaps not as erotic as one of the private sessions in Chicago under the dubious tutelage of Florenz Ziegfeld. To avert any suggestion of improper behaviour, Sandow spelt out to his domestic readers that Mrs Sandow was at his side on his side of the screen, sharing in his amusement at this incident.[128]

Meanwhile, asked by one reporter what would happen if Bengalis took up his system *en masse*, Sandow answered that they would become like himself, "from delicate they will become strong." He had plenty of examples to prove it: Ram Narayan Acharryya, who had been following the Sandow system since the age of 11, had transformed himself from weakling into paragon of muscularity; Chaudra Perk of Calcutta ran a well-attended physical culture class; Surest Chandra Gas Gapta of Bengal managed to increase his chest size from 27 to 31 inches over a year following the Sandow correspondence course. Youths such as these were as brawny as any public school boy at home, he averred. Deploying the language of his campaigns in England, he was offering regeneration for the people of India, a message that was starkly free from racial condescension: he blamed the demonstrably poor physique of the Indian natives on poor diet and want of exercise, rather than any innate limitations of race. "'The native Indians have a foundation for the building of large physical men,'" he insisted, "It is only because of their lack of proper food and systematic exercise that they are thin and haggard." Indians were splendid material to build on, he went on. "They will succeed absolutely. They will succeed more than any nation in the world, because they have perseverance. Look to the welfare of your body, in two hundred years you will have splendid results..."

Sandow was too conservative a figure to be stirring up the aspirations of India's fledgling nationalists intentionally, but his message to the "teeming millions" of native Indians, as he patronisingly called them, was nevertheless subversive. He offered his followers empowerment through control of their bodies – a strange and inadvertent echo of the ideology of Turnvater Jahn, one of Sandow's earliest influences, who had fortified resistance to Napoleonic occupiers by bringing the youth of Germany out to exercise on the heath. Back home in England, where the authorities were still pondering the lessons of the Boer War, it was said (by Lord Meath) that gymnastics had been the first practical step on Germany's road to recovery and now unquestioned rivalry with Great Britain. It would of course be more than four decades before the sub-continent would be liberated from British rule, but Sandow's ideas were taken up enthusiastically. There were many who saw physical fitness as the first step on the road to independence and political power. These included Swami Vivekanda, the Hindu nationalist leader (and exponent of the three Bs: beef, biceps and the Bhagvad-Gita), and Sarala Debi Ghoshal, a niece of Rabindranath Tagore, who, following Sandow's visit, became an extremist leader.

"In India, the name of Sandow represents almost a demigod to hundreds upon thousands of natives, and patients by correspondence are legion," noted the celebrated investigative journalist W.T. Stead a few years later. "Maharajahs have come over from India specially to take his treatment in St James's Street. Other Indian rulers have commissioned Mr Sandow to send out his representatives to look after their physical education." There was a further and more surprising legacy of his visit: Sandow may have inadvertently helped initiate the modern craze for yoga. Part of the appeal of this contortionist pastime to its millions of adherents in the West today is its supposed ancient and mystical Indian antecedents, expressed in the various unpronounceable Hindi names for the postures as well as the trance-like and allegedly Asiatic sense of wellbeing that it induces. In its modern or *asana* form, yoga is fact a recent phenomenon, dating only from the first half of the 20th century. According to some historians, this modern posture-based yoga owes more to Western physical culture (including Sandow's) than it does to Indian tradition. Sandow also gave his name to an early hero of Bollywood: Raja Sandow (1891-1943), so-dubbed because of his impressive physique, was one of the leading actors and directors of Tamil and Hindi cinema in the 1930s and was responsible for pushing the boundaries so that revealing dresses and actual kissing were shown for the first time on Indian screens.

- 13 -
AT HOME, AT LAST

S andow returned to Britain in September 1905, to a reception almost as triumphant as the one that greeted him in Calcutta. A brass band played *See The Conquering Hero Comes* as he and his wife steamed into Dover on 18 September. Blanche had crossed the Channel to meet him after the long separation: he had been away from his children for 18 months. A large crowd, including his two daughters and numerous female admirers, was there to meet him as he disembarked with the rest of his troupe. He was dressed impeccably in black frock-coat, with buttonholes of embossed leather, dark silk waistcoat in black and red, and grey trousers. On his head he sported a black felt trilby hat, under the broad brims of which his blonde hair curled dandyishly.

With consummate lack of political correctness, Helen, now aged nine, asked her father whether he had brought "any little nigger boys for her to play with". Indeed, in the manner of Captain Cook, Sandow had brought back with him human souvenirs of his travels. "I have chosen and brought back with me a native of every country I have visited," he bragged, "thirty-two in all, including Chinese, Hindus, Kaffirs, and natives of the Punjaub [sic]." Most were weaklings, whom Sandow hoped to transform through the proper application of his system, but there was a troupe of wrestlers from India, including two giant Sikhs and a middle-weight called Herichund, who were as fit and strong as any European. With their hair bound in "top knots" and dressed in gaily-coloured shawls, they were soon to be launched on the music hall stage, delighting audiences in locations as far afield as Ardwick in Manchester. But first, they and the rest of the Sandow party had to board a specially chartered train for London.

On arrival at Charing Cross Station, the reception "attained almost to Royal Proportions", noted the *Guardian*. Admission to the platform was by ticket only and a special body of policemen were in position to keep back the waiting (and, it was observed, well-behaved and physically well-developed) crowd of Sandow's "admirers and followers."

> Another noticeable feature of the demonstration was the number of ladies, most of whom brought beautiful bouquets of lilies and chrysanthemums. Mr Sandow, of course, has a popular ladies' school in Pimlico, and almost all the ladies present…were past or present pupils… Anyone who had been unfortunate in the position he chose had to wait quite five minutes before he could even get a glimpse of the strongman, who was undergoing the various processes of making a speech, being photographed, and shaking hands. The enthusiasm reached its height when, after handing his wife and children into his motor car and almost burying them in a mass of flowers, he burst from his friends, sprang up beside the chauffeur, and drove home.[129]

Sandow declared definitively that he would retire, after one farewell tour of the provinces. "I do not consider it necessary again to defend the title which has been given me of the strongest man in the world," he told reporters. "I have done all that, now I intend to devote my life to teaching everyone how to be as strong as myself, and stronger." He would dedicate his energies to creating a new National Institute of Physical Culture – a "huge temple of physical culture" from which he would fight the "degeneration of national physique". But first, it was time for Sandow to settle down: the long years of perpetual motion, of living apart from wife and family like a soldier on some far-flung campaign or a vagabond merchant seaman, had come to an end. At the age of 38, Sandow at last took steps to make himself permanently at home in London, starting with an application to become a British citizen.

In his propaganda as well as in his personal demeanour, Sandow had been presenting himself as a *de facto* English gentleman for years. Despite the curious display of Teutonic allegiance in Australia, he does not appear to have harboured any strong emotional ties to the country of his birth and he had not returned there since he had become famous. So why did it take so long to take the plunge and become British? It is likely that the requirement to disclose under oath the true identity of his parents was the real obstacle. We have seen how he got round that by having his solicitor write a confidential side-letter to the Secretary of State for Home Affairs, in which the shameful details of his origins were adumbrated. These documents remained secret until released recently under the Freedom of Information Act. The process of naturalisation further required that Sandow submit a series of sworn character references to the Home Office and endure a somewhat perfunctory police investigation into his character. The choice of referees is highly illuminating of Sandow's milieu at the time.

One was the Venerable William Macdonald Sinclair, former chaplain to the deceased Queen Victoria and the man who officiated at Sandow's own wedding. Another was Colonel Sir George Malcolm Fox, still the Army's Inspector of Gymnasia and a longstanding proselytiser for Sandow's system within the military. There was a warm tribute from his father-in-law Warwick Brookes, the Manchester photographer, who wrote on his form that he had known Sandow not merely for the eight years since the Prussian had married into his family, but for a full 13 years "during which time our association together has been most close and intimate". The phrase, buried at the bottom of a formal legal document, suggests a profound bond between the two men. Finally, and probably intended as the *coup de grâce* in terms of respectability, Sandow was given a reference by the son of a duke, namely Lord Ronald Sutherland Gower, of Penshurst in the county of Kent.

However, the choice of Gower suggests naïveté on Sandow's part. True, the peer was the younger son of the second Duke of Sutherland and had been brought up at Cliveden and other of the grandest houses in England and Scotland. Close to the top of the heap in Britain's class-bound society, he had been on good terms with Queen Victoria, Gladstone, Disraeli and Garibaldi. He had also served as a Liberal MP and made a successful career for himself as a sculptor, diarist and dilettante man of the arts. But it was hardly a secret that Lord Gower was a homosexual, an ardent *Uranist* in the language of the day, and in all probability the model for Lord Henry Wotton, the hedonistic and effete aristocrat in Oscar Wilde's *Dorian Gray*. Now in his 60s, Lord Ronald (1845-1916) lived quite openly with Frank Hird, a journalist whom the peer had adopted as his son but was reputed to be his lover (and of whom Wilde remarked: "Frank may be seen, but not Hird"). At the time of Sandow's return to London, it was more than 15 years since the nobleman had been intimate with Wilde, who said of his friend at the unveiling of Gower's statue of Shakespeare: "there were few things he did not touch, and everything he touched he adorned". Still further back in time, in 1877, there had been scurrilous rumours in the press about Gower's "moral character" (i.e. his sexuality), but the scandal had been contained. We don't know how Gower and Sandow became acquainted but it seems highly likely that like many other sculptors, Gower was deeply impressed by Sandow's body. That his admiration went further than mere professional appreciation is also probable. If anything, however, Sandow's clumsy choice of Gower as a referee tends to disprove the suggestion that Sandow was himself uranically inclined: if there had been any kind of sexual relationship between the two, Sandow would have done everything to conceal it, rather than flaunt his association with the debauched aristocrat to the Home Secretary.

A policeman came to interview Sandow, then living temporarily at a hotel in central London, and found nothing untoward. "The applicant whom I have seen at the Carlton Hotel, appeared to be a respectable man," reported Sergeant O'Brien of the Criminal Investigation Unit of New Scotland Yard, on 15 December 1905, rather ploddishly. "According to inquiry he has resided in this country for five years within the eight now last past, intends to remain permanently, and wishes to enjoy the rights and privileges of a British subject. He speaks, reads and writes English well."

In the New Year, Sandow became a British citizen at last. The next step in the programme of assimilation was to find a permanent home. "I could never live anywhere but in London, our home and friends are there," Mrs Sandow had declared in June 1903 (in an interview for an Australian newspaper): but here she spoke with her husband's scant regard for the facts. Sandow and his wife had never really had a home of their own and had only briefly resided in London. For more than half their 11-year marriage, Blanche had lived with her parents or out of a suitcase. From 1899 to May 1902, they had indeed lived in rented accommodation at 41 Albemarle Street, just off Piccadilly and within a few minutes' walk from St James's. Before that, however, from

December 1897 to May 1899, they lived with the Brookes family in Manchester. Thereafter they were either travelling together, or Sandow was touring on his own, leaving wife and daughters back in Manchester. In 1906, they acquired the house in Holland Park Avenue that was to be Sandow's home until his death in 1925. If not exactly a mansion, Dhunjibhoy House was a substantial residence on four floors in what was then, as now, a salubrious part of Kensington. Long since broken up into flats, one can see today that the house was entirely appropriate in scale for a prosperous entrepreneur. It had a garden and a spacious drive which would have amply accommodated Sandow's motor cars. In keeping with the belated resurrection of Sandow's reputation, it was only in February 2009 that the house was awarded a "Blue Plaque" to memorialise its by then more or less forgotten former resident.

One wonders about Sandow's life in this home, away from the cheering crowds of women strewing chrysanthemums and men idolising his body. What kind of husband and father was he? Now that he had finally ceased his public performances, did he settle down for evenings in, or was he restlessly out and about? Was he a serial philanderer who retained his charms for the fair sex despite the advance of middle-age? Did he turn his home into an exercise hall, suffering his little girls to exercise with dumb-bells in order to instil physical perfection into his offspring? In keeping with his intense personal privacy, and the presumed destruction of his personal papers, there are so few clues, but imagine my delight when I stumbled on an article in a Chicago newspaper which described his home life at about this time in the following gloriously detailed terms. Under the headline:

How Sandow Is Training His Children to be the Strongest and Healthiest in the World

I read how Sandow's children went barefoot, rolled in the morning dew, slept without covers in the cold weather, lived on vegetables, never took medicines and trained their muscles – all so that they could grow up to share in their father's physical perfection. Blanche was reportedly as hard a taskmaster as her husband. "From their birth, the two youngsters have been taught the value of physical health and prowess," the article went on, "and their athletic mother, no less imbued with ambition than the famous strongman, has spared no pains in the development of her babies' muscles. Mrs Sandow herself was one of Britain's greatest women athletes, a devotee of exercise and outdoor sports since her early girlhood." The children were taught to sustain their own weight on arms and feet before their first birthday, and they were doing one-handed pull-ups by the time they were two years old, all with a view to making them perfect in body and ready for the exigencies of a stage career of their own.

And on it went in this revealing vein – until I realised that the article was entirely made up. The clue, apart from the assertion that Mrs Sandow was a great athlete (this was the first I had heard of that) was not in the date (no, it was not 1 April), but rather in the illustrations, which I had overlooked in my enthusiasm to read through this material. The pictures of the "little Sandows" showed a girl, hard at work on her Symmetrion, and a stocky boy of about eight years old. Alas, the article was a piece of fantasy fabricated to entertain North American readers who would not realise that Sandow had in fact two daughters.[130]

In truth, Blanche did follow her husband's system. Asked by a (real) journalist in Australia whether she "underwent treatment for physical development," she answered emphatically that she used the Sandow developer and dumb-bells every morning. ("Noticing the beautifully moulded figure of the speaker it was easy to believe it," the journalist

THE PERFECT MAN

purred). Helen and Lorraine were encouraged to exercise, but without the fanatical focus on future perfection. Later, when Helen appeared on stage in a comic opera, it was noted as a matter of course that she had an exceptionally well-developed body.

The Sandow marriage itself remains enigmatic. To outsiders, they had seemed a happy couple when they travelled together around the US and Australasia. Asked once how she dared marry the strongest man in the world, Blanche gave a disarming reply. "Oh, he is as gentle as a lamb," she insisted, laughing out loud. "You see, I have been married eight years, and I don't look very bad, do I?"[3] There was a surprising tenderness, even docility on Sandow's part, at the heart of the marriage. Two years and a long separation later, there were public displays of affection as they were reunited. Thereafter, as Sandow himself finally brought his performing career to an end, there was comparatively little occasion for them to be seen together in public and press references to Mrs Sandow dry up until the difficult war years, when the couple found it expedient to present a united front to a hostile world. It has been speculated – indeed asserted as a matter of fact – that by this time the Sandows were estranged and the strongman had embarked on a new career as serial womaniser – perhaps as early as the voyage to Australia in 1902. He himself made light of an incident in Naples, where the *SS Orizaba* docked for a few days early on that trip, when an Italian guide suspected Sandow of paying undue attention to Blanche's travelling companion, a certain Miss Edward. "The guide at once informed Mrs Sandow of her husband's base conduct," Sandow recalled in jest, "but to give Mrs Sandow an opportunity for revenge, he proposed to her an elopement with herself!"

Heaven knows, Sandow had the opportunity to sleep with any number of eager women, but it is unlikely Miss Edward was one of them. But later, during the long periods apart, the temptation must have been acute. Like many an actor on a tour or merchant navy seaman a long way from home, Sandow may well have jumped into bed with an admirer or two. It is a deplorable but proven fact of human nature that men (and women) tend to stray when there is an opportunity to do so and Sandow had more opportunity than most. It was his conscious choice to stay away for so long and this hardly points to the closest of relationships between man and wife. In mitigation, however, Blanche did not marry Sandow so they could spend quiet evenings at home drinking cocoa, even when Sandow started making the stuff: long separations and antisocial hours were par for the course. He was scrupulous in conduct and bearing, fastidious about his personal cleanliness and he also knew that the commercial success of his personal brand was rooted in wholesome behaviour: bluntly, he stood to lose a lot of money if it got out that he was sleeping around.

A further consideration is Sandow's close relationship with the Brookes family. To the end of his days, Sandow remained on excellent terms with Warwick junior and his father. Of course, this is far from conclusive proof that he was faithful to his wife and he was certainly devious enough in other areas of his life (on stage or in business) that he no doubt had the ingenuity to conceal affairs. But he did not behave so outrageously that the entire Brookes clan felt obliged to shun him. All that makes it somehow improbable that he was a consistent womaniser. In making the revisionist case that Sandow was (relatively) pure in thought and deed, I may be naïvely chivalrous. It irks me that his character should be calumniated without a shred of direct evidence.

On his return from his world tour, Sandow had made grand promises to open a new National Institute, but this never came to fruition. It soon became clear that the physical culture craze was abating, in favour of bicycling and other fads, and indeed by 1907, Sandow had shut down both his magazine and his network of Institutes. The last magazine was a special souvenir issue sent to subscribers on July 1907, complete with Sandow portraits and a promise that there would soon be a new Sandow magazine, dedicated entirely to health, which never appeared. Only the original St James's establishment remained and here Sandow spent his days, attending to patients and cooking up business ventures with his brother-in-law. Despite the closures, his business was thriving at this stage. The physical culture part of Sandow's empire generated £7,300 of profits in 1908, more than double that in the following year, and £27,000 in 1909, a staggering amount however one calculates the modern equivalent. In the years 1909, 1910 and 1911, Sandow received "about £10,000 a year in dividends," reported *The Times*.[132]

For now, Sandow was riding high: a rich and famous man, who attended society functions, wearing evening dress without the faintest intention of ripping it off to display the muscles beneath. Staying well clear of the music hall stage, he made ostentatious philanthropic donations which were designed to demonstrate his patriotism as much as his wealth – these included £1,500 donated by way of sponsorship of the Olympic Games in London in 1908 and a munificent £1,000 to Ernest Shackleton's *Nimrod* Expedition of 1907-1909 – the first of the explorer's three expeditions to the Antarctic. The Australian Sir Douglas Mawson travelled with Shackleton and must have been impressed by Sandow (or at least his donation): Mawson subsequently led his own Antarctic expedition, naming a mountain after the strongman. *Mount Sandow* is a so-called nunatak (an isolated peak protruding from, in this case, the Denman Glacier) and reaches 1,380m above sea level.

As tensions with Germany escalated, Sandow responded to Lord Esher's call for recruits to bring the London County Regiments of the Territorial Force up to full strength. "Mr Sandow volunteered at his own expense to provide physical training to all who were desirous of enlisting, but who did not fulfil their physical requirements," noted *The Times* approvingly. "This offer met with so great a response that Mr Sandow, at Lord Esher's suggestion, widened his offer, thereby making himself responsible for giving three months physical training to each of the 11,000 recruits who came forward." (Esher was one of the most powerful men in Edwardian England, an eminence grise and fixer for the King. He was also a closet homosexual: another inconclusive *Uranian* connection.) Demonstrating that he was flush with the profits of his business empire, as well as patriotic pride, Sandow personally offered a cash prize of £1,000 to the men who made the greatest physical improvement under the training. By the time the prizes were presented under the aegis of Lord Northcliffe, the newspaper proprietor, at the Drill Hall in Westminster (on 23 July 1909), each of the 104 winners had added no less than 12 inches to their combined neck, chest, arm and leg measurements, while the outright winner added a magnificent 27 inches, of which 5.75 inches accrued to the chest alone. Later still, Sandow gave free training to the 60,000 boys of the Church Lads' Brigades, with similar success. In March 1911, he gave a lunch for 1,500 naval and military cadets at Crystal Palace, together with an assortment of grandees including the Duke of Argyll and the Duchess of Marlborough, before the boys put on a display. This was one occasion where his wife did make an appearance.

Preoccupied with business and philanthropy, Sandow could afford to laugh off the vestigial establishment disdain expressed in Max

Beerbohm's *Encaenia of 1908*, a caricature depicting Sandow in full academic garb, his muscle-bound arms protruding from underneath his gown to receive an honorary degree from Oxford University. This was a protest at what we would call the dumbing-down of Oxford honorary degrees, after this distinction was conferred on Rudyard Kipling in 1908. Beerbohm objected to Kipling being honoured thus, precisely because he was immensely popular; the other figures gathered around Sandow include Sir Arthur Conan Doyle and Hall Caine, the novelists, Thomas Lipton the grocery magnate (whose name was on at least 600 shop-fronts in the UK), and Little Tich, the diminutive music hall comedian – all heroes or beneficiaries of popular culture. But to be included in this company was of course an enormous, albeit ironic, compliment: Sandow belonged to the pantheon of Edwardian celebrities.

The acme of assimilation came three years later with his appointment as Professor of Scientific Physical Culture to King George V, communicated by means of an article in *The Times* on 28 March 1911:

This is the first appointment of the kind that has been made. The King has long shown keen interest in physical culture and has derived considerable benefit from the prescribed treatments. When Prince of Wales, his Majesty paid more than one visit to the Sandow's Institute in St. James, and appliances for physical culture were fitted in the Ophir when [in 1901] she made her historic voyage to the Colonies... the King is, physically, a powerful man, and, in the training of his children, he had paid particular attention to rational recreation and healthful development...Apart from the purely personal aspects of the appointment, it is a recognition of the value of systematic training in the nation as a whole.

This pronouncement – so gushing it could have been a direct

transmission of a press release issued by the Sandow publicity machine – seems inconsistent with the popular image of the King as anything other than an energetic sportsman. The fawning British media did not choose to comment on this anomaly, but from the other side of the Atlantic, the *New York Times* offered a laconic interpretation of the merits and duties of the appointment:

> Though the King's photographs sometimes give a contrary impression, he is a physically strong man. The honor accorded to Mr Sandow is a recognition of the latter's efforts in improving the physique of the [Territorial Army], rather than an acknowledgement that any personal benefit would be derived by the King from his services.

Still, bizarrely in the light of the monarch's evident portliness, it will become clear that the King did follow a version of Sandow's exercise regime.

- 14 -
THE TONO-BUNGAY YEARS

I n his 1909 novel, *The Secret of Tono-Bungay*, H.G. Wells charts the story of a business venture to promote Tono-Bungay, a tonic which is really just a confection of water and a few dubiously stimulating ingredients, but which is billed as having miraculous restorative powers. Through the power of advertising, and the potency of its catchy but meaningless name, Tono-Bungay is transformed into a mass-market phenomenon, which at first brings its promoters great wealth. Caught up in the "romance of modern commerce," George Ponderevo and his Uncle Edward first subjugate England and Wales; then conquer the Cheviots with a special adaptation containing 11 per cent alcohol, before diversifying with the launch of a "Tono-Bungay Hair Stimulant", followed by Concentrated Tono-Bungay for the eyes…

And we also did admirable things with our next subsidiaries, 'Tono-Bungay' Lozenges', and 'Tono-Bungay Chocolate'. These were urged on the public for their extraordinary nutritive and recuperative value in cases of fatigue and strain. We gave them posters and illustrated advertisements showing climbers hanging from marvellously vertical cliffs, cyclist champions upon the track, mounted messengers engaged in Aix-to-Ghent rides, soldiers lying out under a hot sun. "You can GO for twenty-four hours," we declared, "on Tono-Bungay Chocolate." We did not say whether you could return on the same commodity…

My uncle's last addition to the Tono-Bungay group was the Tono-Bungay Mouthwash. The reader has probably read a hundred times that inspiring inquiry of his, "You are Young, but are you Sure Nothing has Aged your Gums?"

The parallels with Sandow are uncannily direct and not to the strongman's credit. He too was operating a family business – if not with his uncle but rather his father- and brother-in-law. One can imagine Eugen and young Warwick, like the heroes of Wells' novel, sitting round the dinner-table in Holland Park Avenue, or the boardroom table in St James's Street, plotting how to combat the collapse of his core markets. Engaged in what he called "the battlefield of business," Sandow proved (as we would expect) resourceful, determined and full of mountebankish guile. With true Tono-Bungay panache, and a tincture of charlatanism, they too decided to diversify, in the language of today "leveraging the brand" to open up new markets.

Sandow first launched a concentrated embrocation, or ointment, for all manner of ailments ("During my travels that have been world wide, I have collaborated with the finest scientists and herbalists… for the furtherance of my quest," he wrote. The resulting unguent was "infallible for the rapid cure of rheumatism, neuralgia, sciatica, lumbago etc…"). He established a corset division. ("Wonderful new corset," trumpeted his marketing literature in 1910, "as the result of Mr Sandow's scientific labours, it is woman's good fortune to be at last provided with a Corset that is the acme of perfection in the benefits it bestows upon all its wearers…"[133]). This item was launched with an advertising campaign in the *Daily Mail*, the *Daily Sketch*, the *Daily News* and the *Daily Mirror*, featuring a picture of a comely actress, who one might have assumed was wearing one of Sandow's new products:

nothing of the sort, it turned out, and Miss Jones, most recently starring in pantomime in Birmingham, sued Sandow for libel. Eventually, Sandow's corset let him down – commercially speaking, that is.

And then he took the principle of diversification one ultimately catastrophic stage further, by moving into the food manufacturing business, opening Sandow's Cocoa and Chocolate Company from a factory in the New Kent Road, in Vauxhall, south London. Sandow's Health and Strength Cocoa powder was "the most important of all the undertakings he had set himself," the strongman insisted, adopting the true hyperbolic Tono-Bungay tone.[134] This branded powder was launched amid considerable fanfare in October 1911 and, as usual, Sandow cloaked this commercial venture in the language of public-spirited altruism: in a toast to those assembled at the launch party at his new factory premises, he declared that he was launching his new campaign:

> In an earnest endeavour to provide a beverage for the people [which] while nourishing their bodies, [would] stimulate their minds and fit them for their increasingly strenuous daily tasks at a cost which was within reach of their pocket.[135]

Sandow let the more credulous among the press know that, within a matter of days, the demand for his new drink-diet had been overwhelming. "From North, South, East and West – from cities, towns, villages and hamlets through the length and breadth of the Kingdom – from cottager and labourer—from clerk and mechanic ... [to] business and Society ladies...correspondence, inquiries and orders have descended literally in torrents upon Mr Sandow." Somehow struggling free of these torrents, Sandow predicted that before too long there would be few breakfast-tables in the land, nay in the Empire, upon

An advert for Sandow's cocoa, c1912

An advert for Sandow's baking powder, c1912

which Sandow's Health and Strength Cocoa would not appear.[136]

At the same time as he was launching this new business, he found ever more ingenious, not to say shrill, ways of marketing his health regime. REMARKABLE THREEFOLD HEALTH OFFER, screamed the headline of a rare full-page advertisement in the *Telegraph* in April 1912, in which he proclaimed his "practical plan to bring the all-important asset of public health to 100,000 men and women within a few weeks…everyone who is over-stout, 'out of condition', dyspeptic or neurasthenic may benefit by Mr Sandow's offer…" Another campaign claimed to offer comprehensive relief "in cases of indigestion, insomnia, constipation, nervous disorders, weak lungs, sluggish liver, obesity and generally the disorders resulting from a sedentary life". HEALTH BY POST was another full-page advertisement, this time in *The Graphic* of 21 January 1911, in which "MR SANDOW USES THE MARVELLOUS POSTAL ORGANISATION TO SPREAD HIS WONDERFUL HEALTH KNOWLEDGE TO THE ILL AND THE 'UNFIT' ALL OVER THE WORLD…HE WILL SEND GRATIS AND POST FREE A FULL DESCRIPTION OF HIS MEDICINELESS TREATMENT, WHICH IS WORKING SUCH MARVELLOUS CURES IN ALL MANNER OF CASES, WHERE EVERYTHING ELSE HAS FAILED, TO SUFFERERS IN ALL PARTS OF THE UNITED KINGDOM, THE COLONIES AND ABROAD."

He offered personal treatment in St James's, but for those who could not make the journey – including, he claimed, satisfied customers in Jamaica, India, Germany, Australasia, Canada, Russia etc – you could be cured remotely, without the need for medicine, simply by entering into a correspondence course. "You fill up a form, stating your weight, your age, your measurements, and your ailments," Sandow explained, "and if your case is considered one which would benefit, you receive a letter prescribing certain exercises. The intention of the course is not to make you a weight-lifter or a prize-fighter. Indeed the movements prescribed involve no strain, and are performed by the most delicate ladies and elderly people…"

The journalist W. T. Stead dropped in unannounced at the Institute. Stead pioneered modern campaigning journalism – famously arranging to acquire a child prostitute in an attempt to expose the diabolical exploitation of children in the brothels of late-Victorian London. The so-called "Maiden Tribute" initiative had backfired and Stead had been thrown in jail for a few months for his pains. Nevertheless, Stead had unrivalled credentials as an investigative journalist and, as he entered Sandow's Institute, one can assume he had in mind writing at the very least a sceptical article for the readers of his *Review of Reviews*. But any doubts Stead may have had were dispelled almost as soon as he entered the premises. He found the place working like a well-oiled machine. Everything seemed healthy and bright and clean, the journalist remarked. Sandow himself was out, but the attendants were in the pink of life, "peripatetic advertisements of what the system can do". Stead declared himself astonished at the sheer number of people who passed through the doors of the Institute – several hundred patients a day, he was told. There were no beds, but a multitude of outpatients. "Ladies and Gentlemen, old and young were in the consulting-rooms," he discovered. "Patients in the cubicles were going through their exercises; others were having their bath." He quizzed one of the superintendants as to the workings of the Sandow method and was told that patients were carefully screened. Those with certain types of heart ailment were not taken on, however desperate they were for treatment, however much money they were prepared to pay. He was shown draws full of cards detailing the cases of those who were turned down. He was then given a little booklet in which the principles of Sandow's regime were explained, starting with seven exercises repeated eight times a day, increasing to 12 times on the 28th day.

By the time he left, he was a convert to the Sandow system. "There is in the whole place an atmosphere of joyous life," he enthused. "Joyousness…the supreme note of true religion…is recognised as one of the first of therapeutic agents." He likened Sandow and his fellow consultants to miracle workers, casting out the devils of insomnia, nervous depression, indigestion and dozens of other complaints, thereby restoring the joy of life to those to whom it has long been a stranger. He ended his article by urging Winston Churchill and fellow Government ministers to introduce the Sandow system to schools and prisons (of which he had personal experience) and commending readers to call in at the Institute or subscribe to a mail order cure. "Sandow offers you health, happiness, a new body, with as much physical beauty as can be carved out of the rude mask that conceals or reveals your soul…" A ringing endorsement if ever there was one, all the more credible for Stead's credentials as a sceptical reporter.[137]

Stead was not the only journalist to pitch up at the Institute in order to test the truth of Sandow's extravagant claims – a correspondent from Labouchère's *Truth* attended a consultation and also came away favourably impressed. But if the press was easy to convince of the merits of the Sandow system, the medical authorities were not: they mounted a vigorous campaign against Sandow and his Institute. From the very start of his career Sandow had taken pains to keep the medical profession on his side, recognising that doctors' endorsements of his system helped remove any suspicion of charlatanism or mere music hall frippery. But now, all the hard work to win over the doctors proved in vain, for Sandow had committed two unpardonable sins. First, he offered to heal the sick without a proper diploma – and, by the by, seemed to do a pretty good job of it, given that the seriously ill were screened out by the time they got anywhere near the Institute and thereafter anyone stood to benefit from Sandow's exercise regime. And then he advertised, screamingly, wildly, in capital letters, in numerous publications from the *Observer* to the far more down market *Penny Illustrated Paper*, thus deploying techniques that may have been appropriate for Tono-Bungay or corsets, but were proscribed for medical services. So in late May 1911, just two months after the King bestowed his official blessing on Sandow, the General Medical Council announced that it was investigating three qualified doctors who worked at the Institute on suspicion of "infamous conduct". Their offence: to associate themselves in a professional capacity with Sandow and his system, thereby aiding and abetting an "unregistered person". Sandow argued in vain that the doctors were there merely to screen patients and did not participate in the management of the Institute. Two of the three were struck off.[138]

Underlying the GMC's hostilities, one can sense professional frustration at Sandow's absurdly grandiose claims and perhaps envy of the money Sandow was able to make by applying modern business techniques to the provision of medical services. But there is a broader political context to the attacks on Sandow, which helps explain why the affair stirred up such vehemence. The Liberal Government was intent on forcing through the National Insurance Act and the beginnings of state-sponsored healthcare, against the interests and will of the doctors. Sandow was an easier target than David Lloyd George, the reforming Chancellor, and the assault a way for the profession to buttress its crumbling authority. The affair rumbled on until the outbreak of the Great War – attracting international press coverage and even a question in the House of Commons (no doubt orchestrated by Sandow's politically well-connected brother-in-law Warwick Brookes, who would be elected as a Member of Parliament in 1916). Eventually, Sandow and the doctors managed a public rapprochement of sorts: the GMC issued a statement reassuring the public that Sandow had never claimed to be providing explicitly medical treatment and Sandow explained that he thought he had the approval of the GMC for his activities. Sandow took consolation from the fact that many individual doctors, including Conan Doyle, continued to voice their support for him and his System.

In April 1913, there was respite from the pressures of business when his 16-year-old daughter Helen (or now, as she called herself, more pretentiously, Hélène) made her West End debut as the understudy for the lead role in a revival of André Messager's comic opera *Véronique* at the Court Theatre, after the original lead had been taken ill. "This will be my first appearance on any stage, and…I hope it may not be my last," Hélène told reporters. "I am very anxious to become a real actress, and I think father will let me study for the professional stage when my other studies are over."[139] Sandow declared himself astonished at his daughter's talent and application, praising her ability to get up the part at only a day or two's notice. The press noted her blonde-hair, blue-eyes - and her well-developed physique.

In October, Sandow reported to shareholders in his cocoa business that the first year of trading had been largely successful, despite the inordinate amount spent on advertising to generate sales. "Large advertising, successful struggle with competitors," he declared, as if this move into food manufacturing was the commercial equivalent of his contest with Sampson. "A great part of the year was occupied by the directors and management in building up a huge business and in making the products of the company well known," he explained, "as they were certain that the company had in its products articles of the highest standard, and that it was only necessary to secure a proper public test of them to obtain a large and public trade."[140] At the same time, Sandow communicated the fateful decision to move out of the administrative headquarters in Vauxhall and begin manufacturing the product at a new factory at Hayes, to the west of London. With a nominal capital of £300,000 and fully paid up ordinary shares of £175,000, this enterprise required capital investment on a grand scale, particularly when he acquired a secret cocoa formula from a German company. He was moving into direct competition with Cadbury's, Joseph Fry and Rowntree, among the most successful and best-resourced companies of the era, and away from his "core competence", which was in the fields of branding and marketing. It did not help that, at around this time, a German professor whom Sandow claimed to have endorsed the health-giving properties of his cocoa, popped up to deny that he had said any such thing. Dr Otto Hehner launched a lawsuit against Sandow, restraining him from publishing an apparent endorsement of the efficacy of the Cocoa Powder published in a series of advertisements in the *Daily Mail, Daily Express* and the *Sketch*. The combination of formidable competition and a very public association with Germany would sow the seeds of Sandow's personal downfall.

- 15 -
DECLINE AND FALL

A matter of three months or so before the outbreak of war, on 25 March 1914, the Sandow Corset Company held a great "pageant of dress" at the Royal Albert Hall. Just as for the Great Competition, this magnificent venue was once again "packed to the utmost capacity" with a crowd of a rather different complexion than that gathered in 1901 to see the best-developed men in the Kingdom: on this occasion, there were aristocratic ladies like Viscountess Esher, Lady Essex, Lady Pirrie and the Princess Thurn und Taxis, as well as the Japanese Ambassador and his wife, who were eager to see the parade of exceptionally well-dressed ladies who conducted what was in essence a fashion show. There was an overture played by a Viennese orchestra, prizes for the winner of the Queen of the Figure Beautiful competition (sponsored jointly by the Sandow Corset Company and the Daily Mirror), followed by a parade of mannequins who flaunted a succession of couturier gowns on the pre-First World War equivalent of the catwalk, many of which were designed by the Sandow Corset Company.

Presiding over this marvellous event was not Eugen Sandow himself, but rather his daughter Hélène. The would-be actress was mistress of ceremonies at the Albert Hall, giving a word of welcome to the vast audience and championing the latest addition to Sandow's

ever-expanding business empire – a new couturière section in the
"Sandow salons" in St James's Street.[141] The event was a demonstration
of family solidarity as well as commercial self-confidence. Blanche
and Eugen were in the audience to give their support to their elder
daughter; equally, Warwick Brookes Jnr must have been on hand to
supervise the business arrangements. Hélène was on the cusp of
fulfilling her professional dreams, self-confident enough to address
a crowd in an intimidating public setting and helping to expand the
Sandow commercial empire. Not only was she spearheading the charge
into the fashion business, she was also promoting one of Sandow's
more peculiar commercial ventures: the manufacture of spring exercise
dolls for children. Early in 1915, Sandow started advertising children's
classes at the Institute, with the aim of training up 18 to 20 children so
they could give synchronised demonstrations. Hélène became the first
Honorary President of the grandiloquent National Doll League, an
organisation set up to promote the Sandow dolls. In September, there
was even a press conference at the Savoy Hotel when the troupe of
children gave a performance. The initial profits from the sale of these
devices were to be given to the Red Cross.

Although Sandow could not have predicted the murderous extent
of the war, he had in a sense been preparing for this eventuality for
much of his adult life. He had made a clear choice to become British.
He had built (he hoped) a store of goodwill through the work he had
put in to train up Britain's youth, initially for the conflict in South Africa
and subsequently for nothing if not war with Germany. And after war
broke out, he offered up his services once again, declaring himself
on a new mission to make men of the thousands who were below
the physical standard for His Majesty's Army. "At his Institute there
is every facility for the rebuilding of manhood," his publicity machine

insisted. He announced a "Great Campaign" for health and physical fitness. "It is just as patriotic to fight your own illness as to fight the Germans," he exhorted, somewhat tactlessly when his advertisements appeared adjacent to the list of those killed on the western front. Sandow's instinct for the mood of the British public failed him. His assumption that he could present himself as a patriot despite his origins was profoundly misplaced. As it became clear that the war would not be "over by Christmas," and the scale of the casualties mounted, anti-German feeling was understandably profound.

Everyone with German connections, from the Royal Family right down to humble music hall stars, scrambled to distance themselves from their origins. If the Royal family found it expedient to change their name from Saxe-Coburg-Gotha to Windsor, the same sentiment applied in less exalted circles. The mere association with Germany was enough to kill a business or ruin a career, as for example when the high-earning juggler Paul Cinquevalli was banned from performing after the discovery that his real surname was Kestner and he had grown up in Germany; the comedian George Mozart plaintively confessed that his real name was David John Grilling and he had been born in Great Yarmouth; the composer Edward German admitted that his real name was Edward German Smith and had dropped the Smith as it sounded too common – now he added the name back in the hope that his music would be played again. The magician Carl Hertz declared to anyone who would listen that he was American, not German as his name suggested. Meanwhile, Leichner's greasepaint, a great favourite in the music halls before the war, could not speak up for itself and was in effect banned. Viscount Haldane was forced to resign as Chancellor in 1915 because of his alleged pro-German sympathies. After drinking a bottle of embargoed hock wine, Winston Churchill explained that he was merely impounding the banned beverage.

In February 1915, an estate agent in Brighton went into Mr Moseley's shop in West Street and asked if he sold Sandow's cocoa. "No, I do not sell cocoa made in Germany," Mr Mosely answered. Then the customer asked whether there was any Sandow chocolate in stock. No, Mosely replied again, and on being pressed for an explanation, said: "Because they were made in Germany."[142] Sandow himself got wind of this and sued Mr Moseley for criminal libel – it being an immensely serious allegation that the product was manufactured by the arch-enemy – and the case went all the way to the High Court, where it was decided in Sandow's favour, after it could be proved that the cocoa and chocolate were in fact manufactured at Hayes, despite being based on a German recipe. Sandow's heavy-handed response to this incident suggests that, as a naturalised Englishman of acknowledged Prussian origins, he felt his position imperilled. Later that year, he was forced to issue a statement denying that he had been executed as a German spy, advancing some far-fetched but under the circumstances defensible claims about his origins. In the words of his solicitor, Mr Guilford Lewis:

Mr and Mrs Sandow have both personally consulted me regarding a statement which appears to have been largely circulated concerning them, namely that Mr Sandow has been shot as a spy and that Mrs Sandow has been sentenced to a term of imprisonment. The fact that I have personally interviewed both Mr and Mrs Sandow is obviously convincing proof of the falseness of this statement.

I need hardly say that apart from the injury that such a rumour is calculated to cause my client in his business, there is the personal side of the matter, which has affected him and his wife most acutely. I am instructed that, although born just over the Russian border, Mr Sandow's parents were Russians, and that according to Russian law he was and is still a Russian subject, despite the fact that some years ago he became a naturalised British subject.

The object of this letter is to appeal through your columns to your readers to assist my clients to dispel this cruel rumour and to trace it to its origin, and they will be grateful to any person who will assist them with any information to this end by communicating with me at the above address."[143]

The effect of this statement was limited. Just before Christmas, the *Washington Post* reported that he had been executed in the Tower of London after facing a military court on a charge of being a German spy. The currency of such barmy rumours is one reason why after the war many in the US in particular thought Sandow was dead.

So the war was a time of great reversals for Sandow. He was prey to every kind of vicious rumour. The young men who had bought his equipment and subscribed to his regime were off at the front and physical culture was the last thing on their mind – they were busy trying to stay alive or eviscerate their far fitter enemy on the other side of no man's land. And his cocoa and chocolate, either tainted by virtue of its German associations or simply unappetising, ceased to sell. Sandow's business empire unravelled. In April 1915, the Sandow Corset Company announced a closing down sale: corsets and lingerie, made by nuns in the convents of Belgium and France, were offered to discerning customers at knockdown prices, a portion of the proceeds going to help those nations in time of war. The doll venture, and the National Doll League, collapsed amid acrimonious litigation with a business partner. Then Sandow (Limited), the holding company for his business affairs excluding food manufacturing, was subject to a compulsory winding-up order on 27 June 1916, posting a total deficit of £27,857 (along with Sandow, both the Warwick Brookes were directors of this enterprise). The main reason was said to be the non-delivery of corsets due to the war. A month later, Sandow's Cocoa and Chocolate Company (Limited) collapsed with a total deficiency of £351,792 10s and 4d – a monumental sum equivalent to many millions in today's money.[144] "Something like a quarter of a million had been unwisely spent," lamented Sir Vesey Strong – a former Lord Mayor of London, no less – at a shareholders meeting, demonstrating "a lamentable exhibition of commercial incapacity".[145] At a court hearing some years later, a sheepish Sandow explained that the company had acquired the patents for a secret manufacturing process from a German company. "The manufacture was at first a success, but afterwards complaints were received, and the cocoa was returned by customers at home and abroad." It did not help that the raw materials for the product originated in Germany, even if the manufacture took place in West London.

Amid the financial wreckage, the Curative Institute continued to trade and some months later, Sandow was able to buy this business from the receivers. The cocoa factory was bought by Nestlé and nearby there is to this day a Sandow Crescent, the street name commemorating the strongman's unfortunate association with the unlovely London suburb of Hayes. In the absence of records, we will never know the full impact on Sandow and his family's finances. Shares in both the failed companies were publicly traded, with external shareholders who would have cushioned the blow: one estimate suggests Sandow personally lost £15,000 on the demise of the cocoa company, a small proportion of the total.[146] However, looking ahead to his death nearly ten years later, we know that he ultimately left the relatively modest sum of £5,271 13s and 10d in net assets, much of that accounted for by the house in Holland Park and one other investment property. While this did not betoken absolute poverty, far from it – and he may have transferred assets to his wife before he died – it does suggest a drastic diminution of Sandow's wealth. On his return from his world tour, he had been worth tens if not hundreds of thousands of pounds – many millions in today's money. In his plutocratic heyday before the war, he earned twice as much as that a year in dividends alone. A combination of bad luck and execrable business judgement, exacerbated by the circumstances of the war, brought a profound reversal of fortune for Sandow.

The setbacks were emotional as well as financial. He was a man used to emulation and adulation from all corners of the world, now increasingly forgotten – if not actively reviled – by the very people who had once held him in such high regard, confined at home with the wife and two daughters from whom he was growing estranged, and forced to contemplate the effects of age and nature on his body. It was to some extent the journey that all of us are doomed to make, from hopeful youth to middle-age and eventual bodily decrepitude – except that the poignancy of such a decline is so much more acute in a man who for so many held out the prospect of perfectibility, the acquisition of health and strength, and the possibility of slowing down the process of ageing.

Sandow's brother-in-law Warwick was able to make good his escape from the wreckage of the family business empire and went into politics (in 1916 he was elected as the Conservative and Unionist MP for Mile End).[147] The strongman's wife and daughters were not so lucky. Given that tens of thousands of families suffered the loss of fathers, sons and brothers, one should not exaggerate the privations of the Sandow women during the war years. But one senses that they suffered acutely from the change in family circumstances. As the nearest kin of a putative enemy alien and traitor (not to mention a business failure), they must have found themselves shunned and ostracised by former friends and admirers. For Helen, the doors to a show-business career slammed shut and neither the dress business nor the National Doll League survived. After the war, she became (appropriately enough) Mrs Joe Strong and lived in obscurity. Lorraine, a mere 14 years old when the war finished, married a department store owner in 1925 and thereafter (as we will see) behaved in such a way that suggests that she bore the scars of these difficult years.

By 1918, Sandow's Curative Institute was his sole surviving business venture. Apart from dealing with endless litigation stemming from the failure of the cocoa company, his major preoccupation was the work that he hoped to be the final vindication of his life. The enormous *Life is Movement*, first published in 1919 and evidently the result of many years' labour, is a grandiloquent recapitulation of the Sandow system and its claimed efficacy in healing...just about everything:

The whole body must be understood as a great organisation or establishment in which every department and system is inter-related and inter-dependent," he preached, "Each department and being linked up with every other by the blood circulation and the nervous system. By giving movement or employment first to the voluntary muscles, all the other cells of the body are immediately and automatically set moving also, and upon this united and associated movement of all the cells in harmony and balance depends the health of the body and its power in any or every part to resist, conquer and prevent disease...

There is a messianic tone to the book, as well as more than a tincture of pure daftness, as captured in the portentous subtitle:

"The Physical Reconstruction and Regeneration of the People (A Diseaseless World), by Eugen Sandow, Professor of Natural Therapeutics, Instructor in Physical Culture to H.M. the King...this book describes the only natural, radical and permanent method of curing, preventing and eliminating disease...

His ostracism by the General Medical Council rankled and the book strains its sinews to pay homage to the professionals who had treated him with scorn and indifference. Dedicated to the "medical profession throughout the world," the work contained an adulatory preface from Conan Doyle, and later editions listed no less than six pages of "eminent medical practitioners" who have supposedly welcomed the work, as well as page after page of members of Parliament, members of the aristocracy, universities and public schools, leaders of the press, noblemen, cabinet ministers and statesmen (including David Lloyd George), clergy and reigning monarchs including His Majesty the King of England, Her Majesty Queen Alexandra, the kings of Italy, Spain, Sweden, Denmark and Norway, and finally the presidents of the United States of America (His Excellency Woodrow Wilson) and of Switzerland.[148] In addition, the book contains a sequence of photographs demonstrating the development of Sandow's body from childhood to the date of publication, from wimp to Farnese Hercules. Even at the age of 52, it transpires, Sandow was not averse to taking his clothes off. The last photograph, taken by father-in-law Warwick Brookes, is the most strangely intimate of all; it shows him sideways on, sitting down, staring up into space, with the camera at about the level of his shapely right buttock. In contrast to so many of his more contrived poses, this is a conversation piece: he looks relaxed, as if he is chatting informally with his father-in-law on a nudists' outing. He demonstrates a still enviable physique: the only wrinkles to be seen are around his eyes and there is not a hint of flaccidity about the stomach. His biceps still bulge, even when in repose.

Sandow was not forgotten: in 1922, the town of Freezeout in

Texas was renamed Sandow in his honour, advertising the marvellous strength of the local lignite mine. In the same year, James Joyce's *Ulysses* was published, in which the strongman's feats were celebrated. There were still tens of thousands of adherents around the world, even if many of the dumb-bells and symmetrions had been consigned to attics, cellars and dustbins. But Sandow's last years were spent in comparative obscurity: the braggadocio of his early career deserted him, along with his funds, his fitness and his distinguished friends (in 1922, for example, Sandow was not among those invited to celebrate his patron Dhunjibhoy Bomanji's knighthood). He continued to advertise and publish his health guides and deal with patients both in person and by mail order and towards the end of his life was contemplating a return to the international lecture circuit.

Earle Liederman, an American body-builder, visited Sandow at the Institute in St James's in 1924, having been astonished to find that his hero was still alive. "I had been expecting to find a broken down athlete of sixty years, bent from weight-lifting and withered from excessive exercise, some sort of tottering shell of his former self," Liederman recalled. In fact, at 57 Sandow looked about 40 years old, spoke with a vigorous manly voice and had the same broad shoulders and massive chest of yesteryear. "Everything in his manner and bearing indicated not only great physical prowess but strength of character as well." Sandow was not busy with customers on that day, for they spent two hours chatting in Sandow's office, during which (in a surprisingly heavy German accent) Sandow relayed the stories of his youth and eventually allowed his disciple to feel his muscles through his suit. "There is a good vun, feel dat," he exhorted. Overall, Liederman was impressed by his idol's physique, but he noted some signs of bodily wear and tear after all. Sandow's neck was large and flabby and he wore a wing-collar in order to hide the accumulation of wrinkles. He preserved a perfect "six-pack" torso, but some of his muscles were fleshy and running to fat. His eyes were "heavy and tired looking" and he wore glasses which he kept on the end of a black ribbon. "His weary eyes told the story of much glamour, color and adventure along the road of ten thousand yesterdays, and his soul seemed to hunger for that which was forever gone…glory, excitement, youth!"[149]

Sandow asked his young admirer to come to lunch at the Savoy Hotel, where they enjoyed themselves so much that, by the end of the meal, they had negotiated the outline of a business deal. Liederman was to take on the franchise to the Sandow training system in North America for a period of five years and open a Sandow school in New York and Sandow would cross the Atlantic for a nationwide lecture tour. A contract was drawn up, money changed hands (Sandow eventually receiving £1,500 in cash as a down-payment), but Sandow was struck down before he could fulfil his side of the bargain. Early in 1925, he went on a tour of England, Scotland and Wales and it was on this trip that he had the motoring accident that contributed to his early demise. Like his follower Conan Doyle, Sandow lifted up his car after it turned over, a feat carried out more efficaciously by the disciple than the master, for Sandow ruptured himself. He was visibly ill when Florenz Ziegfeld visited him at home late in the summer, albeit still a good-looking man "He received us wearing a brocade dressing gown," recalled Ziegfeld's daughter. "He was still divinely handsome, just as Daddy had always described him." This reunion took place on 28 August. Barely six weeks later, Sandow was dead. He died at home in his bed on the morning of 14 October 1925 and was buried in his ignominious, unmarked grave just two days later.

"I remained a weakling," acknowledged George Bernard Shaw on hearing the news, in a letter to a friend, speaking with the self-satisfied tone of one who resisted Sandow's attempts to get him to take up exercise. "But I am alive and Eugen is dead. Let not my example be lost on you. The pen is mightier than the dumb-bell."[150] Obituary writers around the world were quick to draw their own laconic conclusions about the sudden, youthful death of one who had seemed to offer immunity to disease and ageing. "The strongman yielded to the temptations that come from leisure and inactivity," speculated the *Washington Post* on 17 October. "He no longer was required to keep in condition. It is reported that he indulged in wine and beer and in strong cigars." But the irony was often tinctured by an element of nostalgia for Sandow in his prime. *The Guardian* wrote the day after he died:

> The death of Eugen Sandow sends our thoughts back to the turn of the century, when the amazing physical development of a single individual produced a pretty general cult of the biceps among ambitious boyhood. Sandow was more than a music hall prodigy: his name fought its way into all manner of homes and left them equipped with the apparatus that carried his approval. It might almost be said that he nationalised the dumb-bell, so that numberless young men would harness themselves to their bedroom doors and grip and swing and perspire mightily. Not everyone managed to plod on and keep the passion fresh, but there were the charts and the photographs and the suggestion that the chests and biceps of Olympus were to be translated into Acacia Avenue by mere application of the will, following the purchase of certain equipment…

This sentiment was echoed by the *New York World*:

> Queer memories mutter and stir at the news Sandow is dead. Pondering
> his reign one is back in an almost forgotten age, the plush and pretty
> age of Victoria…an age that called a leg a 'limb' and an exposed calf
> a capital offence, and yet it went stark mad over muscle, pure swelling
> muscle. True to its ideal, it spoke not of Sandow's legs, his arms, his great
> heaving chest, but of his deltoid, pectoral and dormal development of
> his triceps and biceps.[151]

None seriously questioned the official account of his death: that
he had died of a burst blood vessel in the vein, the consequence of
"the shock and strain received in a motor accident" some years before.
The inconsistency in terms of timing – the motor tour was early in the
year – is less telling than anomalies over the actual cause of death. Sir
Thomas Horder, physician to King George V as well as the Monarch
of Muscle, had been attending Sandow in his final illness and declared
the cause of death to be an aortic aneurysm. How Sir Thomas, one of
the great physicians of the day, could have reached this verdict without
carrying out a *post mortem*, remains mysterious. A massive rupture of
the aorta – the vessel channeling blood from the heart to the rest of
the body – could indeed have been caused by the delayed consequences
of Sandow's motor accident. Another, admittedly fanciful, possibility
is that Sandow died because he had been bulking himself up with the
help of what we call steroids: already in the 1920s it was (painfully)
possible to extract testosterone from one's own testicles and inject it
into one's body to increase strength and endurance. Modern body-
builders and athletes have often suffered bodily collapse as a result
of sustained over-exercise and the ingestion of chemical stimulants
– and perhaps this is what occurred in Sandow's case. However, there
is no evidence of this whatsoever. Another possible cause is the

dread syphilis: an aortic aneurysm is one expression of the disease in its advanced stages. This could have been contracted decades before Sandow's death – perhaps even before his marriage – and would help explain the way in which Sandow was treated by his widow. But once again, the evidence is wholly inconclusive.

There is no doubt whatsoever that Blanche moved with unseemly haste to bury both Sandow's body and his memory. Two days after he died, there was a brief, almost perfunctory, memorial service at St John the Baptist's church in Holland Park, near his home, and he was taken off and buried that afternoon. The contrast with the popular send-off given to other music hall celebrities could not be more extreme: when Sandow's erstwhile friend Marie Lloyd died in October 1922, some 10,000 people attended her funeral. Sandow's star had faded by the time of his death, but he still had many adherents and Blanche and her daughters could have rustled up a crowd had they so wished. On 12 November, less than a month after Sandow's decease, it was announced in *The Times* that Messrs. Summers, Henderson & Co of Lime Street, London EC, would be holding a sale of Sandow's home, and the furniture and works of art contained within it, on behalf of the executrix, on 12 December. Blanche sold up and moved back to Manchester by Christmas (both her daughters were married by now, so she was alone). And thereafter, she never granted any interviews and seems to have maintained a policy of deliberate neglect of the grave, as if meting out posthumous retribution to her late husband.

Admirers of Sandow who found their way to Sandow's grave in Putney Vale Cemetery were flabbergasted when they discovered it to be overgrown with weeds and long wild grasses, a scrubby rebuke for some nameless crime. The scene was charged with rather obvious symbolism about the vanity of celebrity and the transience of the flesh, especially such beautiful and once well-toned flesh. Decades later, a friend of Earle Liederman managed to contact Mrs Sandow via the cemetery, with a view to establishing a monument, and was told bluntly that she refused to give her permission. It was not, indeed, until April 2008 that Sandow's great-grandson Chris Davies successfully raised the funds to erect a slab of black marble over his final resting place. So what could possibly have gone wrong?

One absurd thought that came to mind is that Blanche one day stumbled upon her husband and her father engaged in a homosexual act, perhaps in the studio where Sandow was accustomed to take off his clothes in front of the camera. Sandow and the elder Warwick were close, but on sober reflection, not *that* close. Another theory is that Sandow contracted syphilis and had passed it on to his wife – certainly an eventuality that would explain Blanche's behaviour. Perhaps it was the revenge for infidelities – although, as argued earlier, there is plenty of evidence to suggest the marriage was on a harmonious footing until at least as late as the outbreak of the Great War. It is possible that Blanche was driven to distraction by the burden of nursing Sandow in his final months. After the difficult war years and the ruin of the family businesses, she was left to sort out the legal aftermath of her husband's demise. The debenture holders of the cocoa company mounted litigation against the company and its directors, the case dragging on for years. But, in the final analysis, we simply don't know.

While his widow was doing her best to forget him, other more exalted persons had not abandoned Sandow – or at least, the use of his equipment. In the Royal Archives, there is a rather plaintive letter from the Director of Standard Health Appliance Co, Ltd, with which is incorporated Sandow's Developer Co., (telegraphic and cable address: Forearming, London), asking if the firm could be honoured with the appointment as official Suppliers of Physical Cultural Apparatus to His Majesty the King George V. "As Mr Sandow is now dead may we ask that the original appointment be restored to this firm, having regard to the fact that His Majesty has been pleased to place a further order with us." Another letter shows that the King was in receipt of Sandow dumb-bells on November 10, 1925 – less than a month after the strongman's death – with a courtier's note to the effect that the dumb-bells were satisfactory and would be taken to the King for His Majesty's Approval. The King remained loyal to Sandow, even if his widow didn't.[152]

Sandow deserves to be rescued from the margins of cultural history. By virtue of his status as an erstwhile hero of *popular* culture, he has been all but forgotten. His life, from Prussia via London and the Victorian music hall, to wealth, international celebrity and social respectability, followed by decline, provides a rich perspective on late-Victorian and early twentieth-century society. He was intelligent, adaptable, a survivor and a clever entrepreneur, possessing a chameleon-like ability to adapt to the currents that shaped British and American society in the late 19th century and the long build-up to the Great War. His career tells us much about masculinity and sexuality at the *fin de siècle*, and his story resonates more broadly than those of contemporary music hall celebrities who never transcended the milieu that created them. He was intriguingly ambiguous: a man who could be promoted as a paradigm of asexual classical beauty, even as he goaded his audiences to erotic rapture; a pin-up for gay intellectuals, even as he was embraced as the embodiment of idealised manhood; a one-off, who successfully commoditised himself. He was a self-made gentleman who never managed to shrug off accusations of charlatanism; a sincere propagandist for Physical Culture, who never missed a chance to make money; a German-born British patriot, who helped his adoptive country prepare for war with the Fatherland whence he came. He was the self-declared "friend of humanity", the apostle of healthy living whose training no doubt sent many hundreds if not thousands of young men to a grisly and premature death in the trenches of Flanders. He was a self-proclaimed family man, who was apparently disowned by his wife and daughters; the "perfect man", who was clearly flawed. In some ways, he was an archetypal Victorian hero, a sort of Samuel Smiles for the body – a man who through discipline and training turned himself from childhood weakling to icon of masculinity. On the other hand, his is a modern tale of self-invention.

But in asserting that he should be taken seriously as a historical figure, I do not mean that we should take him too seriously. There was always an undercurrent of bathos, as when the strongest man in the world was assaulted in the street by Lurline, the Water Queen, or when the friend of all humanity was pursued in the courts for making allegedly false declarations about his chocolate powder. This is appropriate for a music hall celebrity. For all his self-importance, and his perennial attempts to distance himself from the source of his fame and prosperity, he was first and foremost an entertainer.

Finally, it is not stretching a point to credit Sandow with helping to ignite the passion for physical fitness and bodily self-improvement that is central to western culture today. I have often thought, as I run painstakingly round Wimbledon Common and along the borders of the cemetery where Sandow for so long lay forgotten and neglected, that everybody who goes to the gym to work out or sets out on a jog is taking Sandow as a model, almost certainly unconsciously. All of us who are dissatisfied with the body that we are born with, or seek through exercise to mould a more perfect form or to fend off middle age, are taking our inspiration from Sandow.

- Epilogue -
In the Lion's Den

There is a postscript to this story that provides a distant family connection with the author and links Sandow to another eccentric figure from the margins of British cultural history – indeed, another man who fought with a lion in public, although with a less happy outcome than Sandow himself.

On 7 February 1925, months before his death, Sandow's younger daughter Lorraine married James Douglas Brown, the proprietor of Affleck and Brown, a Manchester department store famed for the quality of its fabrics, and owner of Knockbrex, a stately home on the shores of the Solway Firth in southwest Scotland. Brown was a gruff businessman with a profound interest in local archaeology and cultivating roses but, despite what one supposes to be differences of temperament, it was at first an idyllic life: there were shooting parties, bathing expeditions from the private beach, boat trips on the family's steamboat and a house full of guests all summer long. In time, she had two children and it seemed to be a model union. Until, that is, her husband invited an Oxford undergraduate to come to work with him for the summer in his rose-garden.

Lorraine and the student fell in love. According to family tradition, she ran away with him, abandoning her baby daughters (one of whom is the author's great-aunt Ann), and was never talked of again in the

Brown household (it is tempting to attribute this want of maternal feeling to the circumstances of her own upbringing: perhaps she too was starved of parental affection, for all Sandow's public display of love for his daughters.) The young man was Nugent Davidson, the son of the Reverend Harold Davidson, otherwise known as the Rector of Stiffkey or the Prostitutes' Padre. In a *cause célèbre* that counts as the first sex scandal of Britain between the wars – the great sensation of the 1930s, according to the historian A.J.P. Taylor – Davidson was charged by the Bishop of Norwich under the Clergy Discipline Act, seeking to prove that Davidson's interest in young girls went far beyond the pastoral.

Davidson made a habit of leaving his remote North Norfolk parish on Monday morning for London, returning the following Saturday in time to prepare his sermon for the next day's service. In the intervening time, he would frequent Soho and other nefarious haunts, seeking to engage young women in conversation – and more. "God does not mind the sins of the body, but only those of the soul," was one of his chat-up lines. He had a special penchant for "nippies", the waitresses at Lyons Corner tearooms, whose souls he sought to redeem and whose bodies were not beneath his attention. The Bishop hired private investigators to track the vicar on his wanderings and it was alleged that in November 1931, for example, he embraced a young woman in a public room at a Chinese restaurant in Bloomsbury and that he "habitually associated himself with women of loose moral character for immoral purposes". He would then invite the young women back to his rectory, where he held pyjama parties. In 1932, following a trial that dominated newspaper headlines for several months, he was defrocked after being pronounced guilty of "immoral conduct, immoral acts and immoral habits".

Davidson spent the rest of his life trying to rehabilitate his name. "The trouble is," he reflected, "I carry into my clerical life the unconventional attitude of the stage." With Sandow-like panache, he went to Blackpool, where he sat inside a barrel and charged a penny to tourists who wanted to hear his defence. He exhibited himself next to a dead whale on Hampstead Heath. He signed up to a season at Captain Rye's Pleasureland at the Skegness Amusement Park. On 2 August 1937 Rev. Davidson entered a cage with two lions. It was a busy bank holiday and thousands witnessed Davidson's demise. He died of his wounds, two days after placing his head in the mouth of a lion called Freddie, in what was demonstrably a vain attempt to prove his innocence. As his biographer has noted, he was certainly the last Christian to be eaten by a lion for the sake of his beliefs.[153]

BIBLIOGRAPHY

WORKS BY EUGEN SANDOW

Sandow, Eugen and Mercer Adam, G. *Sandow on Physical Training: A Study in the Perfect Type of the Human Form* (New York: J. Selwin Tait & Sons, 1894).

Sandow, Eugen. *Strength and How to Obtain It* (London: Gale & Polden, 1897).

Sandow, Eugen. *Body Building, or Man in the Making* (London: Gale & Polden [n.d 1904]).

Sandow, Eugen. *The Construction and Reconstruction of the Human Body: A Manual of the Therapeutics of Exercise* (London: John Bale, Sons and Danielsson, 1907).

Sandow, Eugen. *Life is Movement: The Physical Reconstruction & Regeneration of the People* (London: National Health Press, 1918). (Foreword by Arthur Conan Doyle)

NEWSPAPERS AND PERIODICALS

Chicago Daily News
Chicago Tribune
Daily Telegraph
Daily News
The Era
Iron Game History
Le Biceps
Manchester Guardian
New York Times
Observer
Pall Mall Gazette

Physical Culture (magazine published by Eugen Sandow from 1898 to 1907)
Penny Illustrated Paper
Review of Reviews
Reynold's News
Strand Magazine
The Times
Washington Post

SECONDARY TEXTS

Adams, James Eli. *Dandies and Desert Saints: Styles of Victorian Masculinity* (Ithaca and London: Cornell University Press, 1995)

Bailey, Peter. Music Hall: The Business of Pleasure (Milton Keynes: Open University Press, 1986).

Bailey, Peter. *Popular Culture and Performance in the Victorian City* (Cambridge: Cambridge University Press, 1998).

Booth, Michael. *Victorian Spectacular Theatre, 1850-1910* (Boston and London: Routledge Kegan Paul, 1981).

Brod, Harry. *The Making of Masculinities* (Boston: Allen & Unwin, 1987).

Buck, Josh. "Sandow: No Folly with Ziegfeld's First Glorification," *Iron Game History*, Vol.5 No I, May 1998.

Buck, Josh. "Louis Cyr and Charles Sampson: Archetypes of Vaudevillian Strongmen," *Iron Game History,* Vol. 5. No. 3, December 1998.

Budd, Michael Anton. *The Sculpture Machine: Physical Culture and Body Politics in the Age of Empire.* (New York: New York University Press, 1997.)

Bulmer, Michael. *Francis Galton: Pioneer of Heredity and Biometry* (New York: John Hopkins University Press, 2003).

Butler, Judith. *Gender Trouble: Feminism and the Subversion of Identity* (New York: Routledge, 1990).

Carter, Randolph. *The World of Flo Ziegfeld* (London: Paul Elek Ltd, 1974).

Cevasco, G.A., ed. *The 1890's: an Encyclopaedia of British Literature, Art and Culture* (New York and London: Garland, 1993).

Chapman, David. *Sandow the Magnificent: Eugen Sandow and the Beginnings of Body-Building* (Urbana: University of Illinois Press, 1994).

Clark, Kenneth. *The Nude: A Study in Ideal Form* (Princeton: Princeton University Press, 1956).

Conan Doyle, Arthur. *Memories and Adventures.* (London: Hodder & Stoughton, 1924.)

Corley, T.A.B. "British entrepreneurs and brand names," *Oxford Dictionary of National Biography*, Oxford University Press, 2004 [accessed 24 May 2005: http://www.oxforddnb.com/templates/theme.jsp?articleid=92738]

Daley, Caroline. *Leisure and Pleasure: Reshaping and Revealing the New Zealand Body 1900-1960* (Auckland: Auckland University Press, 2003).

Daley, Caroline. "The Strongman of Eugenics, Eugen Sandow," in *Australian Historical Studies*, No. 120, October 2002.

De Frece, Lady. *Recollections of Vesta Tilley.* (London: Hutchinson & Co., 1934).

Dellamora, Richard. *Masculine Desire: The Sexual Politics of Victorian Aestheticism* (Chapel Hill and London: University of North Carolina Press, 1990).

Desbonnet, Edmond, and Roubiet, Dr Georges. *L'Art de Créer le Pur-Sang Humain* (Paris: Berger-Levrault: 1908).

Desbonnet, Edmond. *Les Rois de la Force* (Paris: Berger-Levrault, 1911).

Dowling, Andrew. *Manliness and the Male Novelist in Victorian Literature* (Aldershot: Ashgate, 2001).

Dowling, Linda. *Hellenism and Homosexuality in Victorian Oxford* (Ithaca and London: Cornell University Press, 1994).

Dutton, Kenneth, *The Perfectible Body: The Western Ideal of Male Physical Development* (New York: Continuum, 1995).

Farnsworth, Marjorie. *The Ziegfeld Follies* (London: Peter Davies, 1956).

Gagnier, Regenia. *Idylls of the Marketplace: Oscar Wilde and the Victorian Public* (Aldershot: Scholar Press, 1987).

Gillies, Midge. *Marie Lloyd: The One and Only.* (London: Victor Gollancz, 1999).

Girouard, Mark. *The Return to Camelot: Chivalry and the English Gentleman.* (London and New Haven: Yale University Press, 1981.)

Haley, Bruce. *The Healthy Body and Victorian Culture* (Cambridge, Mass: Harvard University Press, 1978).

Hall, Donald E. ed. *Muscular Christianity: Embodying the Victorian Age* (Cambridge: Cambridge University Press, 1994)

Hatt, Michael. "Physical Culture: The Male Nude and Sculpture in Late Victorian England," in Elizabeth Prettejohn ed., *After the Pre-Raphaelites – Art and Aestheticism in Victorian England*, (Manchester: Manchester University Press, 1999).

Holbrook, Jackson. *The Eighteen Nineties: A Review of Art and Ideas at the Close of the Nineteenth Century* (London: Grant Richards, 1913).

Houghton, Walter. *The Victorian Frame of Mind* (New Haven and London: Yale University Press, 1957).

Hurley, Kelly. *The Gothic Body: Sexuality, Materialism and Degeneration at the Fin de Siècle* (Cambridge: Cambridge University Press, 1996).

Hynes, Samuel. *The Edwardian Turn of Mind* (Princeton and London: Princeton University Press, 1968).

Kasson, John. *Houdini, Tarzan and the Perfect Man: The White Male Body and the Challenge of Modernity in America* (New York: Hill & Wang, 2001).

Kelves, Daniel. *In the Name of Eugenics: Genetics and the Uses of Human Heredity* (Cambridge, Mass., and London: Harvard University Press, 1995).

Larson, Erik. *The Devil in the White City*, (London: Bantam Books, 2004).

le Roux, Hugh and Garnier, Jules. *Acrobats and Mountebanks* (London: Chapman and Hall, 1890).

Ledger, Sally, and Luckhurst, Roger, eds. *The Fin de Siècle: A Reader in Cultural History c.1880-1900* (Oxford: Oxford University Press, 2000).

Ledger, Sally, and McCracken, Scott, eds. *Cultural Politics at the Fin de Siècle* (Manchester: Manchester University Press, 1997).

Lindqvist, Sven, *Bench Press*. (London: Granta Press, 2003).

Mansfield, Harvey. *Manliness*. (New Haven and London: Yale University Press, 2006).

McLaren, Angus. *The Trials of Masculinity: Policing Sexual Boundaries 1870-1930* (Chicago and London: University of Chicago Press, 1997).

McIntosh, Peter. *Physical Education in England Since 1800* (London: G.Bell & Sons, 1952).

Michie, Helena "Under Victorian Skins: The Bodies Beneath" in *A Companion to Victorian Literature and Culture*, ed. Tucker, Herbert F., (London: Blackwell, 1999), pp 407-424.

Mason, Michael. *The Making of Victorian Sexual Attitudes* (Oxford and New York: Oxford University Press, 1994).

Morgan, Kenneth O., 'The Boer War and the Media'. *Twentieth Century British History*, Vol 13, No. 1, 2002, pp. 1-16.

Mosse, George. *The Image of Man: The Creation of Modern Masculinity* (New York and Oxford: Oxford University Press, 1996).

Nordau, Max. *Degeneration* (London: William Heinemann, 1895).

Pearsall, Ronald. *The Worm in the Bud: The World of Victorian Sexuality* (London: Weidenfeld & Nicolson, 1976).

Pearson, Hesketh. *Arthur Conan Doyle: His Life and Art* (London: Methuen, 1943).

Pick, Daniel. *Faces of Degeneration: A European Disorder, c. 1848- c.1918* (Cambridge: Cambridge University Press, 1989).

Price, Richard. *British Society 1680-1880*. (Cambridge: Cambridge University Press, 1999).

Robb, Graham. *Strangers: Homosexual Love in the Nineteenth Century* (London: Picador, 2003).

Saxon, A. H. *The Life and Art of Andrew Ducrow and the Romantic Age of the English Circus* (Hampden, Ct: Archor Books, 1978).

Schneer, Jonathan. *London 1900: The Imperial Metropolis* (New Haven and London: Yale University Press, 1999)

Schueller, Herbert M., and Peters, Robert L, eds., *The Letters of John Addington Symonds* (Detroit: Wayne State University Press 1967-1969, 3 Vols.)

Schwarzenegger, Arnold. *The Education of a Bodybuilder* (New York: Holiday House, 1978)

Searle, G.R. *The Quest for National Efficiency* (Oxford: Basil Blackwell, 1971).

Searle, G.R. *A New England?: Peace and War 1886-1918* (Oxford: Oxford University Press, 2004)

Senelick, L.D. Cheshire, and Schneider, U. *British Music-Hall 1840-1923* (Hamden, CT: Archon, 1981)

Singleton, Mark. *Yoga Body: The Origins of Modern Posture Practice.* (Oxford: OUP, 2010.)

Solomon-Godeau, Abigail. *Male Trouble: A Crisis in Representation* (London and New York, Thames & Hudson, 1987).

Showalter, Elaine. *Sexual Anarchy: Gender and Culture at the Fin de Siècle* (Harmondsworth: Penguin Books, 1990).

Stokes, John. *In the Nineties* (Hemel Hempstead: Harvester Wheatsheaf, 1989).

Sweet, Matthew. *Inventing the Victorians* (London: Faber, 2001).

Tucker, Jonathan. *The Troublesome Priest: Harold Davidson, Rector of Stiffkey,* (Norwich: Michael Russell, 2007).

Useful websites include www.sandowplus.co.uk and Prof. Attila's scrapbook which is available on-line at the H.J. Lutcher Stark Center for Physical Culture and Sports, the University of Texas at Austin. See www.starkcenter.org/research/web/attila-scrapbook.php.

REFERENCES

[1] Lewis Waller, leading Victorian actor. No relation!

INTRODUCTION

[2] See Hesketh Pearson, *Arthur Conan Doyle: His Life and Art* (London: Methuen, 1943), p.149.

[3] Schwarzenegger won this competition seven times: each year from 1970 to 1975, and again in 1980. The Sandow statuette was awarded for the first time in 1977.

[4] *Letters of John Addington Symonds*, Vol 3., ed. Herbert M Schueller and Robert L Peters, letter from Symonds to Gosse, December 28, 1889.

[5] Lady De Frece. *Recollections of Vesta Tilley*. (London: Hutchinson & Co., 1934), p.54.

[6] The picture still exists, hanging in the collection of Joe Weider, the body-building promoter.

1: FROM PRUSSIA WITH MUSCLES

[7] Civilians who survived aerial bombardment and street fighting were driven on a forced march through the surrounding countryside by the Russians. They returned to a nightmare landscape of smouldering ruins, to mass rape and starvation alleviated at times by cannibalism.

[8] With the demise of the Soviet Union, the city and its surrounding areas are today still isolated, both physically and culturally. Its immediate neighbours are now more or less sturdy democracies and members of the European Union, while Kaliningrad itself enjoys notoriety for the sheer number of statues of Marx and Lenin that have been preserved, and for the scale and ugliness of its Soviet-era buildings, chief of which is the 22-storey House of Soviet Culture, which stands derelict and dangerous on the crumbling foundations of the former Royal Palace, a fittingly grim visual metaphor for the transition from one military regime to another. Ill-served by its recent history, the city has been left marginalized and forgotten, finding its way into the news whenever the Russians consider locating nuclear missiles on its ugly

soil, pointing towards western Europe.

[9] In proving that this was impossible, Leonhard Euler is credited with inventing the science of graph theory.

[10] The chief sources for "official" accounts of his early life are: *Sandow on Physical Training: A Study in the Perfect Type of the Human Form*, compiled and edited "under Mr Sandow's direction" by G. Mercer Adam, and published by Gale & Polden in 1894, and the second section of *Strength and How to Obtain It* (1894), entitled 'Incidents of My Professional Career'.

[11] Born Angelo Siciliano, Atlas (1892-1972) was famously inspired to take up physical training after sand was kicked in his face on the beach at Coney Island. Meanwhile Theodore Roosevelt (1858-1919) writes in his *Autobiography* that: "having been a sickly boy, with no natural bodily prowess ...bitterly conscious that I did not have the natural prowess to hold my own, I decided to supply its place with training..."

[12] As relayed in "My Reminiscences" in *Strand Magazine*. Vol XXXIX, January 1910.

[13] Further biographical details, together with excerpts from Prof. Attila's Scrapbook can be viewed online at www.starkcenter.org, copyright the H.J. Lutcher Stark Center for Physical Culture and Sports at The University of Texas at Austin.

[14] The publication is unclear; the article is to be found in Attila's scrapbook.

[15] *The Era*, October 11, 1890.

[16] *The Era*, June 9, 1888.

[17] On 8 February 1888, the Crown Prince underwent a bungled tracheotomy, which did indeed render him speechless for the short remainder of his life and the entirety of his 99-day reign.

[18] Reported in *The Era* on June 15, 1900.

[19] Patent 552,971 for an "exercising apparatus" was granted by the US Patent Office on 14 January 1896, witnessed by Florenz Ziegfeld and Martinus Sieveking. The device is designed to strengthen the muscles of the leg.

2: A LATE-VICTORIAN CELEBRITY

[20] Eugen Sandow and Mercer Adam, G. *Sandow on Physical Training: A Study in the Perfect Type of the Human Form* (New York: J. Selwin Tait & Sons, 1894), p.47-50. See also Chapter II of *Strength and How to Obtain It* (London: Gale & Polden, 1897), pp.93-99 (Strength) and the article "My Reminiscences" in the *Strand Magazine* January 1910, Vol XXXIV. There are many newspaper

articles reporting the contest and its aftermath, see for example *The Times* on November 2 , 4 and 8, 1889.

[21] Peter Bailey, *Popular Culture and Performance in the Victorian City* (Cambridge: Cambridge University Press, 1998), p.140.

[22] See F. Anstey, 'London Music Halls,' *Harper's Magazine*, January 1891, pp. 190-202.

[23] 'At the Empire' by Thomas Wratislaw, cited in *In The Nineties* by John Stokes, p.62.

[24] *Ally Sloper's Half-Holiday*, November 21, 1891.

[25] See Chapter 12 of Houdini's *The Miracle Mongers and Their Methods* (1921), published in New York by E.P. Dutton & Co.

[26] Her second husband Alec Hurley was also a music hall performer (and fellow fitness fanatic) who wrote a popular song about Sandow:

"Up jumped Sandow like Hercules
Lifting up the iron bars
And breaking them with ease.
Sampson looked astonished and said it wasn't fair
But everyone knows Sandow was the winner there."

3: MANHOOD ON TRIAL

[27] Max Nordau, *Degeneration*, (London: William Heinemann, 1895), pp.5-6.

[28] Max Nordau's *Degeneration*, pp. 41-43.

[29] Kenneth O. Morgan 'The Boer War and the Media (1899-1902),' in *Twentieth Century British History*, Vol 13. No 1, 2002, pp. 1-16.

[30] From M. Eastwood, "The New Woman in Fiction and Fact", (1894), excerpt on pp. 90-92 of *The Fin de Siècle: A Reader in Cultural History c. 1880-1900*, ed. Sally Ledger and Roger Luckhurst.

[31] *Pall Mall Gazette*, January 14, 1895.

[32] Quoted in Daniel Pick, *Faces of Degeneration: A European Disorder, c. 1848-c.1918* (Cambridge: CUP, 1989) p.201. As Richard Price noted, working class bodies were singled out as "diseased, degenerate carriers of social disorder." Richard Price, *British Society 1680-1880* (Cambridge: CUP, 1999) p.223.

[33] *The Fin de Siècle: A Reader*, pp. 27-32.

[34] Daniel Kelves, *In the Name of Eugenics: Genetics and the Uses of Human Heredity* (Cambridge, Mass., and London: Harvard UP, 1995), p.33.

[35] Sidney Webb, "The Decline of the Birth Rate", *Fabian Tract No.131* (London:

Fabian Society, 1907) p.19.

[36] It is often forgotten, however, that eugenicist ideas were put into practice in the US before they were embraced by Germany: a laboratory was opened at Cold Springs Harbor on Long Island in 1904 and in time some 35 states, starting with Indiana in 1899, legislated to allow eugenic sterilisation of mentally handicapped people. The first institute of racial biology was established not in Germany but in Uppsala in Sweden as early as 1922. During the 1930s, Hitler's Racial Purity laws led to the sterilisation of 400,000 "unfit" people such as the mentally and physically handicapped, and many thousands were summarily murdered.

[37] "The questions I keep before me are whether or no the British race as a whole is, or is not, equal to its Imperial responsibilities," he wrote, "and again how far it is feasible to make it more capable of the highest destinies that are within its reach, if it possesses the will and power to pursue them. I wish that each one of us should stand aloof from ourselves as a whole, and should watch the conditions and doings of our race, much as an authority of the Royal Agricultural Society might criticise the stock of his neighbour over the hedge. If we do so we may learn in what ways our own stock and its rearing are open to improvement and we may perhaps ensue it."

[38] Galton continued to ruminate on Britain's fitness to rule and some time after Sandow's Great Competition was persuaded to write an article for the *Daily Chronicle*, addressing the masses rather than the august scientific audiences who were the more usual targets of his meditations. The article, published on 29 July 1903, was entitled 'Our National Physique – Prospects of the British Race – Are we Degenerating?'

"As regards the physique of Britons, I think we brag or have bragged more than is right," Galton wrote. "We are not as well formed as might be. It is difficult to get opportunities of studying the nude figures of our countrymen in mass, but I have often watched crowds bathe, as in the Serpentine [a bathing lake in London's Hyde Park], with a critical eye, and have always come to the conclusion that they were less shapely than many of the dark-coloured people whom I have seen."

[39] Pearson himself attempted to codify the extent of the "National Deterioration" by compiling a gigantic series of statistical studies of inherited traits, from nose size and physical defects to scientific, legal and commercial ability, from his base at the Biometric Laboratory. While he never came up with definitive conclusions, he was at least delighted to see how an obscure science became increasingly accepted by the mainstream. "You would be

amused to hear how general is now the use of your word Eugenics," Pearson boasted to Galton in 1907. "I hear most respectable middle-class matrons saying if children are weakly, 'Ah, that was not a eugenic marriage.'" *In the Name of Eugenics* p. 57.

[40] Cited in Mark Girouard *The Return to Camelot*, pp136 and 142.

[41] Hugh le Roux and Jules Garnier, *Acrobats and Mountebanks* (London: Chapman and Hall, 1890), p. 76.

[42] "Sandow in Plaster of Paris: A Unique Cast", in *The Strand Magazine*, October 1901, Vol. xxii No. 130 p.461.

4: Between Titillation and Respectability

[43] Symonds to Edmund Gosse, 12 July 1890, ibid.

[44] Linda Dowling, *Hellenism and Homosexuality in Victorian Oxford* (Ithaca and London: Cornell UP, 1994), p. 28.

[45] "Increasingly, the male nude was not only visible in public sculptures, display pieces and architecture," argues the art historian Michael Hatt, "[but also] in reduced form as statuettes for the home."

[46] New Sculpture thus joined the numerous other "new" fields of cultural activity: new Journalism, criticism, women, unions – all of which points to the 1890s as an "excitingly volatile transitional period" between the Victorian age and the modern.

[47] Josh Buck, "Sandow: No Folly with Ziegfeld's First Glorification," *Iron Game History*, Vol.5 No I, May 1998, p.30.

[48] A. H. Saxon, *The Life and Art of Andrew Ducrow and the Romantic Age of the English Circus* (Hampden, Ct: Archor Books, 1978), pp.151-153.

[49] See John Stokes, *In the Nineties*, (Hemel Hempstead: Harvester Wheatsheaf, 1989), pp. 77-80.

[50] "The nineteenth century homosexual became a personage, a past, a case history, and a childhood, in addition to a type of life, a life form, and a morphology, with an indiscreet anatomy, and possibly a mysterious physiology," the French philosopher Michel Foucault wrote in his *History of Sexuality*. "Nothing that went into his total composition was unaffected by his sexuality." See Elaine Showalter, *Sexual Anarchy: Gender and Culture at the Fin de Siècle* (Harmondsworth: Penguin Books, 1990) p.13.

[51] See Sally Ledger and Scott McCracken, eds. *Cultural Politics at the Fin de Siècle* (Manchester: Manchester University Press, 1997), pages 307 and 311.

[52] See "Sandow in Plaster of Paris: A Unique Cast", in *The Strand Magazine*,

October 1901, Vol. xxii No. 130 p.461.

5: SANDOW TRIUMPHS IN NEW YORK

[53] John Kasson, *Houdini, Tarzan and the Perfect Man: The White Male Body and the Challenge of Modernity in America* (New York: Hill & Wang, 2001), pp.25-28.
[54] *New York Times* June 13 and 18, 1893.
[55] *Strength*, p.129.
[56] "[Schwarzenegger] experimented in an almost scientific way to find an exercise that would separate the pectorals from the deltoid muscles...to develop the inherent potential of a muscle [he] had to devote hundreds of hours to demanding more of it than it is willing to give..." Sven Lindqvist, *Bench Press*, p.28.
[57] *Physical Training*, pp. 131-133.
[58] *Strength*, Chapter VI.
[59] As explained in "The Dead-Weight Principle," an interview conducted with Sieveking by Harriette Brower, a famous musical journalist, contained in *Piano Mastery: The Harriette Brower Interviews*, ed. Jeffrey Johnson, Dover Publications, New York, 203, pp 139-146.
[60] Cited in *Journal of Sport History*, Vol 26, No 2, p 405.
[61] See the *New York Times* July 3, 10, 18 and 25, 1893.
[62] *Sandow on Physical Training*, p. 136.
[63] *New York Times*, June 13, 1893.

6: SEX AND THE CITY OF CHICAGO

[64] Erik Larson, *The Devil in the White City* (London: Bantam Books, 2004).
[65] *Hartford Courant*, October 18, 1925.
[66] *Chicago Daily Tribune*, May 16, 1895.
[67] *Western Daily Mail*, January 5, 1894.
[68] Paderewski, "Piano Playing and Muscle", *Sandow's Magazine*, September 1898 Volume I No. 3, pp.189-191.
[69] The French-language "Programme Officiel" for *Buffalo Bill's Wild West and Congress of Rough Riders of the World* carries an advertisement for Sandow's equipment on the back cover.
[70] See the *Birmingham Daily Post*, January 30, 1895, for an account of the kinetoscope.
[71] *Chicago Daily Tribune*, February 23, 1894.

[72] *Strand Magazine*, My Reminiscences, p.150; see also Chapter IX of Strength.

[73] *The Era*, May 26, 1894.

[74] *Strength*, p.138.

[75] *Pall Mall Gazette*, March 24, 1894.

[76] *Sandow's Magazine* 6 (1901), p.445.

[77] His obituary was published in the *Manchester Guardian* of October 1, 1929, and a fuller appraisal of his career in the same newspaper on October 9th. See also *Photohistorian*, the journal of the historical group of the Royal Photographical Society, Issue No. 82, Autumn 1988.

[78] *Washington Post*, October 19, 1894.

7: BACK IN THE UK

[79] *The Era*, January 9, 1897.

[80] *The Times*, November 30, 1899.

[81] *Reynold's Weekly Newspaper*, August 28, 1898

[82] See Lincolnshire Archives BROG/1/4/3/152/5 June 25 1892.

[83] *Daily News*, April 22, 1899.

[84] Eugen Sandow, *Body-Building, or Man in the Making: How to Become Healthy and Strong* (London: Gale & Polden [N.D. 1904]), p.5.

[85] Eugen Sandow, *Life is Movement: The Physical Reconstruction & Regeneration of the People* (London: National Health Press, 1918), p.8.

[86] *Chicago Daily Tribune*, October 8, 1898.

8: SANDOW'S SYSTEM

[87] *New York World*, October 31, 1925.

[88] *Bench Press*, p.28.

[89] *The Era*, January 9, 1897.

[90] Eugen Sandow, *Body-Building, or Man in the Making* (London: Gale & Polden [n.d 1904]), p.24.

[91] See Chapter 8 of *Body-Building*, the article on the Modern Venus in *Sandow's Magazine*, December 1900, and a further article on Jujitsu for women in the magazine on December 7, 1905.

[92] James Joyce, *Ulysses* (Harmondsworth: Penguin Books, 1980), p. 602. The book was first published in 1922.

[93] Eugen Sandow, *Body-Building, or Man in the Making: How to Become Healthy and

Strong (London: Gale & Polden [N.D. 1904]), p.4.

[94] George Mosse, *The Image of Man: the Creation of Modern Masculinity* (New York and Oxford: OUP, 1996), p.44.

[95] Edmond Desbonnet and Dr Georges Roubiet *L'Art de Créer le Pur-Sang Humain* (Paris: Berger-Levrault, 1911), p.LXIII. "Le but de la culture physique est noble entre tous," he writes. "Elle permet de devenir beau et de jouir d'une excellente santé, de procréer de beaux enfants a que on transmettra les qualités acquises par son propre travail."

[96] Eugene Sandow, "Sandow's Magazine: Physical Culture, What is It?" *Sandow's Magazine*, Vol. I, Number I, July 1998, p.7.

9: JEKYLL AND HYDE

[97] The case was reported in the *Guardian* of November 28 and 29, 1899, and extensively elsewhere.

[98] *The Era*, November 17, 1900.

[99] *Western Mail*, February 1, 1899.

[100] *The Era*, April 8, 1899.

[101] *The Era*, April 8, 1899.

10: FIT TO RULE?

[102] Quoted in Samuel Hynes, *The Edwardian Turn of Mind* (Princeton and London: Princeton University Press, 1968), p.7.

[103] *Daily News*, February 1, 1900.

[104] Jonathan Schneer, *London 1900: The Imperial Metropolis*, p.95.

[105] G.R. Searle, *A New England?: Peace and War 1886-1918* (Oxford: Oxford University Press, 2004), p.285.

[106] *The Era*, October 6, 1900.

[107] Samuel Hynes, *The Edwardian Turn of Mind*, p.22.

[108] G.R. Searle, op. cit., 375.

[109] Samuel Hynes, *The Edwardian Turn of Mind*, pp.22-23; see also *The Times*, August 22, 1902.

11: THE GREAT COMPETITION OF 1901

[110] Pearson, *Life of Galton*, Vol 3, p. 253.

[111] Arthur Conan Doyle, *Memories and Adventures*, pp. 211-213.

[112] See the introduction to Caroline Daley's *Leisure & Pleasure: Reshaping and Revealing the New Zealand Body 1900-1960*.

[113] As this remark from Karl Pearson illustrates:
"The term 'lower races" is very unfashionable at the present time, but it is a pleasing and emotional sentiment rather than real anthropological acumen which asserts that all men are of equal value at birth, or that all races are, physically, mentally and socially, of one standard of fitness. The distinctions between man and man, and race and race, are in the main inborn and not 'innurtured'...Few teachers who have had to instruct young men of many races – and usually the best of lower races – would deny that mentally at least they can be graded. Exceptional men may arise in any race, but it is the averages we have to regard. It was greed that introduced the Negro into North America; it was lack of insight which did not push him northwards in South Africa. In both cases the 'lower race' now forms a grave and almost unsolvable problem for the future."

[114] *Strand Magazine*, "A Unique Cast".

12: IMPERIAL PROGRESS

[115] *New York Times*, March 21, 1902.

[116] Both articles are from the *New York Dramatic Mirror*, cited in *Sandow the Magnificent*, p. 137.

[117] "Sandow in every respect justified all that has been said of his marvellous strength and of his great muscular development", gushed a report in the *West Australian*. "It is claimed that physically he is the most perfect man that ever lived, while anatomists, it is averred, acknowledge him to be the strongest man in the world. It is but natural to expect that such a man would perform feats of strength almost superhuman, and that he did. But he also performs them with an ease and neatness, and with such an absence of indications of great straining, that the onlooker wonders where the limit is attained."

[118] See "My World's Tour" in Sandow's *Body Building*, for this and other newspaper cuttings; also "Sandow's Tour Around the World" in *Sandow's Magazine*, May 1903, Vol. 10, pp.319-324.

[119] *Leisure & Pleasure*, p.256.

[120] *Sandow's Magazine*, November 16, 1905.

[121] H.G. Wells, *The New Machiavelli* (London: J.M Dent, 1994) p.254.

[122] Peter McIntosh, *Physical Education in England Since 1800* (London: G.Bell & Sons, 1952), p.145.

[123] Preface to Sandow's *Life is Movement*, 1919.

[124] See *Sandow's Magazine*, "Sandow in South Africa", Vol 13. July-December 1904, pp.237-241.

[125] *Sandow's Magazine*, September 28, 1905. See also "Physical Culture: Progress in India" from ibid. Vol XIV, March 23 1905.

[126] Sir Dhunjibhoy Bomanji (1862-1937) made his fortune in jute and shipping and was a prominent member of India's Parsee community: over decades he spent half the year in England, chiefly at The Willows on the Thames near Windsor which boasted its own railway line. He was knighted in 1922 after various services to the British Empire.

[127] "My Reminiscences" in *Strand Magazine*, January 1910, Vol. XXXXIX.

[128] "How I Taught Indian Ladies My System", *Sandow's Magazine*, September 28, 1905.

13: At Home, At Last

[129] See the *Manchester Guardian*, September 19, 1905, and "The Return of Mr Sandow" in *Sandow's Magazine*, September 28, 1905, pp. 343-345.

[130] *Chicago Daily Tribune*, September 1, 1907.

[131] *Sandow's Magazine*, June 1903, p.419.

[132] On 30 August 1916.

14: The Tono-Bungay Years

[133] *The Times*, October 1, 1911.

[134] *The Times*, October 11, 1911.

[135] *The Times*, ibid.

[136] *Penny Illustrated Paper*, October 14, 1911.

[137] "As Jolly as a Sandow," *Review of Reviews*, 1911, Vol. 43, pp. 199-202.

[138] *The Times*, May 27, 1911, also reported in the *Guardian* of the same day. Sandow's statement on the matter appeared in *The Times* of December 1, 1911.

[139] Reported in the *Grey River Argus*, May 29, 1913.

[140] *The Times*, October 15, 1913.

15: Decline and Fall

[141] See the *Observer*, March 29, 1914.

[142] *The Times*, February 20, 1915.

[143] *The Observer*, October 24, 1915.

[144] *The Times*, January 25, 1915.

[145] *The Times*, August 25, 1915.

[146] *The Times*, August 30, 1916.

[147] It was a brief and not especially glorious parliamentary career – he was bounced out of his seat and stood unsuccessfully for Preston in the 1918 election – but a vigorous one. Warwick spoke no fewer than 198 times in that short period, popping up to make all manner of speeches, on subjects as various as the causes of the 1916 Irish rebellion and the treatment of enemy prisoners.

[148] *Life is Movement*, pp.1-16.

[149] See Earle Liederman, "Sandow: My Impressions When We First Met," in the April-May 1946 edition of the Canadian magazine *Muscle Power*, also "More about Sandow," in the March 1949 edition of the same. Also accessible on the www.sandowplus.co.uk website.

[150] See *Collected Letters* Vol IV 1926-1950 (Max Reinhardt: London, 1988.) pp. 13-14.

[151] Also published in the *Hartford Courant* of October 18, 1925.

[152] A curt note from Mr Ponsonby, Keeper of the Privy Purse, conveys Buckingham Palace's final decision: "I regret to inform you that it has not been possible to comply with your request…I must therefore ask you to be good enough to return the Royal Warrant of Appointment granted personally to the late Mr Sandow…"

EPILOGUE: IN THE LION'S DEN

[153] See Ronald Blythe, *The Age of Illusion: England in the Twenties and Thirties, 1919-1940* (London: Hamish Hamilton, 1963.)

Acknowledgements

Chris Davies, a professional juggler who has inherited Sandow's talents as a showman, has inspired me with his enthusiasm for the life of his great-grandfather. Prof. Hilary Fraser of Birkbeck read the book in draft and helped me root my subject rigorously in his historical context, as did Prof. Edgar Feuchtwanger. David Chapman, Sandow's first biographer, has generously helped me with his time and insights during the long preparation of this book. My agent Bill Hamilton stuck with it for years, while Catherine Pope of Victorian Secrets has been a wonderful, supportive and imaginative publisher. Others who have helped along the way include: Miss Pamela Clark of the Royal Archives; Robert Kruszynski and Polly Parry of the Natural History Museum; the staff of the London Library and the British Library. Dr Andrew Cull, Jeremy Steele and Prof. Mike Sheaff gave their professional opinions on the causes of Sandow's death. Thanks, as always, to my wife Jane and our three children, who grew up during the completion of this book. Despite good intentions, we never introduced the Sandow regime into our household. Max, Pippa and Munro do not appear to have suffered for not once having picked up a dumb-bell.

About David Waller

David Waller was educated at Manchester Grammar School, Balliol College, Oxford, and Birkbeck College, London. He worked for the best part of ten years as a journalist on the *Financial Times*. David is married with three children and lives in South-West London. He has written two business books but more recently turned to historical biography after the chance find of a treasure-trove of papers in a home counties attic. *The Magnificent Mrs Tennant*, a biography of the Victorian grande dame Gertrude Tennant, was published in summer 2009 by Yale University Press. Reviews have been flattering: the book was compared to "Thackeray at his best" (*Independent*) and Valerie Grove in *The Times* wrote: "Waller's story has terrific pace and wit. It is rich in period detail and places events unobtrusively in context. It is a real discovery."

READING GROUP QUESTIONS

1. What elements of Sandow's story did you find surprising or particularly interesting?

2. How successful do you think Sandow was in maintaining a boundary between his personal and professional lives?

3. Do you think Sandow's public persona was more than just a brand?

4. To what extent do you think xenophobia contributed to Sandow's downfall?

5. Do you agree with David Waller's theory as to why Blanche Sandow buried her husband's body with such unseemly haste?

6. How have notions of celebrity changed, if at all, since Sandow's day?

7. How have ideas of the "perfect" man changed over the last century?

8. Does the biography convince you that Sandow deserves to be taken seriously as an historical figure?

If you would like more information or ideas about using this book as a reading group text, please contact info@victoriansecrets.co.uk.

INDEX

Victorian Secrets

Victorian Secrets is an independent publisher dedicated to producing high-quality books from and about the nineteenth century, including critical editions of neglected novels.

FICTION

A Mummer's Wife by George Moore
The Autobiography of Christopher Kirkland by Eliza Lynn Linton
The Blood of the Vampire by Florence Marryat
The Dead Man's Message by Florence Marryat
Demos by George Gissing
Dorothea's Daughter and Other Nineteenth-Century Postscripts by Barbara Hardy
East of Suez by Alice Perrin
Henry Dunbar by Mary Elizabeth Braddon
Her Father's Name by Florence Marryat
The Light that Failed by Rudyard Kipling
Twilight Stories by Rhoda Broughton
Vice Versâ by F. Anstey
Weird Stories by Charlotte Riddell
Workers in the Dawn by George Gissing

BIOGRAPHY

Notable Women Authors of the Day by Helen C. Black

For more information on any of our titles, please visit:

www.victoriansecrets.co.uk

East of Suez by Alice Perrin
edited with an introduction and notes by Melissa Edmundson
Makala

Originally published in 1901, *East of Suez* was Alice Perrin's first collection of short stories. Her fascinating and thought-provoking tales of Anglo-Indian life rival the best work of Kipling and were hugely successful in their day. Perrin tells stories of illicit love and betrayal set against a beautifully-drawn backdrop of the mystical east, interweaving the supernatural with exquisite details of her characters' lives.

"The volume is beautifully produced and bookended by a learned and perceptive literary introduction to Perrin's work .. and by two interesting appendices depicting the cultural context of the British Raj as the historical frame of the author's body of work. Highly recommended." Mario Guslandi, *The Short Review*

ISBN: 978-1-906469-18-4

Vice Versâ by F. Anstey
edited with an introduction and notes by Peter Merchant

First published in 1882, *Vice Versâ* shows the disastrous consequences of having one's wishes granted. After delivering a pompous lecture to his son Dick, stuffy Paul Bultitude declares his wish to be a schoolboy once more so he can enjoy the carefree existence of youth. Unfortunately for him, he happens to be clutching the mysterious and magical Garudâ stone, and suddenly finds himself transformed into the diminutive body of his son. Dick quickly uses the stone to his own advantage, assuming his father's portly character and swapping roles. While Dick gets the opportunity to run his father's business in the City and wreak havoc on the household, Paul must endure the privations of the brutal boarding school he forced young Dick to attend. Determined not to lose his dignity, Paul retains his former bombastic demeanour, leading to a series of hilarious episodes with the cane-wielding Dr Grimstone.

ISBN: 978-1-906469-21-4

Henry Dunbar by Mary Elizabeth Braddon
edited with an introduction and notes by Anne-Marie Beller

First published in 1864, *Henry Dunbar* includes all the classic ingredients of a sensation novel, including murder, fraud, mistaken identity, and a train accident. The dramatic nature of the tale led to it being adapted for the stage, most notably by Tom Taylor, with Henry Neville and Kate Terry in the lead roles. Some contemporary critics were horrified by this "tale of crime", but modern readers will enjoy a thumping good story and an early example of the great British detective novel.

"I loved the book and strongly recommend reading it in this superior format, with its pleasant typeface and excellent introduction." (amazon.com)

ISBN: 978-1-906469-15-3

The Blood of the Vampire by Florence Marryat
edited with an introduction and notes by Greta Depledge

Marryat's 1897 novel was rather overshadowed by a certain Transylvanian Count who made his debut in the same year. Although there are similarities with Dracula, Marryat's vampire is female and drains her victims' life force, rather than their blood.

Harriet Brandt is the daughter of a mad scientist and a mixed-race voodoo priestess. Brought up on her parents' Jamaican plantation, she is forced to flee to Europe after the slaves revolt. Everyone is initially attracted to Harriet, but people who get close to her seem to sicken and die.

"Marryat has peopled her gothic tale with a delightful mix of upright Victorians and ludicrous eccentrics. The plot is a feast of love conflicts, violated social taboos and medical interventions, nineteenth-century style." (amazon.com)

ISBN: 978-1-906469-16-0

The Light that Failed by Rudyard Kipling
edited with an introduction and notes by Paul Fox

Originally published in 1891, *The Light that Failed* is Rudyard Kipling's semi-autobiographical first novel. Critics who had praised him for *Plain Tales from the Hills* were shocked at the unhappy ending and deviation from his usual style, but none could deny the power of Kipling's writing.

The Light that Failed tells the story of war artist Dick Heldar, his doomed love for childhood sweetheart Maisie, and his descent into blindness. Dick's humiliating relationship with Maisie is based on Kipling's rejection by Flo Garrard, who left him for another woman.

"All in all *The Light that Failed* is a fascinating novel by an important novelist and it's lovely to see an excellent scholarly edition on the market. For anyone interested in the glamorous, wild, dangerous and racy final decade of the Victorian era this is a must." (amazon.co.uk)

ISBN: 978-1-906469-19-1

Demos by George Gissing
edited with an introduction and notes by Debbie Harrison

Thanks to a missing will, London mechanic and ardent socialist Richard Mutimer unexpectedly inherits a fortune at the expense of the presumed heir, aristocratic Hubert Eldon. Mutimer leaves behind his old life to establish a model village for ironworkers in the idyllic Midland town of Wanley. He also deserts the girl who loves him, as he seeks to assume the social status of the middle-class capitalists he once despised. Although Gissing's novel has a purpose, it is also a gripping story of bigamy, bisexuality and betrayal.

"…this detailed edition of *Demos* may earn him new readers." Robert Giddings, *Tribune*

ISBN: 978-1-906469-17-7